ON YOUR O
IN THE W

WN
LDERNESS

by

TOWNSEND WHELEN
and
BRADFORD ANGIER

Illustrated with photographs by the
authors and sketches by Vena Angier

THE STACKPOLE COMPANY
Harrisburg, Pennsylvania

Go and look behind the ranges.

Printed in the United States of America
by The Telegraph Press,
Established 1831
Harrisburg, Pennsylvania

When Brad and I were writing this book we were living three thousand miles apart. He asked me to whom we should dedicate it.

I think it will be plain to every reader that there is one person to whom we owe much for her assistance, for helping to type and edit, for the contributions she has made, and by no means least, for her inspiration.

So entirely at my suggestion this book is dedicated to
VENA ANGIER
A real wilderness wife.

TOWNSEND WHELEN

FOREWORD

THIS IS OCTOBER. Dark spruce greening the lower mountainsides are streaked with the gold of poplars. These stream down the gullies to the parklike valley floor where the little willows the moose love so much have taken on their crimson brightness. Among all this shadows rise, extinguishing color, as the sun is slowly sliced from sight by a saw-toothed ridge. Its final rays momentarily enchant a snow peak to the east to a startling ruby against the rich deep blue of the northern sky.

Our fire leaps at dry spruce logs, as the stars come out one by one. The winds drop at this blending of past day with future night. All becomes hushed except for the small noises of evening. Across a lake, ducks splash in the reeds and quack softly. A great horned owl hoots—who-who-who-ahew-hu-hu.

We eat our moosemeat and bannock, sip our tea, and gaze into the living warmth of the embers. Presently, like a cool sough of air across a glacier, there breathes a sound: softly, hesitantly, sadly at first, soaring and falling and lifting again—a wolf singing of love, of the beauty of the silent places, and of freedom. Over and over again *Mahheekun* howls, so tenderly, sweetly, yearningly. Then we are alone with the stillness.

This is our country. Does it call to you, too? Come with us into it. Let us talk together about how to live in it.

My collaborator and I have had much the same experiences, and this in a way is responsible for this book . . .

Brad was a young Boston newspaperman with a background, starting even before his teens, of year-around weekend camping throughout northern New England and summers of hiking, climbing, and bivouacking in the North Woods—during which he fell irretrievably under the spell of the quiet, beauty and peace of those still almost unspoiled regions where he built his lone campfires.

It was this deepening influence of the Farther Places that later impelled him to extend regular holidays from reportorial and editorial duties with longer and still longer leaves of absence until a couple of months each year he was hunting and fishing with his own little outfit on the upper Southwest Miramichi River in New Brunswick, along the Grand Cascapedia in the Gaspe's wild interior, and in other wilderness expanses not too many wasted hours of travel from his desk.

Finally, the love of nature at her best became an obsession with him. Getting fed up with city-bound existence, the artificiality, and the crowds and noise of Commonwealth Avenue, he decided to make the break. He jumped off to the wildest and one of the most beautiful spots in North America—beyond the end of the last dirt wagon tracks, where the wonderfully lonesome headwaters of the Peace River plunge through the main chain of the Canadian Rockies. Arriving there in the middle of a sub-Arctic winter, he settled down to a thoroughly happy log-cabin life on the sunny north bank of the otherwise vacant, never navigated Rocky Mountain Canyon, a 22-mile wilderness solitude described by Alexander Mackenzie a century and a half before as "one white sheet of foaming water."

There in that vast and primitive region, among hills lean with lodgepole pine and deep spruce-blued chasms, with a background of high snow-coned peaks, he and his wife still continue to reside, living off the country and on the returns from their pens. They tell the story well in their book *At Home in the Woods*. Their occasional and only companions, and it might be said instructors, have been the frugal and competent hunters, trappers, prospectors, and Hudson's Bay men and their pioneer wives. From these sourdough individualists they have learned the art of living economically and comfortably in wild country, and of meeting every situation and emergency successfully with their brains and hands alone.

I, for my part, spent all of my boyhood summers in the Adirondack Mountains, hunting, fishing and camping every clear day; and there I developed a love for the uncut woods, mountains, and lakes that passes all understanding. When I reached manhood all my weekends and holidays found me in little pieces of God's country. Before very long my readings of the Northwest and the illustrations I saw of its high, snow-capped peaks and its broad, deep valleys clad with virgin forests, together with the accounts of the game, so fired my imagination as to act like a lodestone.

So I, too, "jumped off" to the wildest and most glorious country I could learn of—central British Columbia. That was in 1901 at the age of twenty-three. I left the end of the rails alone, with a saddle horse and two pack ponies loaded with grub and meager equipment, and started True North into an uninhabited country I knew nothing of—not even how it looked on maps.

After a few days of wandering unguided up valleys and over snow-covered passes, I came to the bivouac of an old hunter and prospector, one of the very last of the typical Mountain Men of the Old West, clad entirely in buckskin, long haired, and looking as though he had stepped out of a painting of Remington. I camped that night with him. We took a liking to each other and eventually we became partners to hunt, prospect and trap in the wild regions to the north, where there was no civilization between us and the horde who had recently rushed into the Yukon.

There we stuck together for nine glorious months, while that gigantic country cast on me the spell of the North that has remained ingrained in my soul ever since. At the start I was an "innocent pilgrim," but gradually Bones taught me the way of the mountains as only those of the Old West knew it; so very different, so much more efficient than the best methods of the Eastern guides—wilderness technique, we might say, which has all but disappeared.

Since those days, my forty years of service in our Army, including three wars, has afforded opportunity to learn the art of living in and of overcoming the obstacles of strange country. Leaves of absence and vacations invariably spent in the wilds have served to gratify and intensify my longings for the peace and freedom found only there.

Amateur exploration of these regions became my hobby. I usually went alone because finding my own way and overcoming all obstacles without assistance gave me an inexpressible thrill. Sometimes I had a congenial companion, or a canoeman, or a horse wrangler along. Only twice have I employed a guide and that not to show me the way, but rather to permit more time for the intimate study of Nature. I have sometimes been called a "big-game hunter," but I dislike the term. I have been rather a wanderer in and worshiper of beautiful and unspoiled country, what some overcivilized and atrophied individuals call "The Waste-lands."

And so it was that Brad and I came to "savvy the bush."

Each of us in the midst of our life in the open became familiar with the classic writings on woodcraft of George W. Sears (Nessmuk) and Horace Kephart, and we also came under the spell of Thoreau's

Walden. The works were inspirational and revealing, but unfortunately not even these writers knew real, wild, unspoiled country firsthand. Their personal experiences were confined to little stretches of wooded country almost within hearing of the steam whistle. Other more recent writers, with three exceptions, have had rather limited experiences, and their works cover largely the ways of the modern sportsman tied to the apron strings of a guide, of boys and girls camp instruction, and of automobile and motorboat camping.

Gradually, it occurred to both of us that it was well worthwhile to put on record the old but time-tried ways of the wild before they were lost forever in a mass of modern technology based on impractical impediments. We wished to explain what from our experience we'd found to be the best ways of entering wild and unknown country, of finding one's own way through it, and of living there in comfort and safety, enjoying it to the utmost, and inviting one's soul.

When we started to live this life there were no special manufactured and modern conveniences such as exist today. There were not even fairly accurate maps of the wilder regions. Our first outfits were primitive—blankets, home kitchen utensils, ordinary grub, black-powder rifles, lumberman's clothes, and little else.

Since then the production of modern gadgets designed to help one take civilization into the wilderness has reached tremendous proportions. Much of this is just "junk with sales appeal," and in the words of the old timers "not worth hellroom." However, certain pieces of modern equipment serve admirably to smooth the way, to make the outdoor life easier and more comfortable, to lighten the load, and permit more time to be devoted to the worship of nature. We have presented these and explained their uses and advantages.

Some small portions of the text have appeared previously under our names in SPORTS AFIELD and THE AMERICAN RIFLEMAN. We are indebted to the editors of these magazines for permission to include them here. We also thank the U. S. Forest Service, the U. S. National Park Service, the Canadian National Railways, the Canadian Travel Bureau, and the Hudson's Bay Company for a few of the photographs.

A lot of folks dream of escaping to some earthly paradise. Our hopes are that what we have written here may help some of them make that dream come true. Try it first for a holiday. Possibly afterwards you may jump off for good. What Thoreau proved a century ago about returning to nature will still work today.

TOWNSEND WHELEN.

IX

CONTENTS

XII

Gateway to Peace and Utter Freedom

CHAPTER 1

LURE OF THE TRAIL

A LOT OF US are working harder than we want, at things we don't like to do. Why? In order to afford the sort of existence we don't care to live. If one hears the call of the open places, why shall he not answer it as fully as he may while eyes will never be keener nor stride more lusty?

Scientists remind us that nature intended human beings should spend most of their hours beneath open skies. With appetites sharpened by outdoor living, they should eat plain food. They should live at their natural God-given paces, unoppressed by the artificial hurry and tension of man-made civilization.

Yet the mass of city men, stalking their meat at the crowded market instead of in the green woods and cool marshes, put up with existences of quiet desperation. They make themselves sick that they may lay up something against a sick day. Their incessant anxiety and strain is a well-nigh incurable form of disease.

How sensible is it to spend all the best part of one's life earning money in order to enjoy a questionable liberty during the least valuable years? Not everyone may fully heed the summons of the farther places, of course. But many who think themselves shackled to civilized tasks are held only by such deceptive strands as habit, inertia, environment, doubt, resignation, lack of confidence, and often by a general misunderstanding of the make-up of man.

The truth is, Homo sapiens was bred for the tall forests and singing brooks. He was moulded for the wind-rounded desert, the shadowy canyon, and a mountain top where the breeze blows free. Just the thought of the great calling North with its beckoning rivers can cause the most civilized pulse to beat faster. An unseen animal

1

crawling through shimmering grasslands, a lynx crouched in a sun-yellowed tree, and wolves howling beyond the fringes of a small bright campfire beside a lapping lake all have the power to make even the most carefully barbered nape hairs prickle involuntarily.

Man gets along in his steaming asphalt swamps after a fashion. But is it the healthy and normal life? Ask any family doctor, plagued as he is by long lists of complaints—symptoms of nothing so much as man's instinctive rebellion against the race to destruction into which he has pressed himself. Deep down underneath it may well be this very revolt that is driving him more and more toward those atomic weapons of annihilation that can plunge those of us who survive back to the cave, with its roasting haunch of venison sputtering above a simple warm blaze in front.

Beneath pastel shirt and doeskin slacks, even the most unassuming junior assistant is not far removed from the savage. His inherent ferocity is more painstakingly hidden, that is all. If anything, it is potentially all the more violent for having no natural outlet—like that can of beans the tenderfoot buries to heat, unpunctured, in the campfire's embers.

Call it what you will, but each of us still kills to live; though we may hire it done by the stockyard, the tannery, and the pharmaceutical house. As civilization stretches what has been called its gentling influence more benevolently about this battered globe, it is disturbing to have to agree with our military experts that in its ultimate aspects this carnage becomes more wholesale and ruinous. Better the instinct be more nearly answered, as nature intended, by the wholesome hunting and fishing for food and materials with which to remain alive!

The truth of this lies in the observation of Frank R. Butler, long head of British Columbia's Game Commission, that less than one per cent of the disturbingly multiplying hordes of juvenile delinquents have habitually followed hunting, fishing, or other outdoor activities. Commissioner Butler also cites the experience of Judge William G. Long of adjoining Seattle, who, noting that in over twenty years he has handled some 45,000 juvenile cases, recalled that among them there was not a single instance of serious juvenile misconduct involving a youngster whose hobby and recreational outlet was fishing. The inference is obvious.

One reaction crowding on the increasingly restless synthetic heels of formulae, and parities, and nuclear propellents is a yearning to return to the land. This is reflected by the facts that in the United States alone more than 32,000,000 hunting and fishing licenses are sold each year, that over 47,800,000 visitors are now recorded annually at our national parks and monuments, and that never has the demand for outdoor books been more avid.

Modern pioneers of both sexes, jolted from their ruts by cataclysm actual and threatened, want to laugh in farther places where meat is free for the hunting, fish for the catching, fuel for the cutting, land for the settling, and habitation for the satisfaction of building.

Such reversion toward the simple life is as wholesome as eggs and cream. Not everybody realizes that at the start of the last century less than four of every hundred Americans lived in communities of 8000 or more. By the start of the most recent world strife over half the republic's population was so confined.

The cost of a thing is the amount of life required to be exchanged for it, immediately or in the long run. When one has obtained those essentials necessary for well-being—food, shelter, warmth, and clothing—there is an alternative to struggling through steel jungles for the luxuries. That's to adventure on life itself, one's vacation from humble toil having commenced.

Whereas in his tangled metallic thickets a man does well merely to exist, back of beyond he can live—breathing clean air, beholden to none, doing what he wants most to do and giving it his best. That is why the day comes for even the more patient of us when a great town's restless movement becomes oppressive. A lot of inanities begin making even less sense; the remorseless hurry to get nowhere in particular, the hopeless and yet always hopeful bustle, and the more and more deadly boredom of grimly assertive amusements for an unamused multitude.

We all need the tonic of wildness. This is one reason why the hardest and roughest trips often become the milestones by which outdoor careers are later most pleasantly measured. We remember working a canoe, overloaded with game shot along the way, down the uninhabited Half Moon of the Southwest Miramichi River just before one New Brunswick freeze-up. The stinging whiteness of driving sleet became so heavy that it was difficult to pick a channel among the numerous onrushing rocks, to say nothing of retaining a hold with numbing hands on ice-encrusted paddles. Then there was a siwashing trip in a usually semiarid range of the northern Rockies when week after month of rain, attacking from overhead and underfoot and from sodden bush on every side, eventually soaked every portion of our small outfit so that there was no longer any ordinary comfort even in sleeping.

To some extent it is the satisfaction of having overcome such challenges that has emblazoned these hunts in our minds, while many an entirely enjoyable wilderness journey blends almost forgotten with the nostalgic past. Such gratification is based in part on the inhibition-ridding, doubt-dissolving realization that you have proved yourself equal to the worst the elements have to offer. Public opinion is a weak tyrant compared with our own private self-estimations.

It is recollections such as these which, reaching out with unbidden thoughts that quicken the breathing and add a tang of free conifer forests to even the stalest big-town air, keep pulling at us with the tentacles of rearoused racial memories until we break away from civilization's complications yet again.

Everyone answers such urges in his own fashion—with evenings of surf casting, holidays of ice fishing or banging away at clay pigeons, weekends of varmint plinking or making wood and screws spell boat, and in puttering around at odd hours with fly-tying kits or checkering tools. Each of us heeds them most of all with days and weeks of our favorite hunting and fishing or, if you are as fortunate as we two have been, with years upon years spent in the wildest and more stirringly remote areas of this continent.

CHAPTER 2

OUTDOOR OUTFITS and OUTFITTERS

THERE WAS NO SUCH THING as a sportsman's outfitter at the turn of the century. There were not even very many big-game hunters in the strictest sense of the term, although not a few of the adventurers who stampeded throughout the Yukon, British Columbia, and Alaska trailed northward under the flaming aurora as much in hope of bagging moose and grizzly as of finding gold.

Many ranchers, lumbermen, farmers, and others close to the outdoors, together with their fellow workers and occasional guests, hunted in the localities near to them. But most of our city men who could afford long wilderness trips were too busy making money. Comparatively few sportsmen hunted far afield, although this has become commonplace today. It was not until about 1900, as a matter of fact, that the Alaska brown bear and the Rocky Mountain goat became generally known among our North American big-game animals.

In the East about that time were a number of young college graduates, usually sons of rich fathers, who had spent their boyhood summers at camps in and around Maine and the Adirondacks. Here they had learned to love the woods. These young men, more or less under the influence of Theodore Roosevelt and his writings, began to turn their eyes farther afield to wilder country, to the West, and to the Canadian wilds. They formed the vanguard of our present-day phalanx of trophy hunters.

In those days when these adventurous young men wanted to hunt or fish in far regions not known to them, they customarily hired a guide. This guide was perhaps a trapper, logger, miner, or cattleman who knew his own particular wilderness. He furnished his personal

5

things, his blankets and his ax. In the West he often supplied pack-horses and rigging as well. In river and lake country he many times provided canoe, paddles, poles, and the like.

The sportsman saw to nearly everything else—tents, bedding, cooking and eating utensils, and the food. In fact, he usually brought most of this outfit with him from the city.

OUTFITTING

From about 1898, sporting-goods stores in the great cities such as Boston, New York, Chicago, and San Francisco began to furnish outfits to the growing number of outdoorsmen. There were tents of various kinds, duffle bags of one sort and another, grub sacks, a variety of blankets, and shortly thereafter the newly contrived sleeping bags which immediately provoked a stampede of adverse comment and sour looks, especially among oldtimers.

A lot of this particular disfavor stemmed legitimately from the earlier sleeping contraptions themselves, particularly those with waterproof covers which soon rendered all contents, including the occupant, clammy with retained body moisture.

These stores also rigged up a set of aluminum cooking and eating utensils that was so good that it has persisted as a sort of standard until the present day. A kit consisted generally of some three nested aluminum kettles with bails. Inside the smallest kettle went three or so aluminum soup bowls, as well as an equal number of enamel cups with handles open at the bottom so that they also would stack one inside the other.

Room remained for table knives, forks, spoons, a short butcher knife, spatula, dish mop, salt and pepper shakers, and so on, not forgetting the even then inevitable can opener. Nine-inch and twelve-inch frypans with detachable handles fitted on the bottom of the nested kettles, along with aluminum plates. The entire outfit packed into a canvas bag twelve inches high and wide. There were also such auxiliary items as folding aluminum reflector bakers and mixing pans which could be purchased separately.

You can still secure all these articles either in sets or individually, substituting if you want stainless steel cups for the still exceedingly popular enamel. In any event, you will wish to avoid aluminum cups which are as hot to drink from as a tomato can. No better outfit has, in general, ever been devised for the outdoor purpose for which it was designed. This is not true of considerable other outdoor equipment.

I bought a full outfit of this kind when I first started west in

1901. Arriving at my jumping-off spot which happened to be Ashcroft, British Columbia, I purchased a riding-horse, two pack-horses, and saddles. I packed my belongings and grub on the animals and started North alone, so in self-defense I got quite familiar with such a rig.

The cooking kit, it so happens, lasted me intact until 1916. Then a cayuca, a dugout canoe, in which I was cruising along the Caribbean coast got swamped. Everything that I owned went to the bottom except my rifle. But that is another story.

Soon afterward I duplicated the cooking outfit, and it has lasted me ever since. It's still intact and serviceable, and has gone with me on every trip where transportation was adequate.

EARLY OUTDOOR TRIPS

A fishing or hunting foray into the wilds during those early years was relaxingly primitive. In the West, your guide often took along a helper who combined the jobs of cook and wrangler. The guide charged about five dollars a day for himself and maybe three dollars for his hired help. He collected another dollar apiece daily for saddle-horses and half that amount for pack cayuses.

You furnished the grub and most of the outfit. You did as much work as anyone else and maybe a little more. The guide showed the way into game country, and you hunted alone. On moving days, all hands packed and rustled the animals.

Cooking was done over an open fire except when you ran into a top hand with a Dutch oven. The only difference in this case was that he sometimes buried this heavy utensil underground in a safe place where fire would not spread, with plenty of glowing embers above and below. On other occasions, he just set it among hot wood coals, some of which he raked over the top. These cooking fires were usually built in front of a large tarpaulin that was pitched as a lean-to.

Your guide in the Northeast charged about the same but usually threw in his canoe without extra cost. When there was a party, each sportsman customarily had a guide or cook in his canoe. You had to be more or less familiar with this type of watercraft, although as today you could serve an apprenticeship at the bow paddle. You helped over the portages. You pitched in with the various camp chores. You earned your sport and took a just pride in the thus-acquired ability to care for yourself afield under any and all conditions.

MODERN OUTFITTERS

Times have changed since then. Today's big-game hunter usually hasn't been schooled in the camps of northern New England, the Adirondacks, and the Sierras. Hunters and fishermen who can afford to travel to the increasingly distant forests and streams of our shrinking frontiers are in the main fairly successful professional and businessmen who on their first trips often know little or nothing about either wilderness life or outdoor living. Most are in a hurry.

Many of them, for one reason or another, expect to be cared for in every way imaginable. Not a few consider as their rights certain luxuries that the oldtimers not only never dreamed of but would scoff at even today.

And so the sportsman's outfitter has been born. He has crews of guides, cooks, bull cooks, wranglers, packers, and complete outfits of horses, saddles, panniers, and so on; or canoes with outboard motors and boats with inboard motors; or trucks, jeeps, station wagons, and even various types of aircraft.

You need only to provide your personal belongings, your time, and usually your firearms and rods. The latter can be rented instead. You have to give little thought to anything beyond arriving at a specified place at an agreed time.

Depending on where you go and how you travel, you will be provided with a cabin, or possibly a bedroom, or maybe a personal tent. Steps will be taken in cold weather to warm your quarters before you turn out in the morning.

On pack-train trips, for example, there will be a dining tent and often a separate cook tent with its own stove. Meals will include fresh bread and pie and cake baked in a real oven, heavy canned goods, numerous delicacies even to caviar and paté de foie gras—all previously okayed by the client from lengthy grub lists customarily mailed him well in advance.

Gone are the old Three-B days of beans, bacon, and bannock. Gone, more regrettably, is the wilderness life. Civilization has taken to the woods.

THE SYSTEM TODAY

For all this organized service, the outfitter will probably charge you about thirty-five dollars a day for extended eastern trips with canoes, and fifty dollars a day and upwards for western treks with a pack train. In the extreme Northwest and Alaska, expenses and therefore rates run higher. Trophy hunting in the remoter regions of this continent is now pretty much a rich man's game.

This, in general, is the system today, and at first glance it looks mighty rough for the modest fellow who longs for the freedom and the scope of the primitive wilds. The more helpers, animals, stoves, tents, and other equipment the outfitter supplies, the more he must charge. If you don't want it that way, there are plenty of others who can and will pay. By May of recent years, nearly every good outfitter has all his dates secured by deposits for the entire forthcoming season. In many of the more desirable hunting localities, furthermore, local laws require that a nonresident be accompanied by a registered guide.

As far as the outfitter is concerned, this in all fairness should be added. We happen to know throughout the continent a large number of outfitters personally, and not one of these is putting much money away. Most of them have to maintain very costly and quickly depreciating outfits, replacements for which come increasingly high. The productive seasons are comparatively brief.

It seems to us oldtimers that on trips of this kind you don't see or learn much about the genuine lure of the outdoors. You don't get to taste the peace, the contentment, the warm realization of adequacy, and the deep-seated sportsmanship that are revealed only to those who come to personal grips with the farther places. All these things to us old fellows fall within the list of the passions that can not be translated into words, so deeply are they rooted.

OUTDOORSMEN ARE STILL BEING MADE

But the wilderness is still a great educator and leavener. The western dude, or the eastern sport, who starts under these present comparatively luxurious conditions does not long remain a tenderfoot. Either he quits the game when he has a few heads to hang on his wall, or he becomes a real hunter, fisherman, and woodsman in his own right.

If you have red blood in your veins, a love for the beautiful, and a deep-down yearning for freedom and peace, you soon learn to do things for yourself. You take a more and more justifiable pride in your increasing competence. Perhaps you start out hardly able to step over a picket rope and end by hurdling the mountain.

As for the *good old days* that a lot of folks talk about, there are actually hundreds of square miles in North America alone that have never even been walked on yet.

AT HOME IN THE WOODS

There is another way to answer the lure of the wilderness. It is the way my present writing partner took. British Columbia challenged the co-author of this book, too, as it had me years before. There was also the matter of his not being able to afford an outfitter, guide, and pack train.

What he did was pack his outfit in duffle bags and head for a nearly vacant place on the map. For most of the last dozen years he has hunted, fished, camped, prospected, ridden his own horse, and lived in a log cabin on the Peace River where this wilderness stream bursts through the Rockies on its journey to the Arctic Ocean.

Why, asks much of the mail from readers of *At Home in the Woods, How to Build Your Home in the Woods, Wilderness Cookery,* and *How to Go Live in the Woods on $10 a Week,* did he so abruptly quit being a newspaperman and trade-journal editor to go to the woods? As a matter of fact, the transition wasn't so abrupt. Like a lot of others, he had been putting off going for a long time, working harder than he wanted at things he didn't particularly wish to do in order to be able to afford the sort of city existence he didn't care to live.

What finally decided him was a remark Henry Thoreau made a century earlier after living two years in the woods: "If you have built castles in the air, your work need not be lost. That is where they should be. Now put the foundations under them."

Nowhere but there at Hudson Hope, he and his wife have long since decided, can ever be their real home—where they can live deep and suck out all the marrow of life. A lamp is their lighting system, a pair of pails their water system. There are other inconveniences, too. Well, maybe some folks would call them that. They tell me they did before they realized these are also freedoms. If one doesn't have running water, there's no worry about meters and bursting pipes. If stoves crackle with your own wood, high fuel costs and labor management difficulties are something to plague the other fellow.

They, too, learned this by their experiment. If one advances confidently in the direction of his dreams and endeavors to lead the life which he has imagined, he will meet with a success unexpected in common hours.

TIME IS FOR THE LIVING

People have more leisure than ever before. Numerous men not many years ago accepted as an unchallenged fact the pattern of working hard all their lives in order to be able to retire some day to the uncrowded places. The months of countless others were measured by the few days they could snatch from each harried year for the brief free ecstasy of camping, fishing, hunting, or just plain rusticating.

Now the five-day, forty-hour week is commonplace. So are longer and longer annual vacations. Combined with all these are increasingly swifter and cheaper forms of transportation to whisk you where you will.

What you will need if you are going to take fullest possible advantage of the woods and hills and streams is, obviously, an outfit of your own. Not only is assembling such a rig one of the most consistent joys of the outdoorsman's life, but only when you are equipped to camp by yourself will you be in line to lead the simple life to the fullest.

The secret of being miserable is to have the leisure to bother about whether you are happy or not. This is one reason why for many individuals the most relaxing and pleasurable hours of the weeks and months' when they're ordinarily barred from the forests and lakes are those during which they keep busy in going over their outfits.

There are always a few items which, because they were not used during the last trip or even on the one before, you—being a reasonable man—regretfully relegate to the closet. Perhaps, it must be admitted, most of them are returned to the active pile during those moments of weakness, or lucidity, that are almost sure to intervene before the next excursion.

Then there are always those essentials without which you can do no longer, no matter what their purchase does to the budget. After you have gone through this process of adding, discarding, and reconsidering for years, you will have to admit even to yourself that there is no such thing as a perfect outfit. Trying to achieve the near ideal is, however, all the more challenging because of that.

It is some advantage to live a primitive life if only to learn what are the necessaries. Most of the luxuries and many of the so-called comforts are not only dispensable, but positive hindrances. Our life is frittered away with detail. To maintain one's self on this earth is not a hardship but a pastime, if we will live simply and wisely.

OLD TECHNIQUES OFTEN IMPROVED

A lot has happened since I first hit the trail. Scurvy, which was still taking a lot of outdoorsmen those early days, we now know can be simply and easily conquered back of beyond without the cost of a single penny. Several insect repellents that really work are available which have it all over the old tarry, smelly, and ineffective dopes.

All the shelter necessary for many an outdoor trip can now be carried in a shirt pocket.

On the other hand, good wool socks have not only never been surpassed, but they are still the only ones satisfactory for hiking. There are still a lot of downright harmful boots and a few very good ones. Much of the outdoor clothing made from synthetic fabrics is uncomfortable and even dangerous to wear. Some of the nylon tents can freeze you to death. Plastic dishes are no equal for the familiar old nested aluminum and steel favorites.

Techniques, too, have often been improved. That most conservative of all classes—we outdoorsmen—do not always hear nor are always told of these changes, however. For example, a recent observation of mine in one of the big outdoor magazines drew the following thoughtful, courteous, intelligent and, incidentally, characteristic letter:

"You say, 'The pack sags down into the hollow of your back and over half its weight rests on your hips. The notion that the pack weight should be carried high up on your shoulders is all wet.' We now turn to what is practically Holy Writ for the outdoorsman. Kephart states, 'Worse still, the pack rides so low that it presses hard against the small of the back, which is the worst of all places to put a strain on.' And speaking of the *Nessmuk* packsack, 'This packsack carries higher, and hence more comfortably, than a rucksack.' It would be blatant impudence on my part to criticize any of these statements. But I would be less confused if someone would equate all the above excerpts!"

KNEW NESSMUK AND KEPHART

My answer was: "I fear the authorities you quote on back packing are rather out of date. Nessmuk's *Woodcraft* dates back about 65 years, and Kephart's *Camping and Woodcraft* about 40 years. Lots of water has gone over the dam since then."

Except for a ten-day trip in Michigan some 70 years ago, the only back packing that George W. Sears (Nessmuk) ever did was across short carries between lakes in the Adirondacks. I met Nessmuk when I was a small boy; came on him in a small cabin on Eagle Lake in the Adirondacks one day. I remember him as a very friendly old man.

Kephart I knew personally and corresponded with a lot. A very fine man indeed! His is still the best book on its subject, but it is weak in parts, and Kephart did not have very extended field experience. In fact all his experience was confined to the Great Smoky Mountains in North Carolina and to some of the swampy country on the

Mississippi River below St. Louis, in neither of which places could he have acquired much information or experience on back packing. Kephart was well read, but there were relatively few books by specialists in outdoor living in his day. In Sears' time there were practically none.

Back packing is still being done over the whole world wherever there is country without road and river communications. In each locality the method is different, or at least slightly so. A man who has seen it only in one region is liable to be prejudiced by the method there used. But there is no locality where so much attention has been given to it by fairly educated men of ingenuity and resourcefulness as that country in our western mountains from northern California clear to the Arctic Ocean, and also among Alpinists the world over who climb high peaks for sport.

Here these men of long experience—hunters, trappers, prospectors, and sportsmen—have, in recent years, come in almost all cases to prefer either the Alaska packboard or the Bergans type of Alpine frame rucksack, and they invariably let the shoulder straps out so these packs sag down slightly. I have done most of my packing in this country (and in the wilder portions of Panama). I have been more or less associated with these men, and I have adopted their method because it has proved best.

If you tighten the shoulder straps on a pack so it rides high on the shoulders, the weight is both on top and on the front of your shoulders. The weight and pressure of the shoulder straps on the front of your shoulders tend to pull you backward. So you lean forward, and tighten up your stomach muscles, and this to some extent interferes with your breathing. The shoulder straps are so tight they cut into your shoulders. The weight, being carried high, tends to make you top-heavy, and you are not as surefooted. You have more or less trouble getting your arms through the straps and the pack up on your shoulders where it must be.

If you let the shoulder straps out slightly so the pack sags down a little toward and almost on the hips, then the weight comes almost entirely on the top of the shoulders. There is no weight or pressure on the front of the shoulders, and the pack does not pull you backward. The pack being lower, your center of gravity is lower. You are in better balance, and you are more sure-footed. It is far easier to put the pack on your shoulders and your arms through the straps. It's just like putting on and taking off a pair of suspenders.

WILDCRAFT

As each of us observes the world from a different trail, it is only natural that points of view will vary. Take for example three sportsmen approaching a water hole. One will see only the disappearing cubs. Another will see only the large bear hurrying nearer. The third will see both cubs and mother. All three will have seen what they were looking at, and all three will have been right.

We do not, for a moment, suppose that our ways are the only ways, but at least it may be helpful to know the other fellow's points.

CHAPTER 3

THREE GREAT CAMPING AREAS

DO YOU WANT a great new experience in camping? Throughout all tropical America, from central Mexico to southern Brazil, you will find vast stretches of unspoiled and practically uninhabited wilderness. Part of this is in grass and plains. Other portions are dense with thickets of so-called second growth. The biggest segment, however, is primeval rain forest thought of by most northerners as jungle.

Actually this is a true forest not much denser than many in the eastern United States, but with exotic growth and with many trees of remarkable size and height that stretch up and up before spreading their tops and hiding the sky. Beneath this canopy it is shady and cool. There is little underbrush, only some small palms and plants.

LIVING OFF THE LAND

This is an entirely different world from what most northern sportsmen are used to. It shelters a multitude of animals, birds, and freshwater fish that are more or less strange to the majority of us. All, incidentally, are good to eat.

This rain forest may not be particularly attractive to a hunter interested only in big game. The only fairly large animals are small deer, peccary, tapir, puma, and jaguar. These are all somewhat difficult to find, see, or hunt in the prevalent cover. But here you will find many species of small mammals, more birds than anywhere else in the world, and an exciting abundance of fish in the streams.

This is not a region, either, for sportsmen who expect to have their work done for them. There are few outfitters, guides, or even camp helpers. But if you are a lover of nature and if you like to wander through wild and unspoiled country, finding and winning your own way, the ancient wilderness of tropical America has a particular fascination.

Added to this, it is the easiest type of country that I know for camping and roaming. You can siwash there almost indefinitely, living off the land at scarcely any expense. The most valuable factor, as a matter of fact, will be your time. You'll find yourself becoming stingy with every hour.

CAMPCRAFT WITH A DIFFERENCE

It is always summer here. The climate within the prehistoric rain forest, however, is not nearly so hot and humid as that of many of our own southern states. Contrary to usually accepted notions, too, the forest is as healthy as any place in the world.

It is entirely practical to enter this pristine wonderland with only what you can easily pack on your back, to hunt and fish and photograph and live with nature for almost as long as you will, and all in all to have a glorious and totally different adventure that you'll never forget.

I know, for I have spent two years in doing just that.

The dry season and the wet season are all there are hereabouts. The arrival and the duration of these differ in various localities. You will naturally take them into account when making your plans. The vacationist will ordinarily prefer the dry months, of course, when it hardly ever rains. But actually the only difficulty that rainy weather presents is that of finding dry firewood.

For either season, only a very few precautions need to be taken, even less now than when I was there because of the tremendous advances in medicine during the past few years. Some of these simple safeguards are discussed in the chapter on camp pests. Your doctor can advise you of others. You should camp at night at least a mile from any native habitation so as to avoid mosquitoes that may be infected with malaria. You should always have a mosquito bar at night. Malaria carriers, as you are aware, do not attack until sunset.

Any skin abrasion or cut should get prompt attention. As this country is largely uninhabited, the water is likely to be pure. It is always well any place in the world, however, to take the usual brief precautions with drinking water that are considered in detail elsewhere in this volume. Rivers and small streams are found almost everywhere. A bath every evening followed by a change of underwear is, therefore, less a chore than a pleasantly awaited refreshment—and highly desirable.

In the tropical camp, shelter from rain, mosquitoes, and ants only is necessary.

PACKING

Climate and terrain make it an easy matter to camp, travel, and live in comfort with a surprising minimum of effort. Not even bedding, which comprises the heaviest and bulkiest essential camp impedimenta in the north, is needed here. Only the lightest shelter is required. There is even usable firewood everywhere without having to be cut.

You have your choice of two ways of traveling and living in this country. The first is to go afoot and pack everything on your back. This procedure sounds like a lot of work. Really, there is no way easier. Then you are absolutely foot-loose and free to wander wherever you like. Foot travel with a thirty-five-pound back pack is just as uncomplicated and practical here as in our own Appalachian and Pacific Coast regions where thousands of more or less inexperienced campers and hikers do it every year.

Since you largely eliminate bedding and shelter in the ordinary sense, your basic outfit is amazingly light and compact. This permits you to carry some twenty to twenty-five pounds of store grub. Hunting and fishing along the way you can make journeys or sojourns of up to a month and more, independent of all commercial sources of supply, entirely feasible.

Excellent packs are the frame rucksacks of the Alpine type and the pack board. These don't heat up your back. They are so adaptable that with them you can carry almost any amount or type of outfit.

MAKING CAMP

For combined bedding and shelter, you have a mosquito bar about seven by three by three feet. To the bottom of this is sewed a light waterproof ground cloth. This is left loose on one side so that you can crawl under the netting, then tuck it beneath the floor cloth to make a mosquitoproof and antproof shelter. Over all this is stretched the lightest fly you can get, possibly a section of plastic sheeting weighing three or four ounces.

To pitch camp you merely clear off a piece of flat ground, cut a dozen large palm fronds which are everywhere, haul them to the

On the trail in Panama. The little white roll contains shelter and bedding, and the author's rucksack holds all other equipment and grub for ten days, allowing meat or fish for one meal a day to be obtained from the country.

cleared place, and then with your machete lop off leaflets until they pile a foot deep. You stake down the ground cloth over this heap, and the green stuff mats down to a springy mattress six inches thick.

Support the corners of your mosquito bar with sticks, stretch the fly over all, and your camp is up. At night you crawl inside, strip off your clothing, and go to sleep on the floor cloth. I invariably slept raw, but one or two of my men preferred to take an ordinary sheet for cover.

A minimum of cooking and eating utensils will suffice, such as two small nesting pots, a frypan with folding handle, an enamel or stainless steel cup, and a few implements. You'll want a tiny first-aid outfit and a small toilet kit, as well as a few personal items. You'll pick up a machete instead of an ax, the latter being entirely unnecessary here. This with the bedding is all the basic outfit you will need or can reasonably use. It shouldn't weigh more than ten pounds including the pack, and you'll still have plenty of room to stick in this book if you want.

For food, take mostly items such as flour, cereals, edible fats not requiring refrigeration, salt, sugar, baking powder, powdered milk and eggs, instant tea or coffee, dried fruit, and so on—grub, in other words, that goes well with fish and game. As an emergency ration, you may care to include two pounds of rice. With all that, matches, compass, fishing and hunting equipment, and a good light knife, you can live in the rain forest for a long time.

For your sporting outfit, I would suggest a rifle for a load like the .22 Hornet, with a supply of full-charge cartridges for the larger game and, for smaller prey, reduced loads having ballistics similar to those of the .22 long-rifle cartridge. You'll also want fishline, snell hooks, and sinkers. A good 35-mm. camera, film in sealed waterproof cans, small exposure meter, a tiny clamp holding device, red and yellow and polarizing filters, and a self-timer will also be very desirable.

All you need in the way of clothing are khaki trousers and shirt, summer underwear, a broad brimmed hat, and rubber-soled basket-ball shoes with six-inch canvas tops. The shoes will last from two weeks to a month depending on how much wading in streams you do. Take a change of underwear and several pairs of light woolen socks, and each evening wash the ones you have worn during the day.

BY DUGOUT CANOE

If back packing doesn't appeal to you, the other way to enter such country is by paddling, poling, wading, and occasionally lining a dugout canoe called a cayuca up one of the smaller rivers that uncoil like lustrous threads from uninhabited country. On such a trip you can take more equipment and grub.

You can also substitute a jungle hammock for the previously described shelter. The hammock, though, is too heavy and bulky for back packing. It is no more comfortable, furthermore, nor is it easier to erect. Its bottom is a canvas sheet. Above this, rope supports a waterproof fly with net sides which lap over each other on the hammock to provide a mosquitoproof enclosure.

Don't get the idea, however, that mosquitoes infest this area in great numbers. They are all night flying only, and usually you'll run into only enough to make it potentially annoying when sleeping. As for snakes and venomous reptiles, they are no more plentiful than in our own South.

MAKING FINAL PREPARATIONS

Don't forget a compass. Often you won't be able to see the sun for hours because of the leafy ceiling overhead. Your compass is very necessary, too, for keeping oriented in cloudy weather. In a level country you might walk in circles and easily get lost. Often in such terrain I have found it necessary to keep a scratch map of my route, orienting and drawing in the back trail every mile or fifteen minutes, so I would know exactly where I had been and would be able to follow my route back.

If you keep your outfit with you always, however, you may elect to get lost promptly, keeping only enough track of your whereabouts so as to be able to steer your way back to civilization within some four or five days when your trip nears its end.

When you come out, what a tale you will have to tell about this entirely different world you have been in. Anyone who has sat by a fire at night in a camp deep in the jungle wilderness wants to go back. I hope that someday I can.

Such a trip naturally takes careful planning. You may want to handle the details yourself or to get help from a travel agency. If you're doing the job on your own, a good way to start is either by writing directly to the country you're interested in, or by visiting or otherwise contacting one of its local consulates. If none is in your area, write the consulate in Washington or in New York City. You will probably wish to ask for information on any regulations covering hunting, the bringing in of firearms, fishing, camping, and traveling in general. You may want to know if native helpers are available.

And when your planning is done and you are ready to head into the tropical mountains and valleys, you will be in for adventure and sport that's different from anything you've ever known.

THE APPALACHIAN TRAIL

There is a footpath extending 2,050 miles from Mount Oglethorpe in Georgia to Mount Katahdin in Maine. It crosses the restful wild areas along the crests of the Great Smoky, Blue Ridge, Allegheny and Catskill Mountains; ambles leisurely through the Berkshire Hills, the Green and White Mountains; and finally sashays through the sparkling lake and mountain country of Maine to its northern terminus. It is the free, serene, and slightly incredible Applachian Trail.

Among the feeder paths to this great wilderness thoroughfare is the Horseshoe Trail which starts at the historic Valley Forge battlefield and joins the main Appalachian Trail at Manada Gap, Pennsylvania. The Horseshoe, unlike the parent route, is a riding lane as well as a footpath. There are also numerous motor roads that cross the summits of these mountains, thus tapping the Trail and providing easy access to it from any of our eastern states.

This wilderness way twines for the most part, at elevations of from 2000 to 5000 feet, through high wooded mountains with many open crests and stirring panoramas. It passes, enjoyably, through a well watered country. There are campgrounds with fireplaces and a number of lean-tos along it for those who do not pack their own shelter. Camp spots innumerable exist everywhere for the more experienced.

Weather and travel conditions are best from about the middle of June to late September. The climate at these high altitudes offers a blessed relief during these months from the swelter of the lowlands, and the noisome smells and the grime and the nervous vaca-

On the Appalachian Trail.

tion traffic of the thronged, hot cities. Camping and hiking under almost arctic conditions is possible for the more strenuous during the snowy months. In fact, the region has often served as a laboratory for both of us in experimenting with winter camp equipment.

Here and there along the Appalachian Trail will be found an occasional lodge and small vacation resort. As a rule, however, it is all wilderness that is free for the enjoying. Those who plan to take fullest advantage of the outdoor opportunities the country affords must pack shelter and food on their backs, as it is a hiker's route and not a horse trail.

It is unnecessary to overburden one's self with weighty equipment and food, however. The mild summer nights require but a minimum of bedding, except in the unforgettable White Mountain areas above tree line where weather is unpredictable. A very light down bag is ideal. Every three or four hiking days along the Trail there are branch paths and sometimes roads winding down to farming land and small villages where country stores afford a chance to replenish food supplies.

FISHING AND HUNTING

Good fishing abounds in many of the streams that splash from the crests. Much of the Trail crosses national forests where hunting is permitted in season, always in conformity with state laws. Some of it passes through National Parks where fishing is permissible but not hunting nor the carrying of firearms unless these have been sealed or otherwise rendered inoperative.

I have had many pleasant hikes and camps along the Appalachian Trail, mostly in the Blue Ridge country and in the Green and White Mountains. It passes within three miles of my Vermont summer home in the Green Mountains.

The Appalachian Trail is a volunteer recreational project. It is supervised and maintained by the Appalachian Trail Conference with headquarters at 1916 Sunderland Place, N.W., Washington 6, D. C. This is a federation of organizations, mainly outing clubs, and individuals interested in the footpath. Its objectives and activities are entirely voluntary. Having no salaried employees, it disseminates complete information about the Trail by means of its pamphlets, guide books, and maps. A small charge is made for these. The funds so derived are used to republish the literature.

The data these contain is complete, and no other information is there available. Upon receipt of thirty-five cents in coin, the Conference will mail a pamphlet: *Suggestions for Appalachian Trail Users.* This gives general information and lists the other available

literature and guide books. The Conference has neither funds or facilities to answer correspondence except in this wise. All the information anyone needs is contained in their publications.

THE PACIFIC CREST TRAILWAY

The Pacific Crest Trailway extends from Canada to Mexico along the crests of the Cascade, Sierra Nevada, and Sierra Madre Mountains. Its some 2,156 miles stretch through many of the national forests and parks of the Pacific slope where it skirts such famous mountains as Rainier, Adams, Hood, Shasta, and towering Whitney.

This plainly defined course passes through Yosemite and Sequoia Parks. Often historic paths of many names are incorporated in its system, including the famous John Muir Trail. It has been largely built by the U. S. Forest Service and the National Park Service who maintain it. Only 160 miles in fact are outside our government forests and parks.

The long path from the Republic of Mexico to the Commonwealth of Canada is not a rustic lane for picnic parties. It is, in its rugged country-wide slash from dusty cactus to murmurous lodgepole pine, a wilderness route for expert outdoorsmen. This does not imply that numerous scenic portions of the Trailway, particularly in California, are not entirely feasible even for families with eight-year-old children and eighty-year-old grandparents. They are.

To publicize this true nature trail, the Pacific Coast Trail System Conference has been organized with headquarters in Pasadena, California. The Sierra Club, 1050 Mills Tower, San Francisco 4, California, is the organization that has done the most work in bringing the Trailway to the attention of the public and in fostering all that it stands for. Founded in 1892 with John Muir as its first president, the Sierra Club with its present thousands of members has devoted itself to the study and protection of the natural scenic resources, especially those of the mountainous strongholds of the western coast. Each year it organizes summer trips into the high hills and along the star-scouring trails where it maintains numerous camp sites, huts, and cheerful lean-tos.

PACK TRAINS

Much of the robust coarse, where not too steep or bare, is suitable for well shod pack animals as well as for hikers and back packers. Most of it passes through very wild country with considerable distances between supply points. For traversing many of the long stretches, animal transport becomes in fact necessary, since an individual with a pack can not reasonably carry more than about two weeks' grub.

This is a more challenging route, steeper in spots, than the Appalachian Trail. Some of it zigzags to altitudes one and two miles

On the Pacific Coast Trailway.

above sea level. Because of snow in the high country, portions are not always penetrable until well into July, and also the loftier passes can not usually be crossed until late September. Only those individuals capable of mountain travel in high altitudes should undertake trips in these rough places without either a guide or a companion familiar with the conditions that may be met.

Only a few railroads and highways cross the main Trailway. All along the mountains, however, there are many numerous roads entering from the lowlands. These bring you to it after one or two days of travel from traffic-clogged highways. Some of these side trails are, as a matter of fact, equal in scenic and recreational features to the north-south wilderness path itself. At the ends of many of these approaches will be found outfitters with pack animals and supplies for trail travel.

The outfitting business here is in the main well organized, with dozens of outfitters banded together in several associations. You can arrange for a packer with his train to take you along the trail as far as you wish, perhaps going in over one lateral road and coming out along another.

The more popular plan is to have an outfitter pack your duffle into a more or less permanent camp in some favorably situated locality and then take you out on some prearranged date. In the meantime, you can explore the region with a back pack. The country is so vast, and in most areas the scenery is so varied and grand, that you can easily spend a month or more taking short trips to and from an established camp and never exhaust the possibilities for variety and enjoyment.

MAPS

The best maps are those of the national forests published by the U. S. Forest Service, Washington 25, D. C. If you will mention the particular sections of the Trailway in which you are interested, this division of the Department of Agriculture will suggest the names and the very low prices of maps showing these.

The supervisors of the various national forests can furnish both planimetric maps of their particular areas and the names of outfitters in the regions you wish to penetrate. The two U. S. Forest Service regional headquarter offices covering the Trailway area are located at 630 Sansome Street, San Francisco, California, and in the Post Office Building, Portland, Oregon.

Forest Service maps, however, rarely include contours. Such information, showing the rise and fall of the land, can be invaluable in mountainous regions. If you are interested in contour maps of many areas, you can best contact the U. S. Geological Survey, Department of the Interior, Washington, D. C. They publish free index sheets of individual states and from these you can determine if the topographic maps you want are available.

SUGGESTIONS TO USERS OF BOTH TRAILS

As neither trail nor the country adjacent to it can be easily negotiated nor thoroughly enjoyed without some back packing, a readily carried outfit containing equipment and food for each person is very desirable. Large tents and other heavy rigging are both unsuitable and handicapping, except for extended and rather expensive pack-train trips along the western pitches. For back packing, everything should be cut down in weight and bulk to absolute essentials. Food should be largely water free.

Briefly, the total weight of the back pack for mountain travel in spring, summer, and fall should not exceed about thirty-five pounds for young and strenuous men. This maximum should be pared down to some fifteen to twenty-five pounds for women and juniors. As for proportions, the equipment proper in the largest pack should not weigh over fifteen pounds, thus allowing a food load of at least twenty pounds.

Ample subsistence for one man for one day is contained in two and one-quarter pounds of carefully selected and reasonably water-free foods. The thirty-five-pound pack, therefore, allows one to carry grub enough for over eight days, not including the day going in and the day coming out. Therefore ten days is on the average the practical duration of a back-packing trek between sources of supply, except when rations can be supplemented with wild edibles like fish and berries as one goes along.

The Pacific Crest Trailway is the rougher. Too, the nights there are apt to be cooler than on the Appalachian Trail. In the west, therefore, some of your equipment should approach that of the Alpinist. Strong mountain shoes, preferably with cleated rubber soles, are highly desirable. You'll also probably appreciate a warm jacket, shirt, or sweater for the evenings. Bedding should be a little heavier than along the Atlantic rim of the continent. A down sleeping bag, a mummy type weighing not over five pounds, will be excellent.

Along neither route is a regular tent essential during moderate weather. A compact plastic poncho, weighing less than a pound, will pinch-hit perfectly for both raincoat and shelter.

A compass is always desirable, as it is everywhere in wild places. Although both of these wilderness trails are well marked, it is easy to get mixed up on directions in the haze and clouds often encountered at high altitudes.

CHAPTER 4

THE MOST INEXPENSIVE VACATIONS

BACK PACKING—where you carry all necessary equipment on your back and wander, travel, and camp where you will in sheer wilderness, along hiking trails, or in the little woodland stretches near home—is one of the pleasantest ways of spending a vacation in the open. It has two advantages over all other ways of vacationing afield.

First: you are absolutely foot-loose, free, and independent to roam and pitch your shelter where you will. You need to rely on no one, and you have none of the bother and expense of automobiles, boats, and pack animals.

Second: it is the cheapest of all ways of vacationing. Once you have assembled your small and inexpensive outfit and have arrived at your jumping-off place, you can hunt and fish and prospect at no further expense other than for food—for less than it costs to live at home.

There is nothing particularly new about hiking and camping with only what we can easily pack on our backs. Our early frontiersmen traveled that way whenever they entered the wilderness. Daniel Boone spent two whole years more or less alone in the virgin wilderness of Kentucky, living off the country, with no outfit except that which he had been carrying when he left.

Modern equipment and improved methods have been developed that rid the pastime of its drudgery and hard physical work. It will pay us to look carefully at these methods and equipment, for they are based on experience. Those who have never done any back packing in the right manner with a good outfit have the idea that it is the toughest kind of toil. We often hear the expression, "I do not propose to make a pack horse of myself!" It is a lamentable fact that about half of those who attempt such a vacation never repeat it because they have found it too much like hard work, due entirely to improper equipment and mistaken technique.

Done right, there is nothing hard about it. You wander free and unfettered, with just enough easy exercise in the pure air to make the life thoroughly enjoyable, and with so much hearty and healthy pleasure that you repeat such excursions year after year. We propose to show you here the right way to do it.

WHO CAN GO?

Those who have adopted the best methods of back packing, formerly known only to a few, are returning to the trails and bringing others with them. Many are combining the satisfactions of hiking and camping with hunting and fishing in unspoiled wilderness, all this at costs that elsewhere they could not even approximate.

Such trips are not only for the strenuous young man, but for anyone healthy and fairly vigorous. They can be equally enjoyed by wives, by teen-agers of both sexes, and by the older among us. In fact, one of the last hikers I have encountered who has traversed the entire 2050 miles of the Appalachian Trail in a single season was a gentleman seventy years old—George F. Miller of Washington, D. C. He covered every foot of it in 1952, carrying his pack and camping out almost every night. One day that summer my grandson, Townsend Whelen Bowling, was fishing in a wild spot near our Vermont home and came across Miller who had missed the trail and was seeking information. Towney brought him back to me, and I had the pleasure of entertaining him and setting him on the path again.

At the other extreme, parents can even take their little tots along.

WHERE TO GO?

"Along where?" you may ask.

Carrying your all on your own back, you can journey in any sparsely settled and fairly well watered country. In the little hilly spots of rambling woodlands close to our big cities. In the glorious rolling and mountainous regions along our entire eastern seaboard where the Appalachian Trail wends from Georgia to Maine, and in the broad wild stretches adjacent.

Toting everything you need, you can rove along the Pacific Crest Trailway from northern Washington to the Mexican border. In any of the National Forests and National Parks scattered all over the

United States. In the woods of all of our Atlantic States. In the forests of northern Michigan, Wisconsin, and Minnesota, and in the Ozark Mountains. In the pinon and cactus highlands about Taos, New Mexico, where Kit Carson made his camps earlier.

If you live near crowded New York, there are the Catskill Mountains only three hours away by auto. North of Boston, beyond the inviting roads of Essex and Gloucester, are the White Mountains with the Little Imp and other unforgettable trails. Just east of Philadelphia are the South Jersey pine barrens. From the capital of our country, the cloud-scoured Blue Ridge is only two hours distant.

Two things only are essential: fresh water, which you can purify if you must, and country where you can pitch camp without trespassing.

Spring, summer, and early fall are the usual recreational seasons, but winter weather is no deterrent to those fairly conversant with wildcraft. One mid-January morning we left Washington, D. C., and three hours later said good-by to noise, gasoline fumes, and crowds. Shouldering our pack, we swung off toward the horizon to spend two delightful weeks in the lovely mountains just west of the Shenandoah Valley.

WHAT ABOUT WEIGHT?

A basic consideration is how much weight can we carry, all day long if necessary, over the fairly rough and perhaps steep trails we may strike in wilder terrain. Typical country of this sort is encountered on the Appalachian and the Pacific Crest trails. Each summer along these wilderness routes thousands, young and old, pack their every necessity on hiking vacations of from several days to a few weeks.

It is on these proving grounds that the experienced and enthusiastic members of the Appalachian Trail Conference, the Sierra Club, and allied mountain-climbing groups have developed a modern technique vastly superior to older haphazard methods. These procedures are thoroughly in accord with the modern practices of scalers of the world's loftiest mountains. They coincide, too, with the down-to-earth practices of the hardy trappers, prospectors, and hunters of the really wild and remote regions of Alaska, British Columbia, the Yukon, and the jungle country of Central and South America.

All this experience has clearly indicated that a young, vigorous, and athletic man should not attempt a backload of over thirty-five pounds for his first year or two of packing over fairly rough country.

This is for hikes of two or more days, averaging from five to fifteen miles a day in fairly good weather. After the first year or two his own experience will be his guide as to how much he can pack without undue fatigue and without making his trip anything but a pleasure. The limit for the similarly vigorous and athletic young woman is about twenty-five pounds.

These weights must be graded for others, as youth, age, and physical condition impose limitations. All this is for all-day hiking. It has no reference to what it may be possible to pack a few miles to a more or less permanent camp. It has no connection with the loads that can be wrestled a mile or so across a canoe portage. We are not discussing that kind of packing at all.

Almost every hiker in the past has overloaded himself, at least at first, under the impression that he needed a lot of stuff if he was to avoid hardships. If you take the right articles and use them in the right way, there are no hardships. There are two slogans which the back packer should adopt: "Go light but right." "When in doubt, leave it out."

MILEAGE

Mileage depends on such concrete factors, among other things, as the country, the roughness and steepness of the trail, the climate, and particularly the temperature. Experienced hikers of average good physique, carrying a pack of a weight commensurate with their capabilities, should average from two to fifteen miles a day in good, reasonably cool weather. This they should do without becoming exhausted to a point where hiking is no longer a recreation. At the end they should arrive in condition to make an agreeable camp and enjoy their supper and a wholesome night's rest.

Never press if you can avoid it. Let the mileage depend upon the condition and steepness of the trail. Some day you may be up against an exceedingly steep and hard climb up a mountain the first thing in the morning. The two-mile struggle to the top leaves you dripping with sweat and feeling quite exhausted. If you are in good physical condition, a short rest will be all it will take to make you feel tops again. But after such an exertion it will usually be unwise to attempt more that day, and you had better stop and camp at the first half-decent spot. On the other hand, on a fine brisk day over a good trail, fifteen miles may be just a delightful jaunt, particularly if the scenery is stimulating.

THE BASIC PACK

In dry temperate weather a hiker on lonely trails can get along all right for a night or so lying by a fire without bedding or shelter and eating food either uncooked or roasted on a forked stick. But on an extended trip he must carry an outfit which will insure adequate protection from rain and wind, undisturbed sleep, and good nourishing meals. Anything less then this spells discomfort, needlessly wasted energy, possible injury to health and, decidedly, no fun.

Detailed experience by those who have long specialized in back packing indicates that for summer and early fall the lightest practical camp and trail outfit, not including food, will weigh about fifteen pounds. Every effort should be made to keep it below this maximum. For colder weather, where night temperatures approach zero, the basic weight should be increased by an additional two pounds of waterfowl down insulation in the sleeping bag.

Your basic pack should contain all the necessary provisions for shelter, warmth, dryness, comfort, and for the preparation and eating of meals. If the total load is going to be limited to thirty pounds, for example, this then will permit the carrying of fifteen pounds of food.

A stalwart individual, doing hard outdoor work such as hiking and back packing, needs just about two and a quarter pounds of well selected and reasonably water-free grub per day to maintain energy. If the hiking country through which one journeys does not permit replenishment of food, fifteen pounds of provisions will suffice for seven days not including breakfast at the start of the first day. With a total load of thirty pounds, in other words, the duration of one's trip is limited to about one week by the amount of food that can be included.

This week can be extended almost without limit if there are stores, towns, or farms along the trail where victuals can be restocked from time to time as needed. Such supply points exist every ten to thirty miles along many of our more popular hiking ways, either alongside the particular route or a mile or so off it.

LIVING OFF THE LAND

It is also interesting to note that in a wilderness, laws permitting, one can replenish his food not only with wild fruits and vegetables as he goes along, but also with fish and game. In fact it has been proved hundreds of times that if a man is a competent woodsman, hunter, and fisherman, he can thrive indefinitely in a good game country just by living off the land. It is entirely possible to subsist for months and even years on fat rare meat alone, as a matter of fact, and yet maintain perfect health and vigor.

The basic outfit must then include preferably the firearm most suitable to the region, sufficient ammunition, fishhooks or a fish net, snare wire, and an adequate supply of matches. Clothing, as it is worn out, can be replaced from the skins of the animals secured. Not even salt is essential. After you've gone without salt for a few weeks, you'll very possibly find it not even particularly desirable once you've tried it again.

Living Off the Country by Bradford Angier, and published by the Stackpole Company, covers this vital and engrossing subject in detail.

WHAT SHELTER WILL YOU NEED?

Some kind of shelter is usually essential for overnight camps on hiking trips as protection from rain, wind, and possibly even snow or mosquitoes. You seldom get the last two together, as a matter of fact. A tent is usually thought of in this connection. But especially during the warm months, a tent is usually not only unnecessary, but is needlessly costly and bulky.

One outfitter furnishes a waterproof and bugproof tent, intended for Alpinists and back packers, that weighs three and three-fourths pounds, rolls into a bundle eleven inches by five inches, and costs thirty-five dollars. In some country and during some seasons such a piece of equipment is a fine thing to have along.

The expense and weight of a tent can be dispensed with in almost all temperate North America from the middle of June through the first half of September, however. One's bed can be sheltered instead with a simple tarpaulin, about five feet by seven feet, stretched as a lean-to with its back toward the direction from which storms are likely to come. For cheerful warmth, a fire built five feet or so in front of such a lean-to will reflect light and heat into it.

Such a tarp, made of nylon or very light plastic sheeting, need weigh only a few ounces. The commercial Koroseal Poncho, obtainable from most dealers in camp supplies, measuring sixty-six inches by ninety inches and weighing fifteen ounces, is excellent for this purpose. It will also serve as a raincoat, covering both person and pack. It can be used, too, below the bedding to keep out dampness from the ground. In the unlikely event of a wind that blows the rain into the lean-to, the bed can be protected by a roof of spruce boughs thrown up in front of the shelter which will cause the drops to fall straight down instead of driving in on the bed.

Such an arrangement makes a very practical and comfortable bivouac at savings of about thirty-one dollars and two and one-half pounds as compared to the previously mentioned tent.

SLEEPING WARM

Your bed will be the bulkiest and heaviest article in your pack. In summer weather when night temperatures do not ordinarily go below forty-five degrees Fahrenheit, an all-wool blanket weighing about three pounds will suffice for more sturdy outdoor individuals. The Army and Marine Corps blankets to be had from dealers in surplus goods are fine, or a blanket can be requisitioned from a home closet.

There are two secrets for keeping warm on cool nights with light bedding. One is to turn in dry and fully clothed, except for shoes. Garments and bedding can, of course, be dried before the campfire if necessary. The other prerequisite is to have a soft mattress so that one's weight will press only a minimum of the insulating dead air out of the coverings. This mattress can be made of spruce or other evergreen boughs, shingled on the bed space as described elsewhere. Pine needles, leaves, or grass gathered close by can also be used.

A typical back packer's bivouac. The thin plastic tarp, pitched as a lean-to, gives protection from rain, and reflects heat from the fire on the bed. Weighs less than a pound. The sleeping bag, insulated with two pounds of goose down, weighs about four pounds.

Also, a plastic air mattress of Vinylite is available in sections each two feet square and each weighing fourteen ounces. Two sections snapped together makes a mattress twenty-four by forty-eight inches, which is ample. While this means additional weight of nearly two pounds, plus some bulk, the result is an extremely comfortable bed at every camp.

The very best bedding of all for the back packer, particularly where night temperatures are liable to be rather low, are the light mountain sleeping bags insulated with pure waterfowl down, discussed in the chapter on beds.

If the hiker is using a frame rucksack—one of the only two really satisfactory types of packs for back-packing vacations, as we will consider pro and con in the following chapter—the bedding is rolled into a bundle about five inches by eighteen inches with the poncho on the outside. This bedroll is strapped on the top of the rucksack, perhaps under the flap which closes the main sack.

With the pack board—the sole remaining candidate and in some respects the most ideal pack for such use, although in a few other characteristics not quite as fine as the frame rucksack—both poncho and bedding are laid flat. The other contents of the pack are stacked atop them. Then everything is rolled into a bundle about fifteen inches by thirty inches with the poncho outside. If several short lengths of light rope or cord are used for binding this, these will come in handy for such camp uses as lashing together the pole framework for the lean-to.

WHAT'S FOR SUPPER?

Cooking utensils are the next consideration in the outfit. One must have appetizing, well cooked, and nourishing food when doing strenuous work outside. This usually means for each meal something boiled in a kettle, a hot drink, and something cooked in a pan. For the lone camper, therefore, the minimum is two small kettles, always with covers and with bales by which they can be hung above a wood fire, a small frypan with folding handle, a tablespoon, and either an enamel or stainless steel cup.

The frypan will serve as a plate, and cereals can be eaten from the cup. One's pocket or sheath knife can be used whenever needed. A forked stick will do for a fork. One Hudson's Bay Company trader one of us has eaten with on the trail did surprisingly well for a Scotsman with a couple of peeled green sticks, which he wielded like chopsticks.

Two nesting alumnium kettles, the larger holding a quart and a half and the smaller one quart, together with an eight-inch aluminum frypan, are available from dealers in camping goods. Weighing twenty-five ounces, these take up no appreciable bulk in the pack, for grub and other essentials can be packed inside them.

Contents of back pack, with shelter, equipment, and grub for a week, Weight about thirty pounds. If two packers share cooking utensils the pack of each is reduced about two pounds. If camera, ammunition, or fishing tackle is included the weight is increased about two pounds. High-altitude country necessitates an increase of a pound of down in the sleeping bag.

When there are two or three persons in the party this same outfit of two kettles and frypan will suffice, plus a light aluminum plate, stainless steel or enamel cup, and a spoon for each person. All these utensils can be divided among the hikers.

For packing such articles as cereals, flour, and sugar, small plastic bags with tie strings can be used. If the plastic is transparent, most of the contents can be recognized at a glance. A small aluminum jar will do for items like butter and lard. Bacon may be wrapped in aluminum foil. Matches should be carried where they will be safe both from moisture and from the teeth of small animals such as squirrels.

A small dishcloth is a convenience. You can conserve soap by washing your dishes at the creek or lake edge, using a bunch of grass with earth attached to the roots for scouring. This and other related subjects are considered in detail in the chapters on food.

WHAT ELSE TO TAKE

Other desirable and essential additions to the camp outfit, depending to some degree on the individual and the country, may include: A small hand ax weighing, with sheath, a pound. The smallest toilet outfit you can get along with, containing perhaps a toothbrush, comb, hotel-size cake of soap, safety razor wrapped in a light crash towel, and mirror, together with any other necessities. A small medicine kit with usually just a cathartic, a few small adhesive bandages, some foot powder, several aspirin tablets, etc. Perhaps the smallest available flashlight although this is not indispensable. Writing materials. A map of the locality.

Some extra clothing will be welcome but should be held to a minimum. After a strenuous day on the trail, the hiker is apt to arrive at his campsite pretty well damp with perspiration. A rubdown and the donning of dry underwear and socks will pay off in refreshed well being. One set of light underwear and one extra pair of socks are therefore necessary for keeping a change freshly washed at all times.

One usually wears something such as a light khaki overshirt when hiking in warm weather, and then a medium weight wool shirt will be desirable for wear after nightfall. In colder weather, a poplin or similar light jacket to go over the wool shirt will add the warmth appreciated on cold nights.

In his pockets each individual should have a filled, unbreakable, waterproof match case. He should also have a small luminous compass, watch, sturdy pocketknife, handkerchief, sunglasses perhaps, and if he has to wear corrective spectacles an extra pair of these. Include smokes if you are addicted to the weed.

Almost always a camera is desired. One should suffice for a party, each hiker using it for such pictures as he wants. Ideal are the best light and compact 35-mm. jobs. We both eventually managed along the way to come by Leicas.

It is usually best for each hiker to carry his own shelter and bedding and to make his own individual camp each night. He then gets it exactly as he wishes, and he alone is responsible. Incidently, two lean-tos pitched facing each other, with the fire between, make a particularly snug camp in cool weather.

Now let us enumerate all this equipment in the form of a check list, suggesting the weights of each article and the total weight of the basic pack.

BASIC PACK

Frame rucksack or pack board	3 lbs. 12 oz.
Plastic tarp and Koroseal poncho	1 " 5 "
Blanket or down sleeping bag	3 " 8 "
Cooking utensils as above *	1 " 12 "
Hand ax with sheath *	1 "
Underwear and socks	12 "
Wool shirt, jacket, or sweater	1 " 8 "
Toilet articles	8 "
Flashlight, whetstone	6 "
Medicines, needles, thread, buttons	4 "
Total weight without food	15 lbs.

* In a party of two or more these articles will be used in common, each individual carrying his share. Add a plate, cup, and spoon to cooking utensils for each additional man.

FOOD

You can now figure on adding to the basic pack sufficient food to bring the total weight up to the determined maximum which, as previously explained, should not ordinarily exceed twenty-five pounds for the more athletic women and youths, nor thirty-five pounds for vigorous outdoor men. About two and one-quarter pounds apiece per day will be eaten, indicating the number of days the grubstake will last without replenishment.

Many like to balance this in the following proportions by weight: starches 25%, sugars 15%, fats 10%, proteins 30%, fruits 15%, beverages, seasoning (and matches) 5%. This very important subject of rations for outdoor living is covered in detail in later chapters.

ENCHANTED AND ENCHANTING

And so at the end of the paved trail—shouldering your pack and striding into enchanted and enchanting country—you leave behind the unhealthy tension, bustle, noise, fumes, expense, and frustrations of civilization. There is no other kind of vacation that will compare with these; none that will take you so close to peace and utter freedom.

Footnote:

Those desiring to take up back packing often find it difficult to obtain the desired equipment, particularly some of the articles mentioned in this chapter.

The Potomac Appalachian Trail Club, 1916 Sunderland Place, Washington 6, D.C., publish an informative pamphlet called *Hiking, Camping, and Trail Clearing Equipment,* which they sell for fifty cents to defray cost. It gives the names and addresses of firms selling equipment for back packers and the items available together with prices, dimensions, and weights.

The following are the names of some of the catalog publishing firms specializing in back-packing and Alpine equipment. One or more of them handle the articles mentioned in this book.

D. T. Abercrombie Co., 97 Chambers Street, New York 7, N. Y.

Abercrombie & Fitch Co., Madison at 45th St., New York 17, N. Y.

Camp & Trail Outfitters, 112 Chambers St., New York 7, N. Y.

Gerry, Box 910, Ward, Colorado

Holubar, 1215 Grandview Ave., Boulder, Colorado.

Le Trappeur, Inc., 438 Stuart St., Boston 16, Mass.

Norm Thompson, 1805 N.W. Thurman, Portland 9, Oregon.

Smilie Outfits, 536 Mission St., San Francisco 7, Calif.

Trailwise, 1615 University Avenue, Berkeley 3, Calif.

THE TWO GOOD HIKING PACKS

CHAPTER 5

WHAT TYPE OF PACK should you use to carry outfit and grub on your back? The answer is as significant as that one about whether or not you can kill a grizzly with a .22 short fired from a single-shot rifle, this sort of low-powered armament being carried a lot in country where red squirrel also abound.   These little rim-fire cartridges put out about 80 foot-pounds of muzzle energy, whereas the ordinary 30-06 cartridges develop closer to 2900.

Two of our friends have done it, one to save his pack dog and the other by reflex action resulting from sheer surprise when a curious grizzly reared up practically above him in thick bush. Neither has ever chosen to attempt it a second time.

Each year we see dozens of enthusiastic hikers, on our popular trails and in our national parks, struggling along with poor packs that are continually distressing them to such an extent you can tell they're not having much fun. You know, too, that it is unlikely that they will repeat a back-packing vacation the following year. If they do, in all probability they won't do it with the same outfit.

One camping outfitter lists nine models of back packs in his catalog. Some of these are terrible punishers. Others are good only for portaging heavy loads over short carries on canoe trips. Only two are satisfactory for comfortably packing one's duffle day after day over trails and through wilderness country.

The ideal packsack or pack board should be strong and durable, should accommodate all your camp outfit and grub, should neither abrade nor overheat shoulders and back, should be easy to put on and take off, and should support the weight rather low on your back so that you will not be top-heavy and so uncertain of your footing on rough ground.

Again we turn to the experience of our old and seasoned back packers, as well as to Alpinists who have to carry their equipment and food in high and steep country all day long. These individuals have found that only two types of packs are really satisfactory for back-packing excursions.

FRAME RUCKSACK

The first of these is the Bergans type of frame rucksack. This is the type preferred by almost all Alpinists. It consists of a waterproof canvas sack with a large central compartment for the bulky and heavy articles, a flat back pocket, and two smaller side pockets for odds and ends. Flaps buckle protectively over all pockets. Rings or loops provide for the strapping on of additional articles around the outside.

On the back of this pack is a triangular metal frame to which the two leather shoulder straps are attached. Across the outwardly curving base of this often tubular form is stretched a web band which rests against the lower back or top of the hips.

This rucksack should be adjusted to ride a little low on the back. It should not be carried tight and high up on the top of the back,

Alpine frame rucksack. The roll of poncho, shelter tarp and sleeping bag is shown carried under the flap of the large compartment.

as is often seen, but rather sagging down a little so that considerable of the weight rests low on the broad of the hips. The center of gravity is thus kept low and any unstable feeling of top-heaviness avoided.

The pack will not then actually touch the body. It will droop slightly away, with the result that there will be a circulation of air between the pack and the back, preventing overheating and chafing. That portion of the weight borne by the shoulder straps will come straight down on top of the shoulders, instead of pulling back on the front of the shoulders and making one lean forward in a rather exhausting manner to overcome the back pull.

This type of pack is usually thought to be slightly superior to the pack board in that the articles one is likely to need during the day can be stowed in the small pockets, where they can be reached without unpacking the entire load.

Excellent models are made by at least four firms catering to back packers (D. T. Abercrombie, Camp & Trail Outfitters, Trailwise and Norm Thompson). Others have long been imported. During World War II it was used considerably by our mountain troops, and after the hostilities the Army disposed of their excess to surplus dealers, from whom one can still occasionally be purchased at a very reasonable price.

THE ALASKAN PACK BOARD

The second type of pack that has been found eminently satisfactory is the Alaskan pack board. The nucleus of this is a rectangular wooden or fiber frame about fifteen inches wide by thirty inches long, over which a canvas is doubled and tautly laced. There is about a two-and-one-half-inch space between the two areas of canvas which, because only one expanse of canvas rests against the back, insures a free circulation of air. The effect is exactly as though you were lying on your back on a canvas cot.

There are two cross members to this frame, the top one being about six inches below the top of the form. To it is attached, closely together, the two broad leather shoulder straps. These pass through a slit in the canvas on the side towards the back and their lower ends are fastened to the lower outside corners of the board.

Your outfit and grub are tightly wrapped in a tarp, tent, or poncho so as to form a compact bundle about fifteen inches in diameter and some thirty inches long. This is lashed to the outside of the pack board by several short ropes. Because the load does not touch the back at all, being held away by the space between the two cover-

Underside of Alpine frame rucksack, showing metal frame, shoulder straps, and band that rests on hips.

ings of canvas, you can pack anything from a bag of ore to an outboard motor without bruising or chafing.

The pack board should have its shoulder straps adjusted so that it sags down just a little and some of the weight comes on the lower back of the hips. The shoulder straps will then bear straight down on the top of the shouders instead of pulling uncomfortably backwards, the same as with the frame rucksack.

The commercial model of the Alaskan pack board, known as the Trapper Nelson Pack Board, is furnished by almost all dealers in camp equipment. Three sizes are made. The medium size, fourteen and one-half inches by thirty inches, is right for sportsmen. The small size, thirteen inches by twenty-six inches, is excellent for women and youths.

It can be had with a large canvas dunnage bag that laces to it. This is only extra weight, however. It is usually best to purchase the pack without the bag and to tie your outfit on in a cover that has some other use, and so pays for its weight and bulk.

The Army also used a similar pack board for heavy mountain carrying in World War II. This is strongly and substantially made over a fiberboard frame. Some can still be found in surplus stores.

MAKE AN ALASKAN PACK BOARD

The following instructions are based on the Alaskan pack board as made in Juneau, Alaska, the model suggested having been perfected by J. C. Liston in collaboration with my good friend Jay Williams, formerly of the U. S. Forest Service and later one of the leading outfitters and guides in the Territory. Both are now across the Great Divide.

Procure some strips of Sitka Spruce, oak or other strong wood, 2½ inches wide and 1/2-inch thick. Cut two strips 28 inches long for the sides of the frame. Round the top ends but leave the bottom ends square.

Cut two other strips for the crosspieces, one 12 inches long and the other 15½ inches long. Join the two sidepieces by the two cross-pieces, making a frame as shown in Fig. I. The top of the upper cross member should come 6 inches down from the top ends of the side-pieces. The bottom of the lower cross member should be 3 inches above the bottom ends of the sidepieces.

The edge of the sidepieces and the flat of the crosspieces face the packer's back. (See Fig 1, and Fig 3.) Notice that the crosspieces are flush with the edge of the sidepieces farthest from the packer's back.

The crosspieces must be fastened to the sidepieces very accurately and strongly. Use angle irons with two wood screws in each face of the irons. These can be bought in the size you need at most hard-ware stores.

Alaskan pack board. Contents is wrapped in poncho, tarp, and sleeping bag, and lashed• to the outside of the canvas-covered board frame.

The resulting frame will be 13 inches wide at the top, 16½ inches wide at the bottom, 28 inches high, and 2½ inches thick.

LACING ON THE CANVAS

Over this frame you lace a cover of twelve-ounce canvas, cut and made as shown in Fig. 2. It is 28 inches wide at the top, 35 inches at the bottom, and 25 inches high, and covers the frame to within 1½ inches of top and bottom.

Hem it all around and insert seven brass grommets along each side edge for lacing. These are obtainable from many outfitters and from all tent and awning makers. The latter two will insert them for you if you wish. One outdoor supplier, for example, sells grommets at a cent apiece and will install them for an additional five cents apiece. On the side edge hem the cover with two folds, fastening the grommets through both folds so they won't pull out.

Three and a half inches down from the top edge there should be a horizontal slit, 8 inches long, strongly reinforced at the edges. This is for the shoulder straps to pass through.

Do not make the mistake of using too light canvas—twelve ounces is right. This canvas cover is laced around the frame, drum tight, by means of strong cod line or leather thong passed through the grommets. The slit comes on the side toward the packer's back, and the lacing on the side of the frame where the crosspieces are flush with the edges of the sidepieces. (See Fig. 3.) The grommetted edges of the cover should not meet by about 2 inches so the canvas can be laced up very taut with the cord or throng.

THE SHOULDER STRAPS

The upper ends of the shouder straps are secured around the top crosspieces of the frame at its center. They pass through the slit in

Under side of Alaskan pack board.

the canvas, then around and over the packer's shoulders, and finally are secured to the outside of the sidepieces of the frame 6 inches above the lower ends of these members as shown in Fig. 4. A piece of leather with 1-inch buckle is screwed to each of the sidepieces for this purpose.

The straps are best made of heavy chrome tanned leather, saturated with neatsfoot oil. They should be 2 inches wide at the top and where they go over the shoulders, tapering to an inch wide at the bottom where they are secured to the buckles.

Holes are punched in the straps to provide for their adjustment for length. It is not necessary to have any snap fasteners at the bottom of the shoulder straps.

PUTTING IT ON

After these straps have been adjusted for length, they can most conveniently be placed over the shoulders just as one puts on his coat or suspenders. Stand the loaded pack board upright on the ground. Sit down, and place your arms through the straps. Run your thumbs under the straps to make sure they snuggle right into the shoulders. Then stand up.

Figure 3 shows a section as viewed looking down from the top. Figure 4 shows a side view with the shoulder straps in position and with a load lashed on the board. Holes are drilled in top and bottom of the sidepieces of the frame, to which to attach the lashing ropes.

TUMP LINES

In other portions of the world, natives frequently with little ingenuity and with few materials at their command use all kinds of back packs dictated by their customs for many generations. Such packs are good, bad, and indifferent; mostly the last two. But in the northern portions of North America, away from roads and horses, packing is done largely by red-blooded and intelligent Americans and Canadians. Their inventive genius, coupled with experience and fierce free feeling of independence, has developed the very best back-packing contrivances.

For canoe country where the freighting is over portages seldom as long as a mile, the tump line passed around a bundle wrapped in a tarp, or a combination of Duluth or Woods packsack with tump line attached, is generally used.

But such a pack heats and galls the back after an hour or more of packing. With head and neck immobolized by tump line, one can not look around, enjoy the scenery, or easily use gun or rifle

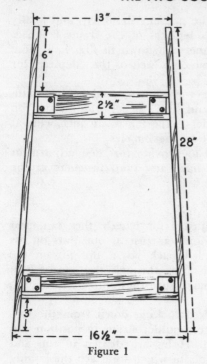

Figure 1

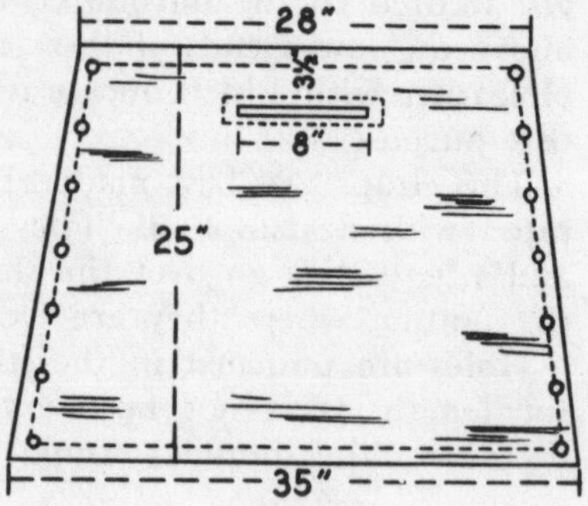

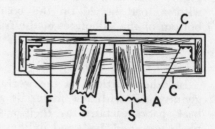

Figure 2

Figure 3
F-Wood frame. A-Angle iron. C-Canvas
cover. L-Lacing of cover. S-Shoulder
strap.

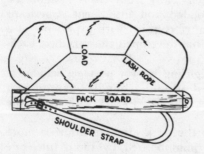

Figure 4

if desired. Neither can he examine the country ahead for the least restricted way through a thicket.

His eyes are glued to the portage trail, and for the time being he is just a beast of burden with a tump line a tight band over his forehead. Having ourselves found it useful for such carriers, we are in no sense criticizing the tump line for heavy packing over short portages. For such it has shown its worth over centuries.

SOURDOUGHS USE IT

In Alaska, northern British Columbia, and the Yukon the old sourdough trappers, prospectors, and hunters not infrequently have to back-pack all their outfit from where their boat (or now often airplane) takes them to their trapping, prospecting, or hunting country. Many have to fight the brush and steep mountain slopes for miles and miles, for one to ten days of continuous travel. They constantly have to see ahead where they are going and uphill as well as down.

They may be packing only their blankets, or a sack of potatoes or traps, or a hot and wet quarter of moose meat. The load must not dig into, gall, or heat the back. Frequently they may wish to take a shot at a grouse, ptarmigan, or even big game while the pack is in place. They have evolved the Alaskan pack board as the best contrivance for such packing.

THE CHEECHAKO, TOO

Some sportsmen hunting in these far northwest game regions have to reach their general destination by polling or "put-putting" their canoe up some swift mountain river and then, from the valley where they have to leave their boat, by toting their outfit and grub up and back five to fifty miles into the mountains where the game is ranging. For such carrying the back board is also by far the best arrangement, as it also is for bringing out heads and meat.

For the vacationist who elects to take his holiday traveling on foot through more or less wild country, packing his home on his back and camping where late afternoon finds him, the problem is much more like that of the northern sourdough than of the Canadian canoe voyageur. For him the Alaskan pack board is, many times, the best contrivance. If it isn't, then the frame rucksack of the Bergans type will be.

CHAPTER 6

THE HUNTER'S PACK

WHEN YOU LEAVE CAMP for a day of big-game hunting, the chances are that you are carrying about ten cartridges in addition to those in your loaded rifle, a knife, watch, compass, waterproof match box, a small tea pail maybe, and a lunch. A camera in its case may hang over a shoulder.

You may also have along a binocular or a good telescope, for either will help you to determine, while there's still time to do something about it, if certain suspicious objects are game or not. Likely there will be other items bulging from your pockets: handkerchief, map, notebook, pencil, tiny first-aid kit, collapsible drinking cup, exposure meter, extra film, sunglasses, small mirror, piece of cord, and carborundum stone.

CACHE OR CARRY

A lot of hunters, if the weather is at all cold, start off in the chill of the morning in a heavy mackinaw. Many in addition so stuff their pockets and weigh down their belts that, particularly if they push through any tamarack with its shedding needles or past burned spruce, they soon look and feel like an overloaded Christmas tree.

They puff, and grunt, and perspire along in a bulky jacket as they top hills and breast thick bush. The straps of camera and glasses continually hang them up. The pull and strain of loaded clothing becomes more and more uncomfortable. The chances are that by now they would like to shed that coat, but they have nowhere to carry it.

All or most of this impedimenta is often desirable on a day's hunt. That particular system of carrying it, however, is unnecessarily handi-

A simple tarp is about as good a shelter as a more elaborate and much more costly tent, and easier to heat than most.

capping and unduly out of date. I started out more than sixty years ago lugging my stuff more or less in this fashion until I noted that most of the world's most experienced hunters, except those accompanied by guides or gunbearers, toted such articles in a rucksack on their backs. I thereupon adopted this method and have adhered to it ever since.

ALL DISCOMFORT VANISHES

Once you have carried a light rucksack for three or four days afield, you will never thereafter notice you have it with you. All discomfort is gone. Nothing dangles or catches. Your belt does not restrict you the way it did before. Your pockets do not bulge or press.

As you warm from exercise, off comes the jacket or extra shirt and into your rucksack it goes. If you stop to glass a promising slope or to enjoy lunch, or if you begin threading along a windy ridge, there is your extra clothing to put on again. You can get at everything quickly, and the rucksack is no burden at all.

The pack does not have to be anything elaborate. In a pinch, a gunny sack with the middle of a short rope tied to its mouth and the ends knotted to the lower corners to serve as shoulder straps will fill the bill. It will be easier to keep such knots in place, incidently, if they are tied around bulges made by some handy light objects such as potatoes. The ropes will ride better, too, if something such as gloves or birch bark is placed between them and the shoulders. But the point is, the pack does not have to be expensive or elaborate.

Camp outfitters stock many models, but those rucksacks having two small pockets on the outside of the big central sack are most desirable, particularly if they have leather instead of web straps. Such models are usually made of a light waterproof duck. If the color is too near that of a game animal, simply baste a red bandana handkerchief over the outside when hunting in frequented forests.

SHOULDER STRAPS

My rucksacks have all been of this type, my present one being made of tanned moosehide of my own killing, and thong sewed, but that is perhaps a pardonable affectation.

The shoulder straps should be let out so that the pack sags down into the hollow of the back with more than half of its weight resting on the hips. Thus, its burden is not felt on your shoulders, and your center of gravity remains low enough to assure better and safer balance. You can get in and out of the harness as easily as you can your suspenders.

The widespread and persistent notion that a pack should be carried high on the shoulders is all wrong and likely originated with some writer who never in his life hefted a pack for more than an hour or two. At least, all light- and medium-weight packs used in rough country should be carried low down with most of the weight on the hips. The extremely heavy loads borne short distances over portages and freight trails are another story.

For ordinary one-day hunts, your pack and its contents should never weigh over ten pounds. Even when you anticipate the desirability of staying out from your base camp overnight, the pack need not weigh in excess of fifteen pounds. Such cargos are scarcely felt after you have accustomed yourself to carrying a light load on your lower back. Packing of this sort is, indeed, not nearly so tiring as hiking in boots that weigh a pound more than your city shoes.

MAKING YOUR HUNTING PAY OFF

Before we inventory the desirable contents of this rucksack, let us consider two kinds of big-game hunting. The first and the more common variety is when you leave your base after a good breakfast, well after daylight, and then hunt and tramp until late afternoon except for perhaps taking a stand during midday on a good lookout. You wend your way homeward in time to reach camp and supper before dark.

This is the average day's hunt, and it is not productive of much success except by sheer good luck. Big game feeds and travels abroad mostly between the last hour before sunset and the first hour after sunrise. These two extreme hours are worth more than all the rest of the day combined so far as spotting and bagging game is concerned.

If you hunt in the usual way, you are probably spending these two really productive hours either in camp or within a mile or so of there, where game is surely disturbed and alerted if not actually driven out by noises and smells.

With the other method, often used by the more experienced still hunter, you breakfast long before dawn. You leave camp when just enough pale light has smudged across the eastern horizon to enable you to see well enough not to run a branch into an eye or step into a hole. By the time it's light enough to make out your rifle sights, you are well away in undisturbed country. Throughout the daylight hours you hunt and watch in the bedding or feeding grounds of the game. You turn homeward when the shadows become long and black.

WHY NOT SLEEP WHERE YOU ARE?

Or maybe along toward late afternoon, you see ahead a basin or a range that looks like a mighty good game prospect. Perhaps with your glasses you even make out a buck or a berry-gouging bear several miles ahead. So you elect to make a bivouac where you then are, preferably in some sheltered spot near water, and to resume the following day your hunt in this more promising game country—country that from your base camp you could not reasonably expect to reach and cover, and then return, in one day.

Such a decision to remain out overnight may also be forced on you when you kill a large animal near sunset, miles from camp, and in the interest of good meat or a fine trophy have to dress and butcher without delay. This task may occupy you well after darkness has set in so blackly that you have to build a fire to see to finish the job.

In many such cases, the chances are that you may even have to make a second camp on your final way back to the base and thus to be two nights out. This is real hunting as distinguished from a day's tramp, and of course it pertains more to unspoiled wilderness than to the more populated deer forests adjacent to eastern farming country.

To be completely factual, there is an exception to this pale dawn to dim dusk hunting. This is in the open country of the Canadian Northwest where you find sheep, goat, caribou, moose, and bear. These animals here feed and bed largely in the open. They can be seen near noon almost as often as in the wee hours, although if you seek them at watering spots, the early and late portions of the day are still most productive. We often locate game here with glasses and then stalk them rather than still hunt.

In such open country, too, you and perhaps your horse can customarily travel long after the sun goes down. In Northern British Columbia, the days become so prolonged that during June it is possible in clear weather to read outdoors comfortably at midnight. Hunting in such regions may be considered as a third kind.

For the first and third kinds of hunting, you require only some of the articles already mentioned. Unless you are traveling in the saddle or with a pack dog, these items can be most easily and satisfactorily carried in your rucksack. Probably the entire load will be considerably less than ten pounds.

The Hunter's Pack.

WHAT TO TAKE

For the second type of hunting, you need to carry food and shelter that will enable you to remain out two nights if necessary. This entire outfit need not weigh over fifteen pounds. Let us inventory this kind of a hunter's pack.

Take the ammunition first. In addition to the cartridges in your rifle, you should have at least two or three rounds in your handiest pocket. These can be wadded in your handkerchief so that they will not rattle. The more convenient and practical way to carry them is silently and compactly in a clip. This way, paying attention to their continued accessibility, you can have out and headed in the right direction with a single motion.

Then in your rucksack carry a full carton of twenty, five of these being small-game loads. The latter may come in handy for grouse and small mammals you may want to collect either for the pot or, unless prohibited by local law, for their pelts. Why so many cartridges? For one reason, you can never tell when some emergency may arise, nor when signal shots may be highly desirable.

Your watch, compass, and waterproof match box go along, certainly, probably in your pockets unless the compass happens to be one of the convenient pin-on variety. In the rucksack, perhaps, you have a sharp skinning knife and a whetstone with which to keep it that way.

If you expect that you may shoot a moose or other big animal, it will be a good idea also to include one of two things. A small, keen hand-ax weighing not more than a pound is a great aid in butchering large game. So is a light folding saw if you can locate one of sufficiently good quality. If not, a small hacksaw will get through bones a lot more neatly than an ax.

CAMERA AND GLASSES

Almost certainly you will want to bring back some record of your hunt, whether it is successful from a trophy standpoint or not. Photographs of animal tracks, new country, and of your bivouac will help you to relive your trip and share it with others for years afterwards. So you will very possibly wish to include a small camera, an exposure meter, spare film, and a clamp-on holder which with a self timer will let you get into the picture. This equipage also goes into the rucksack.

Binoculars, however, should be suspended by the leather thong around your neck so that they will hang in front, just below your collar, where you can bring them to your eyes instantly. There is no need to wear a case. So that the glasses won't bounce around too much or get in the way when I lean forward, I shove mine inside my shirt.

CLOTHING

For clothing, you may need some kind of warm garment for the chill of the morning, to put on while watching on a stand, or to don at night. A mackinaw or similar coat, if you're walking, is ordinarily too heavy and unwieldy in ratio to the warmth it affords. A down insulated jacket is a better choice in cold weather. Otherwise, it is also apt to be unduly bulky.

During many years in the wildest and occasionally the coldest portions of the continent, we have both found the best extra garment is simply another good woolen shirt. When it becomes too warm, stow it in your rucksack along with a light pair of gloves perhaps, or, during colder weather, woolen mitts one of which has a flap-covered slit in the palm through which the trigger finger can be extended.

Another item we would recommend is a poncho. You can secure one weighing only a pound which will fold up as small as a bandana handkerchief. It will keep even your knees bone dry in snow and rain. It is protection in a cold wind. It will even serve splendidly for a lean-to shelter when you remain out overnight.

For sleeping you may like to consider one of the very light down-filled mummy sleeping bags that weigh only some three or four pounds. These are a little bulky, and if you roll one inside your poncho, it will make a bundle about six by fifteen inches which will probably have to be tied on the outside of your rucksack.

GRUBSTAKE

Next we come to grub, briefly because of the detailed chapters on the subject of sustenance toward the end of this book. You are going prepared to spend two nights—seven meals, that is—away from your base camp. You will need sufficient nourishment to keep you warm and stoked with energy. This food should be reasonably free of water and not bulky.

Our own tastes have always been quite simple. We have relied mostly on small waterproof bags containing such staples as rolled oats, corn meal, whole milk powder, whole egg powder, flour and other ingredients mixed in the correct proportions to provide bannock dough when water is added, sugar, salt, bacon, figs, dates, raisins, chocolate, tea, and the like. Experiment with these at home, why don't you? to get an idea of how much it takes to make seven meals that will reasonably satisfy an outdoor appetite. You will probably be surprised at the scant weight and bulk.

For cooking and eating utensils, you will need a small pot with a bail. If you don't want to bother carrying it back, a large fruit-juice can with an attached wire bail will do. You'll also probably want either an enamel or stainless steel cup. An army aluminum mess pan which will provide both frypan and plate. Any greasy food may be carried inside of this, incidently.

Add a spoon. You already have your knife. A stick will make a suitable fork, although taking a light stainless steel fork offers no trouble, either. Include, too, a plastic bag about fifteen inches square which will be handy for carrying back any liver, heart, kidney and tongue.

So that is the whole cheese, the maximum hunter's pack. It will probably weigh somewhere between ten and fifteen pounds. The bulk will be slight. If you carry it in a rucksack low down on your back, you will scarcely notice it all day long.

SIWASHING IN COMFORT

But how can you be comfortable siwashing out in the hills and woods on a cold night with so light a rig and without a tent? This is not nearly as difficult as it may seem. When you decide you are going to make a night of it, begin looking for a suitable place to bivouac.

There should be water, of course. Ordinarily, however, you will not bed down close beside it. You will generally find that climate more comfortable a hundred feet or so higher on a bench or hill. There it will be warmer, dryer, quieter possibly, and the air drift will be much less. Try to find a small clump of spruce, balsam, or at least some thick bushes in which your bed will be sheltered from any wind.

For the bed, clean off a level space about three feet wide and a foot longer than your height. Scratch depressions several inches deep for your shoulders and hips. If you want to take the trouble, cut four poles and stake them in place around the edge of this bed. A mattress can be made of shingled evergreen boughs, as described elsewhere, or you may simply gather together dry forest litter such as leaves and pine needles. As a matter of fact, the latter will be warmer.

Then haul in a lot of firewood, enough to last all night. This does not have to be short, and you don't need to spend a lot of time working it into any particular lengths. Unless there is a fire hazard, fairly big logs ten to fifteen feet long are fine. You can place the centers in the fire, let them burn in two, and then move the ends in easily.

UNFORGETTABLE CAMPS

Locate your fire downwind from your bed, lengthwise to it, and about three feet away. Stretch your poncho above the bed as a reflecting tent if you want, and your little camp will be all ready for supper and a night's rest. After you have fueled up on grub, take time to dry out your underwear and socks. Put on the extra shirt. Arrange the rucksack for a pillow if you want.

Build up the fire with the big stuff so that it will hold, and lie down and let your thoughts drift you as lazily as the clouds scudding across the yellow moon. In two or three hours, maybe the cold will awaken you. Don't just lie there and shiver. Hunch up and build the fire up again. While you're getting warm, listen to the night noises, the sweetness with which a whippoorwill's call sounds, the wildness of the echoes set vibrating by a dark loon's laugh.

Perhaps you'll detect the faint distant cries of migrating swans, of wild wings flapping exultantly nearer, and of tremulous notes that mingle vaguely with the music of wilderness water and the melodic muttering of trees. Perhaps you'll even hear, as few do, the swishing of northern lights and see them in bands, curtains, arcs, beams, and coronas of mingling colors among which, likely as not, the silvery green of chatoyant jade will be dominant.

These small, heartening, one-night camps are among the most memorable you will ever experience, particularly if you are fortunate enough to have a congenial companion along. They will live longer in your thoughts than those spent in the base camp with its comparative conveniences. And at the first platinum streak of dawn, you will be rested, fed, and in the best hunting country.

	CAMPING
CHAPTER 7	WITHOUT
	A TENT

WE CAMP OUT to get close to remote woods and waters that offer the best sport; to relish the fresh air, freedom, and the good fellowship available • nowhere else; and to get far enough away from the restraint, noise, and crowds of the big towns to enjoy the friendship of the seasons. If our camp is comfortable, so much the better. There is no reason why it should not be.

As the Hudson's Bay Company says after nearly three centuries in the farthest and most primitive reaches of this continent, "There is usually little object in traveling tough just for the sake of being tough."

Rough it, sure, if you want to prove to yourself the actually very important fact that you can rough it. One day, it's true, anyone at all may be thrown entirely upon his own resources and forced to get along the best he can with a minimum of comforts.

But as far as the preference goes, roughing it is a development stage. Once we've successfully tested our ability to take it, a whole lot of doubts and inhibitions disappear. We find ourselves realizing that the real challenge lies in smoothing it. We come to appreciate that making it easy on ourselves takes a lot more experience and ingenuity than building it through the tough way.

WHY A TENT?

In one sense a tent may be said to be a portable house, made of cloth, that we take with us when camping. We may wish it to shelter us from rain, snow, or wind. In public and frequented places, we may appreciate the privacy one affords. A tent may seem almost a necessity to keep us warm in cold weather and, for that matter, cool in a hot climate. It may be invaluable at times as protection against mosquitoes, bugs, and other pests.

A tent does not necessarily have to do all these things. In fact, if despite expense one was fashioned to do everything, it would be unnecessarily heavy, bulky, and difficult to erect.

When we first began to design tents, we tried to make them so that each would serve many purposes. Today we have better learned the wisdom of having many different types of tents, each for a special use or for a certain kind of country.

BIVOUACING

A tent is not always a necessity for camping out. Shelter may often be better extemporized from materials we find in the woods. But there are certain fundamental techniques for doing this.

When our forefathers came here to the New World, the majority of them were from families that had been living in cities and towns or on farms for hundreds of years. Very few knew a thing about either camping or the woods.

When they went out hunting, exploring, or Indian fighting, they seldom took anything with which to shelter themselves. At night they simply lay down on the ground, perhaps under a tree, and tried to go to sleep. If it was cold and if danger was not too great, they lay close to a fire. If it rained, the chances were that they soon became soaked.

We think of them as hardy souls, able to rough it and to take it. As a matter of fact, nearly all had rheumatism as a result of exposure, and they usually died young. But they and their sons and daughters eventually learned from the Indians how to obtain shelter, warmth, and food. So let us start with the most primitive and simple of all shelters that a woodsman makes when he has nothing better.

If a fellow knocks around in the open long enough, the time comes sooner or later when he has to spend a night or more outdoors without any shelter except what Nature can be persuaded to provide. Perhaps you have been hunting, fishing, or tramping. Before you know it, twilight finds you far from base camp or human habitation. Perhaps you've become slightly turned around. You realize you can not reasonably expect to get back before dark.

TRAVELING IN THE DARK

It is hazardous to attempt to travel through the woods or over rough country at night without a light. You are liable to run a twig or branch into an eye, or fall over a cliff, or to get mixed up in direction and perhaps even bogged down. An electric flashlight will serve to help you pick good footing ahead, but this is often behind in camp.

The temptation to stay in good country as long as light remains is inevitable. In the north woods where white birch trees are plentiful, a birch bark torch has often brought me safe and sound to camp.

One of these is made easily enough by stripping off a piece of birch bark a foot wide and about three feet long. Fold this in three layers lengthwise, making a three-ply strip about four inches by three feet. Split one end of a three-foot pole for carrying, the cleft of the pole engaging the bark about eight inches from one end and keeping it from unfolding. Light the short eight-inch end.

If you want more illumination, turn the lighted end downward so the fire will burn up on the bark. If it burns too fast, turn the flaming end upward. As the bark is consumed, pull more of it through the split in the stick handle. Such a strip will last fifteen to twenty minutes and will light all the ground, trees, and bushes within about twenty feet. When the bark is about half consumed look for another tree from which to get more fuel.

Late one afternoon in the Rockies I was fortunate enough to shoot a fine ram. It was coming on night by the time I had it dressed, a cloudy night and pitch dark. Camp was four miles off down a steep mountainside. Against my better judgment, lured by the prospects of a good meal and a soft bed, I was enticed to try to make it. I cut a pole about ten feet long and with it felt the ground in front of me to be sure I would not go over a ledge or cliff.

It was an exceedingly slow and risky journey, but I finally arrived about two a.m., woke up my companion, and we had a fine meal of moose meat and boiled creamed cabbage. Unbeknownst to me, he had saved the latter for the evening I shot a ram.

If you are ever in the same fix, and are tempted to try to reach camp in the dark through trackless woods or rough and steep ground, my advice is to forget it. It is far safer to find a sheltered spot, drag in a lot of firewood, and spend the night in comfort and safety.

AGREE BEFOREHAND

Whenever you find that you can not get back to tent or road before dark, the most sensible thing to do is to stop while a little daylight remains, make a bivouac, and lay up wherever you happen to be. There is nothing difficult or perilous about this. There are no wild animals in North America that are dangerous when unprovoked. At the very worst you may miss a meal or two, or perhaps you may become a bit thirsty unless you happen to knock off near a spring or stream.

As far as your companions are concerned, a prior understanding may well have been agreed upon for the safety of all involved. Otherwise, you may feel obliged to press on and they to get out unnecessarily and search. On sporting trips we have made with others back of beyond, there has always been a prior understanding that anyone should camp out any night he felt this advisable and, unless he signaled for help, no one should do anything about it until at least noon of the next day.

No wilderness nights are more memorable, as a matter of fact, than one or two spent under these circumstances alone in the bush. In a wooded country whatever the weather, you can always manage to get a fair amount of slumber. If the approaching darkness promises to be warm and clear, simply select a dry and level spot for your bed, scrape slight hollows for shoulders and hips, cover the resting place with grass or pine needles or any soft dry forest litter, and then lie down and sleep the night out.

WHEN IT'S COLD AND STORMY

Often, however, the night is apt to be cold or at least cool, and there may be rain or snow. A campfire will then prove to be the most congenial of companions, affording both warmth and cheer.

A big tree with thick foliage will ward off a lot of snow and rain. One of the easiest and best overnight niches can be quickly made, as a matter of fact, by stripping off enough lower branches of a short thick evergreen tree to form a small cubbyhole. These branches, supplemented with more from other trees, can be used to make a soft dry flooring and to thatch the roof and sides.

An evergreen bivouac of this sort is so easily and rapidly fashioned that both of us have often made them so as to enjoy more fully the noon tea pail and not infrequently some sizzling kabobs and bannock as well. In any event, the tree chosen should first be shaken free of any snow or rain. If a storm has settled in heavily, a few pieces of birch bark or similar forest material will shed a lot of moisture.

If the dusk that is quickly dropping over the forest is bringing with it a deepening cold, try to select your bivouac site in a thick clump of small trees. If possible, let it be halfway down the lee slope of a hill, as this is the warmest spot in most country. During the daylight that is left, haul in all the dead and dry firewood you can find in the immediate locality. You may need a lot to last the night out. Include a few damp or rotting stumps and snags if possible, and perhaps a recently fallen big green limb or so, as these will be handy for holding a more even heat and for retaining the fire.

If time is pressing, kindle your fire at nightfall and complete your preparations by its leaping illumination. Make everything as ready and comfortable as you reasonably can. If your clothes are damp, get them dry before trying to sleep. This you will probably be able to accomplish faster if you take most of them off and stretch and hang them on sticks not too close to flames or sparks.

Then put the heaviest and longest lasting wood on the fire, arranging them so that the blaze will be at least as long as your body. Stretch out beside the dancing warmth. Relax and let the hoo-ho-ho-hooooing of whisper-winged owls, the yipping of coyotes, and if you're real lucky the sweet violent chorus of timber wolves lull you to sleep.

In several hours or so, the coldness will of its own accord awaken you. The fire has burned to embers. You grope carefully for the woodpile and toss some sticks into the coals. The pieces flare up quickly, flicking light across your bed and vitalizing it with fresh heat. You hunch up on an elbow, the living warmth of the blaze cheerful about you. We've both experienced this feeling you get; amid frozen beaver ponds in New Brunswick, high by the Continental Divide when pinons made strange shapes against the desert moon, and in the velvet British Columbia night.

There is a wind high up in the trees, maybe, whirling splinters of ice from stars that shiver in a glacial blue-black sky. Some bird you've never heard before calls in the distance, like a moonbeam turned to sound. You lay back finally, all tension slackening. Almost at once it is morning, and you are ready to travel again. Put your fire dead out.

IN COLDER WEATHER

It is not enough in colder weather merely to build a fire and stretch out beside it. Unless other provisions are made, such a blaze would warm you in front, but those parts of your body facing away from it would be so uncomfortably cold that invigorating sleep would be impossible. Under such conditions, you need to consider ways of confining and reflecting the heat and of keeping the frosty breezes away.

One very easy solution is to arrange some sort of a ridgepole about four feet off the ground, laying it perhaps between rocks or trees. Lean poles or sticks against this at such an angle that they will reach the ground along the long back edge of your bed. You are, of course, going to make your fire so that it will warm the entire length of your body from feet to head.

On these poles, shingle or lay a quantity of spruce boughs, leafy branches, bark, and the like. You can even lean small evergreen trees in place, hooking alternate ones across the ridgepole so as to present a thick uniform wall against the night. The result, in any case, will be an open-faced camp with the first built along the front of it. Shingle in the ends of your lean-to also, or pile a few small balsams or firs there, too.

If you can kindle your fire against some reflecting surface, so much the better. The snugger you make your camp and the better the firewood you haul in, the longer will be your naps. There is no sense in being cold in a wooded country. Nothing is more enjoyable under favorable conditions than hobbling your cayuse and rolling up in the saddle blanket on star-silvered needles from nearby lodgepole pines. There are many other nights, however, when a half-hour occupied in readying a bivouac will be vastly repaid in convenience, ease, and refreshed well-being.

There are no set rules governing siwashing. You do the best you can, as soon as you can, with the materials at hand. A shallow cave may be nearby where, heated by a fire in front, you can rest as cosily as did your earliest ancestor who sought shelter in such a place.

Two or three boulders may be so grouped that, once a bough roof is thrown across them, they will afford snug sanctuary. A crude

The making of an overnite shelter with poles and pine or spruce boughs.

Umbrella tents at a public camp ground.

triangle stamped in deep snow, with the larger end floored and roofed with evergreen boughs and with the remaining corner reflecting a small fire, will provide warmth and shelter even if one is without bedding. The main precaution in this latter circumstance is to keep dry, as clothing which becomes damp or frozen loses its qualities of insulation in direct proportion.

CAMPFIRE SHELTERS

Based on joint experience accumulated during many years in the wilderness, our reaction to closed-in tents is not particularly enthusiastic. These do have their uses, of course, especially during intense cold, in mosquito country under certain conditions, in construction and other work camps, and at public camp grounds where fires may be restricted and where certainly privacy is highly desirable.

Too often with such a shelter, however, you are needlessly shut up in a canvas shell that not infrequently is stuffy and poorly ventilated. You are closed in from the fresh air, the scenery, the delicious unspoiled odors, and the voices of the saucy chipmunks and birds and the other little dwellers of the wild places. We go camping largely to enjoy the congenial vigor of a wood fire, and, across its ever changing pattern, the contemplation of miles of beautiful country from the front of an open tent pitched on an attractive site.

We are lulled by the unforgettable way wind sings through dislodged and disintegrating bark up near the timber line, and by the startling booming of live trees as freezing sap harmlessly bursts their innermost fibers. We're reassured somehow by the lap-lap-lap of tiny waves on the lake shore, the slap of a beaver's tail, the evening conversation of two loons, the whistling wings of ducks, and the leaping of what can be nothing less than the granddaddy of all trout. We yearn to be awakened many more nights by the horse exchange of bull and cow moose and by the way a solitary wolf lets its wavering voice lift and lower, rise and fall again, and then soar another time in three crescendos. All these you sense in a campfire tent.

This form of tent is very simple, consisting essentially of a canvas roof that is suspended and stretched from a ridgepole at an angle of about forty-five degrees. Large enough to shelter the beds of two sleepers from rain or snow, it is entirely open at the front. The campfire is built from four to six feet in front of the peak of the roof, whose angle is such that it reflects both heat and light into the interior and down onto the beds.

CAMPING WITH A TARPAULIN

The simplest form of campfire tent is merely a tarp or a rectangular sheet of canvas or light waterproof cotton. The minimum effective size is about nine feet wide and fourteen feet long. Erected with the nine-foot length to the front and with the peak about seven feet above the ground, such a covering will shelter the beds of two campers who are sleeping with either their heads or feet to the front. It will allow, at the same time, about two and one-half feet of clearance above the ground at the inner ends of the beds.

Made of six-ounce waterproof cotton, such a tarpaulin will weigh about six pounds. Sewed of eight-ounce canvas, it will weigh closer to nine pounds. When pitched, it will be entirely open at the sides. If rain, wind, or snow blows in to a disagreeable extent, which seldom happens, the sides may be closed in by whatever way happens at the time to be most convenient. Heaping up a number of small evergreen trees, or any bushes with leafy tops, has proved adequate for us in bad weather ranging from blizzards to rainstorms of tropical intensity.

Such a simple terpaulin is, as a matter of fact, about as good as any of the more elaborate lean-to tents. It is easy to put up. It is far less costly than more complicated structures. It is the most used of all shelters by the oldtime woodsmen of the north, partly because cooking over the fire in front is easy except in an exceedingly heavy rain. Furthermore, a tarpaulin has a multitude of practical uses besides that of a shelter for sleeping.

The Baker form of tent, featured by most of our better tent makers, is merely an elaboration of the already described tarpaulin arrangement. It has side walls in addition to the roof. There is a low wall at the rear of the roof. An awning attached to the peak can either be tied down to close the front completely, or it can be stretched out to form a canopy. The Baker is a fairly good tent. However, there are other ways, as we will consider in a moment, in which the same amount and bulk of canvas can be used to make a more effective and comfortable shelter.

CHAPTER 8

TENTS FOR WILDERNESS CAMPERS

I SPENT ALL my boyhood summers in the north woods. There the almost universal camp was the log lean-to, with its sloping and reflecting roof and its open front before which a cheerfully big campfire was kindled. The last thing at night, heavy logs were heaped on this. By the time the forest was becoming silhouetted against the lemonish smudge of an eastern sky line, often ghostly with streamers of early morning mist from lake and river, these snapping guardians against the cold had usually shaken apart into hot coals ideal for cooking.

This type of permanent lean-to, still to be seen in our forests, was a direct development evolving from the open-face camp that our early frontiersmen used when away from their backwoods cabins. From these early bivouacs have come, too, our most agreeable and functional modern tents.

The Spanish-American War instilled in me a strong desire for army life. When I was mustered out of the service in the spring of 1900, a second lieutenant in the First Pennsylvania Infantry with five hundred dollars in my pocket, I learned there would be no opportunity for examinations for entrance into the army for a year. So I determined to have a grand hunting trip in the meantime. I'd been dreaming of such a hunt ever since getting my first rifle in 1891, a .22 Remington rolling block with which, the following year, I was fortunate enough to win my first rifle match for guides in the Adirondacks and to shoot my first deer unaided and alone.

So I gathered a small outfit. June found me in British Columbia, at the southern terminus of the Telegraph Trail to Alaska. There I bought three horses, rigging, and grub, and I started toward the top of the continent, not to return for nine glorious months.

Following the lessons derived from my boyhood experiences, the only shelter I had was a tarpaulin. Ten feet long and eight feet wide, this was made of light and closely woven cotton. I had sewed it myself, as a matter of fact, and had waterproofed it with paraffin.

TARPAULIN SHELTER

The fifth day on the trail I ran into Bones Andrews, an old mountain man. We figured we might as well string along together for a few days. This association developed into a close friendship, and we agreed on a partnership to "hunt and prospect."

Bones had a dilapidated A-wall tent eight feet square. Not only was this full of holes, but it was heavy and difficult to erect. It wasn't long before we came to prefer my tarp, easily pitched as a lean-to. Bones finally traded his tent to some Chilkootin Indians for a ground hog, or what it is also known thereabouts as a marmot or whistler, robe.

From then on—all through the warm summer, and fall when birches and poplars turned an incredible yellow, and the sometimes blusterous winter—we used my tarp. We put it up at an angle of about forty-five degrees. We filled in with boughs or small spruce trees at the ends whenever the weather was cold or stormy. Firewood was plentiful everywhere, just as it still is in that country, and we had a comfortable and cheerful camp even when temperatures dropped so low that Bones remarked that what we needed was a three-foot thermometer with zero at the top. We cooked, ate, worked, and just loafed in perfect ease.

TEPEE

In the years that followed I experimented extensively with shelter and camp equipment, partly because—as a result of such assignments as Director of Research and Development at Springfield Armory, Commanding Officer at Frankfort Arsenal, and Ordnance representative on the Infantry Board—experimentation in achieving greater perfection in performance became pretty much second nature with me.

On two long trips in the Northwest we used an Indian tepee, which is an exceptionally pleasant and functional conical tent. The nomads of the entire northern world have used it, or slight modifications of it, for many centuries. It was often their only shelter and home, and in it they raised families and grew to an old age.

The tepee is an all-weather shelter. Used closed, with a little wood fire in the center which serves for cooking and heat as well as for light, it will take you through even an Arctic blizzard in perfect comfort.

The two major drawbacks of a tepee are its weight and the difficulty of finding and cutting eleven or more long straight poles. In those early days we used the tepee in mountain country that was fragrant with lodgepole pines. At innumerable places suitable for a camp, we'd find quantities of tepee poles cut and stacked up against trees. The Indians who originally hunted this range had left them there.

On a trip through the same area some years later I found these lodgepoles all gone, burned up by modern campers in their confounded tin stoves. Where my present writing partner lives, beside the great Peace River in the Canadian Rockies, one still comes across quantities of such poles, however, mostly along old trails that now are nearly forgotten.

The tepee today is impractical except as a permanent camp.

ONE-MAN TENTS

When a fellow camps by himself and does all his own work, there are certain features that he appreciates in a shelter. He wants a tent that is neither ponderous nor bulky. He likes something that is simple to erect.

The tent, furthermore, should be ruggedly capable of sheltering him from rain and snow. It should warm up quickly and easily from a wood fire in front, no matter what the direction of the wind. It should be so arranged that moisture beating by the open front will not reach the bedding.

The immediate front of such a tent should provide a comfortable place in which to cook, repair equipment, oil rods and firearms, skin animals, and just plain lounge. Cooking in any weather short of a torrential downpour should be possible without getting wet. There should be convenient places to store the various classes of duffle, to dry clothing, and to hang a mosquito bar if desirable.

Such a tent should be laid out so that the camper will sleep lengthwise across the front, parallel to a long fire. His vital organs will thus be nearest the heart of the vitalizing heat. It will also be easy for him to get in and out of the sleeping bag. He will be able to see out of the tent while in bed, and hear also, and the genial warmth and light of the campfire will be at hand to be enjoyed and regulated if need be until sleep drops its nightly curtain.

SLEEPING IN VERY COLD WEATHER

In very cold weather a fire will not warm the back interior of any tent, but it does always warm a tent of this sort for at least four feet back from the front. The habit, almost a religion among some, of sleeping with the feet toward the opening and the fire is all wrong. This places head and shoulders inconveniently back in the dark and poorly ventilated portion, makes it unnecessarily difficult to get in and out of bed, and pens one in needlessly.

When we've been forced because of unexpected crowding to bunch up in a tent, as a matter of fact, both of us even during our greener years automatically chose to sleep with head and shoulders toward embers and outdoors. During more than one night, we've been aroused by other occupants following suit.

It has often been said that if the feet are warm, the entire body will be comfortable. As a matter of fact, it is more important to have the vital organs near the center of the body warm, and if they are, the whole body will indeed be at ease provided you don't turn in with wet socks.

With all these factors in mind, and after a lot of experience and experiment, I thought out what I called a Hunter's Lean-to Tent. This I had made up by one of our leading tent makers who, incidentally, has been marketing it since as the Whelen Lean-to. I have used it in the north for twenty years, and it is the best design I've ever found. Two old sourdough friends, Jay Williams and Hosea Sarber, now both across the Great Divide, likewise used it exclusively in Alaska for many moons and swore by it.

THE WHELEN LEAN-TO TENT

This design would not be satisfactory for a group of sportsmen with guides and cooks. For such a party I know of nothing that will equal a big tarp, twelve by fourteen feet or larger, pitched as a lean-to. But for one or two hunters, fishermen, or woods loafers who do their own work, including cooking, and who travel by pack train or canoe, shifting camp often, I know of no shelter so convenient and so comfortable in any climate where firewood is plentiful—with the single exception of tropical mosquito country.

This tent in principle is somewhat like the Baker tent. It, too, has a steeply sloping shed roof. The side walls, instead of being perpendicular, splay outward and forward at the bottom. Their angle is such that the front end of each of those walls stakes down about two feet outward and two feet forward of where a perpendicular would reach the ground if dropped from the ends of the six-foot tape ridge.

Thus the walls slope at such an angle that they will reflect heat and light into the tent. They extend forward so as to keep winds and cold breezes from blowing around in front and making the little living sanctuary there chilly. With the walls spreading out in this way, a storage space is created at the head of the sleeping bag for personal effects, while another is provided at the foot for cooking utensils and grub.

The fact that there is no wall at the back of the roof simplifies both construction and pitching. It reduces cost. The low area beneath the roof at the rear can be utilized for stowing duffle not in use.

Loops are attached to the tape ridge through which the ridgepole is thrust. On the under side of this six-foot tape ridge are two other loops which will support a short pole on which clothing may be hung either to be out of the way or to dry.

A thirty-inch-wide awning is sewed to the ridge. This can either be thrown back over the ridgepole or extended out to prolong the roof. In case of storm, for example, the awning is stretched out forward and downward from the ridge so that it shelters the ground in front, keeps moisture from driving into the tent, and creates a dry space in which to sit and cook over the fire.

To extend the awning in this fashion, you don't have to use always bothersome guy ropes. You simply cut a pair of poles about six feet long and sharpen both ends. Stick one end of each in the large grommet at each outer corner of the awning. Plant the other ends at the foot and at the head of the sleeping bag. The weight of these will keep the awning extended and taut without any guy lines being in the way to snag you or trip you. The front edge of the awning

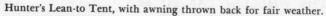

Hunter's Lean-to Tent, with awning thrown back for fair weather.

Hunter's Lean-to Tent, with awning extended for rain or snow, The weight of the poles hold it out without guy-ropes.

will then be about four feet above the ground where heat and light from the fire can still come in under it.

PITCHING THE WHELEN LEAN-TO

To pitch this tent, cut a ridgepole about ten feet long. Thread this through the loops of the tape ridge. Support the pole by trees or sheer poles, as suggested by the illustrations, about six feet above the ground. Then stake down the back and sides, and your tent is ready for occupancy.

The tent shown is one-man size. It will comfortably accommodate two campers, sleeping side by side parallel to the front. The man whose turn it is to build the fire in the morning snoozes on the outside. He can then lean out of his bag, place shavings and split wood in the fireplace, touch a match to them, and get up ten minutes later in the reflected warmth.

Made of Aberlite or Green Waterproof Egyptian cotton running approximately six ounces per square yard, the Whelen Lean-to Tent weighs about seven pounds. It is also available in an Extra Light long stapled cotton weighing five pounds. It is seven feet deep, six feet wide at the rear, and about ten feet wide in front. This front can become the cosiest and warmest living room easily available in the farther places. The sides somehow do much to keep smoke from blowing into the tent and, in fact, eradicate this nuisance entirely if you have a tier of back logs a foot high behind the campfire.

It is not adapted to temperatures of twenty degrees below zero and colder, for it would then take too many hours of ax work to get in the fire wood necessary for heat and for cooking. When such frigidity endures for any considerable time, you need a closed tent with a stove. Besides an ax, you should also have either a bucksaw or a swede saw to cut the wood into the short lengths necessary to feed the firebox.

ONE-MAN SHELTER

In cold weather, the solitary back packer on a brief outing will not want to carry a bulky tent stove. He must depend, therefore, on the campfire to keep him snug and warm in the face of wintry blasts.

The best plan is to build a blaze about as long as you yourself are in front of the open end of a lean-to tent. This fire may well be laid between two dry logs that have been placed about a foot apart. You will not doubt want to lie lengthwise beside this fire, of course.

Even this small a lean-to tent promotes cheerfulness, comfort, and enjoyable convenience. Not only do you profit to the fullest reasonable degree from the fire while asleep, but when you awake in the morning, there is the sky to study for weather hints and the surrounding country to scan.

When you are seated before the fire, preparing your meals, you will have plenty of room for food and utensils on either side. As you recline after supper, you can bask in the hearty warmth of the campfire and see between the tongues of flame, perhaps, some of the magnificences reserved as special rewards for those who venture into distant and deserted places.

The original tent, made in 1926 of Abercrombie's Green Waterproof Egyptian cotton, is still being used in 1955 after at least 400 days of camping. I know of no better tent for one or two men, doing their own camp work, except for bad mosquito country, or at temperatures lower than 20 below.—T.W.

For the simplest shelter you need carry only a simple tarpaulin corresponding in shape and design to shelter cloth illustrated here. This will serve to protect your bed from rain, to act as a windbreak, and to reflect heat from your outdoor fire.

So that it will add a minimum of bulk and weight to your pack, the tarpaulin should be made of one of the lighter waterproof cottons. You can, of course, waterproof the fabric yourself as described in the following chapter. The main section of the shelter cloth illustrated measures six feet high by seven feet wide. The triangular ends form side walls when the shelter is erected.

The side-view drawing shows the bivouac in place. Such a tent can be easily erected in a few minutes. I usually look for a tree to support one end of the ridgepole and use a couple of poles tied together as shears at the other end. A bough mattress for your sleeping bag can be spread between two logs which, at the same time, will provide a deacon seat across the front of the tent.

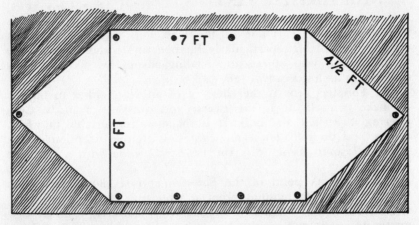

Diagram of small shelter tarp for bivouac. Make it of light waterproof material or light plastic sheeting.

I usually cut a fair sized log and stake it down at the back of the tent, tying the lower part of the rear wall to this rather than bothering with stakes. Not only is this technique generally easier and quicker, but it makes a more substantial job as well as serving to keep out furtive drafts. In very cold weather, imitate the trapper and choose a cubbyhole as your campsite—a sheltered spot among thickly spreading spruce or, perhaps, a tiny clearing in the center of a thick fir grove.

Simple over-night bivouac using small shelter tarp.

THE FORESTER TENT

If your problem is to cut weight or costs, the Forester Tent is a good solution. It is one of the best tents ever devised for a chronic woods loafer, particularly for one who wishes to live close to nature and who objects to spending any of his outdoor hours confined in a closed canvas cell.

The Forester Tent is the cheapest of all tents either to buy or to make yourself. It is the easiest and quickest to pitch. Considering its weight and bulk, it is the most comfortable in which to live and do your few camp chores. With the exception of the Whelen Lean-to Tent, it is the easiest to warm with a campfire in front.

The one weak point of the Forester, at first glance anyway, is that if you try to mosquitoproof it, you ruin its inexpensiveness and its functional simplicity. In bug time, however, it is an easy matter to secure a mosquito bar for a dollar or two and to hang or stake this net enclosure over your bed.

The Forester Tent is triangular in shape. The smallest practical dimensions for one man, or for two who do not mind a bit of crowding, is about seven feet wide at the open front, three feet wide at the back, and seven feet deep from front to rear. The peak of such a model should stand about six feet above the ground in the front, while the triangular rear wall will be about three feet high. With the entire tent open to the fire in front, the angles will be such that heat and light will be reflected throughout the sheltered area.

The tent is usually pitched with three poles and eight sticks cut at the campsite. The ridgepole should be long enough to extend from the peak and to pass down and out through the hole at the top of the back wall at such a tilt that it will rest on the ground about three feet behind the tent. Two shorter poles are arranged in front as shares and holding the ridgepole at their apex, run from the peak to the front corners.

PREVAILING WIND

You pitch this tent with its back to the prevailing wind. If the wind shifts around to the front and it comes on rain or snow, however, the front of the tent and the more exposed parts of the bedding can get wet. This is why some tent makers sew a hood to the front of the shelter that can be stretched protectively out in case of storm. A poncho or any small piece of canvas can be used to close the top of the open front, too.

In any event, the entire front should not be closed all the way down to the ground. If only the top part is shut, moisture will be kept out. It will still be possible, at the same time, to cook comfortably during a storm. Another advantage inherent with this particular type of tent is that one is so easy to handle that only a very few minutes will be required to strike and then erect it again with its back to the new wind direction. Made in this small size of almost any of the light waterproof tent fabrics, such a tent will not weigh more than four or five pounds.

Forester Tent.

EXPERIMENTAL WINTER CAMP

My first experience with the Forester dates back to about thirty years ago when I was experimenting with various types of camp equipment. I took a Forester Tent with light back-packing equipment and climbed up to the summit of the Alleghenies one January. There by a litle stream, high up on a peak in a rather exposed spot, I pitched camp and lived for a week.

The climate gave the tent a rugged test. I ran into rain, sleet, and snow. There was wind. Temperatures dropped way below freezing at night. At first, in the cold and gusty weather, I needed only a brisk fire four feet in front of the tent to afford me perfect comfort. When it began to blow and storm I erected a pile of rocks in back of the fire as a reflector, and I heaped up a lot of brush at the sides. Thereafter, despite blizzard and severe cold, I remained perfectly reposed. These were unusually tough conditions, and never thereafter did I have to resort to closing in the front area in this way.

Trips since then, made under usual summer and fall conditions, have shown that a moderate fire warms and lights this type of tent so that it becomes an extremely enjoyable and jolly abode. The sloping and the outward splaying of the side walls contribute a great deal to heating and illuminating this little shelter.

The walls seem to serve these purposes much better than does the sloping roof of the conventional Baker form of lean-to tent. As a matter of fact, it was my experience with the walls of the Forester that led me to incorporate the same principle in my Lean-to Tent.

On this winter test trip I just mentioned, I was also experimenting with bedding. I laid a browse mattress on the frozen ground and covered the spruce boughs with a light poncho. Then I spread my sleeping bag on top. This bag, also experimental, had an outside cover of unwaterproofed, unbleached muslin. Within this were two bags. The outer consisted of three pounds of wool batting, quilted in light wool flannel. The inner was a two-and-a-half-pound woolen blanket. The entire arrangement weighed ten pounds.

I slept in all my day clothing with the exception of moccasions and mackinaw coat. The latter served for my pillow. On the frostiest and most tempestuous nights, I woke up two or three times with the shivers and had to pile out and rebuild the blaze. On still nights I slept soundly all the way through, although the campfire went out sometime during the small dark hours.

PATTERN FOR MAKING WHELEN LEAN-TO TENT

For one or two campers, sleeping with their sides to the front. Make of closely woven waterproof cotton about 5 to 7 ounces per square yard, and cut and sew to the shape and dimensions shown, allowing 1 inch around the edges for hemming.

A A—Tape ridge with outside loops for ridge pole, and two loops on under side for clothing pole.

B B—Loops or cords sewed to outside of roof in which to insert poles when necessary to take "belly" from roof in snow or heavy rain.

C C—Large grommets, 1″ diameter, in which to insert sharpened poles which keep awning extended to the front when desired.

D D—Loops sewed inside at junction of roof and walls to hang mosquito bar from when needed.

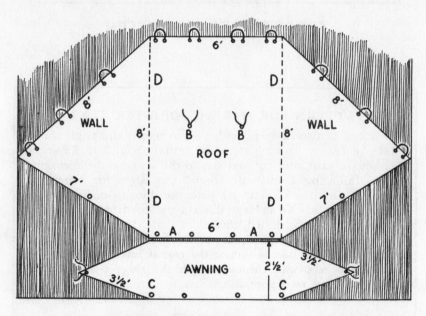

A study in camp comfort in cold weather.

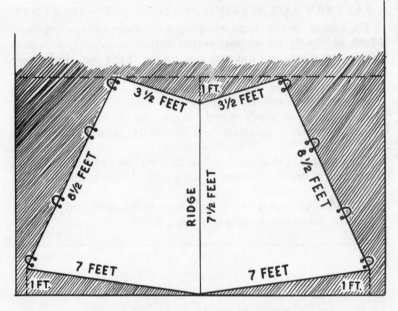

FORESTER TENT PATTERN

PATTERN FOR MAKING FORESTER TENT

For one or two campers, with beds arranged along side walls. Make of closely woven waterproof cotton about 5 to 7 ounces per square yard, and cut and sew to the shape and dimensions shown, allowing 1 inch all around the edges for hemming. Note how bottom of sides set back one foot to make tent sit right on ground. To manage this cut pattern from rectangular canvas as shown by dotted lines, then angle the front and back. The rear wall is cut off square at top, and when this is sewed to the main body of the tent at the rear it leaves a hole at the top of the rear wall through which the ridge pole is stuck. Total weight 4 to 5 pounds.

THE FAR NORTH

Several years later this same bag served me on a two-months fall hunting trip in the northern Canadian Rockies where occasional night temperatures dropped almost to zero. I slept in a tepee on a balsam mattress with two horse blankets spread between boughs and bag. No attempt was made to keep the fire up all night. I was perfectly snug, although on the coldest nights I would not have been so if it had not been for the gear underneath.

This same little Forester tent has gone with me, too, on many of my trips into the Far North. It has often been used there by my companions while I was sleeping in my Lean-to Tent. The two shelters pitched ten feet apart facing each other, with a fire flickering between, make about the most comfortable camp imaginable.

"Most men are needlessly poor all of their lives because they think they must have such a house as their neighbors have," an old woodsman said more than a century ago. "Consider how slight a shelter is absolutely necessary."

A lean-to and forester tent pitched facing each other with fire between in a a grove of thick spruces.

CHAPTER 9

MORE
TENTS
and
MATERIALS

TENTS THAT SHUT UP all around are sometimes most desirable. In intensely cold climates where weight is not too great a factor, a lot less chopping is required to warm a closed tent by means of a wood-burning stove than to keep the chill out of an open shelter. Where mosquitoes actually blacken the humming heavens as in some Arctic and sub-Arctic regions in summer, a tent with a net front and either a sewed-in floor or a sod cloth will provide welcome sanctuary.

A closed tent is usually preferable at crowded camping grounds and similar public locations, particularly when women are along. Not only do they afford privacy but, depending on the model, one can cook on a stove either inside the shelter or under an attached awning. Wall tents have long been the favorite at mining, construction, and other work camps. When one is climbing in high mountains where wood is not available, a very small closed tent with floor cloth is indicated. This need hold little more than the compact sleeping paraphernalia it shelters from the wind and weather.

THE A-WALL TENT

The commonest, oldest, and still the most widely used closed tent is the rectangular A-Wall with side walls some two to three feet high and with a ridge roof under which it is usually possible to stand erect. The sides and ends of the better models can be rolled up, opening the tent all around upwards to several feet from the ground and affording a welcome circulation of air in hot weather. This tent is also well adapted for heating and cooking with a portable stove. It is, therefore one of the best tents available for both extremely hot and very cold weather.

What about size? One that is seven feet square will accommodate two campers with their cots or sleeping bags placed along the two sides. There will not be much room for any duffle, however. The model with floor space nine feet square will hold three campers without crowding or inconvenience.

If a stove is to be used inside, however, the tent should be some nine feet wide and twelve feet long. This will allow the heater to be placed so that it will not be closer than eighteen inches to the canvas while still affording room for two campers to sleep without their beds coming too close to the hot metal.

FLOOR OR SOD CLOTH

The wall tent should be fitted with a sod cloth or a sewed-in floor. The sod cloth is usually preferable. This is a strip of canvas, usually some nine to twelve inches wide, stitched to the bottom of the walls all around. You stretch this over the ground around the inside of the tent. By weighing it down with baggage, poles, or whatever may be handy, you make the bottom of the tent both windproof and reasonably insectproof.

It is best to have an easily replaceable waterproof ground cloth which, lapping the sod cloth, will cover all the area inside the tent. Part of this flooring can be folded back to expose a safe base on which to set a stove. When necessary, it can be easily taken up entirely for cleaning or drying.

The sewed-in floor is not quite so functional because, for one reason, it precludes the use of a stove unless special precautions are taken, such as the carrying of an asbestos mat. The sewed-in floor, furthermore, is difficult to keep clean even with a broom. If left on the ground too long, it becomes damp and eventually rots. To take up a sewed-in ground cloth for airing and drying, you of course have to take your tent down.

For trips when camp is moved frequently, the A-Wall is not too suitable, if only because more time and labor are required for erecting it than is the case with most other models. It is usually made to go up on a wooden ridgepole supported by two uprights. All three are long and heavy enough to make them hard to transport. Metal poles, jointed for easier packing, are available for automobilists and others who have the means to carry them.

ADAPTING WALL TENT FOR LOCAL POLES

Most campers in wooded country where cutting is not prohibited

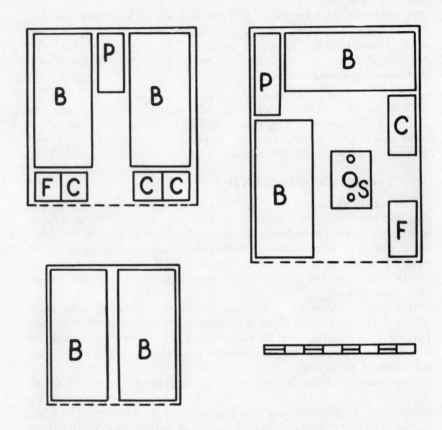

FLOOR PLANS FOR CLOSED TENTS

B—Each bed occupies 7' x 3'
C—Cook kit and Grub.
F—Firewood and kindling.
P—Personal effects.
S—Sheet iron stove.

7' x 7' —No room for anything but two beds.
7' x 9' —Room for everything except stove.
9' x 12'—Stove can be safely located with two campers.

Note:—The 9 x 12 foot tent will be three times the bulk and weight of the Whelen Lean-to Tent, and the stove will double this. Only advantage over lean-to is privacy and better for heavy rain and extreme cold.

prefer to drop their own poles on the spot. If it seems desirable to take advantage of locally secured supports, the tent should if necessary be adapted for their use. One way of doing this is by providing a tape ridge with outside loops through which to thrust the ridgepole. An easier procedure, if you are going to do the job yourself, is to cut holes six inches in diameter through the apex of each end wall. The circumferences of these may be reenforced with narrow canvas strips.

For the ridgepoles, lop off a pole some four inches in diameter and three feet longer than the tent. Shave this reasonably smooth

Pitching tents with poles cut locally. The "A-Wall" tent on the right has the ridge run through holes cut in the peaks. The Forester tent has a tape ridge with outside loops.

and then push it through the holes until it extends about one and one-half feet outside the tent at each end. Support the extremities of the ridgepole with sheer poles and arrange guy ropes to hold the tent firmly erect. As you know, shears are made by tying two poles together near their upper ends and then resting them in their spread heels so as to provide a crotch at the top.

Or, better, back the tent up to a tree and there lash one end of the ridgepole, whereupon guys will be unnecessary. A tent can also be erected with a rope ridge passed through the holes and suspended between two trees, two shear poles, or a combination of both.

A rather large number of stakes are required to pin down the bottom of the tent and to guy out the tops of the walls. These may be purchased with the tent or, if weight is a factor, cut when needed.

FOR AUTO AND FAMILY CAMPING

The most popular tent today for auto camping, for public campgrounds, and for trips when the family goes along is the Umbrella or Marquee Tent. This is extremely easy to pitch in a hurry. It is the more roomy for the ample head room it affords, enabling campers to walk erect throughout it. The area one requires is no larger than that covered by the floor.

No guy ropes are ordinarily needed. This can be a disadvantage, however, particularly in areas where there may be strong winds. The addition of guys will be a simple and a sensible precaution under such circumstances.

This widely manufactured model is available in a variety of sizes, including those running from seven feet square, measured by the floor space, on up through twelve feet square with nearly perpendicular walls five and six feet high topped by a pyramidal roof. They are neither light nor inexpensive, one ten-by-ten Umbrella Tent weighing ninety pounds complete and costing better than two hundred dollars plus express charge. You can, of course, find others affording the same amount of living space if not the same quality for on down to about one-fourth as much.

A single center post and a sewed-in floor are usual. You simply stretch the floor cloth out evenly on a flat patch of ground, stake down the four corners, and then with center pole in hand lift the tent and go inside. Once you have stuck the pole in place and run the four arms attached to it out to the tent corners, the shelter is up.

Some campers object to the center pole's taking up what they consider is too much room. This central support can be eliminated by four telescoping corner poles from which depends an umbrellalike frame that holds the pyramidal roof in place. The tent then costs more and is a little harder to erect. On the whole, the center pole is the better arrangement. It can be furnished with a strap to which hooks are attached, giving it the usually appreciated utility of a clothes rack.

These Umbrella Tents usually have a net door, often supplemented by a flap that can be tied out of the way when not in use. Screened windows are a great aid to ventilation. Without them, hot air has a tendency during the summer months to accumulate and press downward from the peaked roof. The tents can be secured with front awnings under which the campers can lounge in the warmest weather. Although the tent is not well adapted to heating by a wood stove, a gasoline stove can be conveniently and safely used under the awning. As these tents are frequently used in localities where wood for cooking is not available, both the awning and the gasoline stove may be very desirable adjuncts.

CANVAS COTS

Canvas cots can be set around the walls of the closed tent, or air mattresses and sleeping bags can be laid on the floor. When bulk and weight are not important factors, as is often the case when such tents are used, the cots are usually more preferable in warm weather at least if only for the additional storage space that is thus afforded beneath them.

If the weather is at all cold, however, some insulation such as a kapok mattress must be added. Even one of the heavier sleeping bags is cold when used atop bare canvas when temperatures approach freezing. But still cots are often very desirable for women, and when used with mattress, sheets, and blankets, make comfortable camp beds.

CARBON MONOXIDE

A wood-burning heater should be used when artificial warmth is desirable in the A-Wall or Umbrella Tent. Such tents do not warm well from a campfire in front. A gasoline stove can not be used inside for this purpose with any real comfort or safety. Such a stove generates quantities of the deadly carbon monoxide gas, to avoid the poisonous effects of which the tent should be kept very thoroughly ventilated—to such a degree, in fact, that much of the heat escapes.

There is even a certain generally unrecognized danger from carbon monoxide with a wood stove, as considered in some detail in the chapter on first aid.

MOSQUITOES AND FLIES

There are times and places where mosquitoes, black flies, and other winged biters can take much of the immediate pleasure out of life unless we are ready for them. Especially in the Far North during the long days when dusk blends imperceptibly with dawn, mosquitoes are often to be encountered in such air-darkening clouds as to be absolutely unbelievable to a southerner.

A great deal has been done to lick these abhorrences since the building of the Alaska Highway and since the activity in Alaska dating from the Second World War. A lot of people who could do something about it learned at first hand in those practical laboratories that mosquitoes can be a lot tougher obstacle than even the sub-Arctic's incomparable mud and muskegs.

There are four easy ways in which the camper may combat the pernicious activities of these pests. One, or in extreme cases a combination of all four, is sure to be so successful that no one need longer dread the critters.

Tents may be protected by screened doors and windows in addition to sod cloths or sewed-in floors. Individual mosquito bars are, along this same line of defense, very effective. Annoyers that still manage to get inside enclosures can be killed or immobilized by insecticides that to some extent will discourage them in the first place. Exposed portions of the body may be kept so coated with harmless and not unpleasant repellents that usually no insect will land on them for more than an instant. Biteproof clothing, extending even to gloves and head nets in drastic cases, may be worn.

The subject is, as we both can testify from long and considerable personal experience, a broad and important one. It is covered at length in a separate chapter on "Mosquitoes, Flies, et Al."

TENT MATERIALS

The best small tents are generally made of lightweight, closely woven cotton fabric that weighs some five to seven ounces per square yard. These materials ordinarily are waterproofed by a patented process peculiar to the individual tent maker.

Outfitters sell such tent materials, whose widths vary, by the running yard, to those who desire to make their own shelters. If the tent is larger than about nine by nine feet, however, it should be made of cloth that weighs from eight to ten ounces per yard, as in such expanses the lighter materials will not always stand the strain of tight pitching and high winds.

These standard tent cloths are very desirable because usually they are absolutely waterproof, do not absorb moisture and so become very heavy when wet, and are less vulnerable to mildew and rot. Any tent made of natural fabrics should, however, always be most thoroughly aired and dried before it is packed away at the end of a camping trip if mildew and rot are to be prevented.

A SIMPLE WAY TO SLACKEN A TENT

Ordinary old-fashioned canvas and duck, if fairly heavy, is intrinsically waterproof without special processing. There is this exception, often learned at a very young age, that if the inside of the roof is touched during a rain, water will drip through at that spot.

It will also shrink when it gets wet. When the tent is made of some such material, therefore, it is imperative to loosen guy ropes so that the shrinkage will not result in the pulling out of tent stakes. An easy way to avoid the necessity of rushing around during a sudden storm is to dig a small hole, four inches deep, beside where each upright pole stands on the ground. The pole can then be instantly lowered into this hole, automatically loosening the entire tent.

WATERPROOFING

Closely woven cotton material can be easily waterproofed at home. If you have a five-by-seven tent, for example, pitch this tight and taut some sunny morning.

Take two pounds of paraffin. This is usually procurable in cakes at most grocery stores. Cut it into shavings and dissolve these in two gallons of turpentine. The process can be hastened by placing the can in a receptacle of hot water. Keep it away from fire, however, as it is quite inflammable.

Paint the fabric liberally with the solution, preferably while it is warm, and let the tent stand until thoroughly dry.

This, however, will not work on nylon tents. If one of these develops leaky areas or seams, one answer is to cover offending spots with any thick paint and at the end of the season to throw the thing away. Waterproofing compounds for all fabrics are obtainable, too.

TENTS OF NYLON AND OTHER SYNTHETICS

Since World War II, there have appeared on the market a variety of tent designs employing nylon, Dacron and other synthetic fibers. Owing to their light weight and waterproof qualities, these tents have become quite popular with the modern mobile camper. A nylon tent, however, is very airtight, and unless the flap is left open, moisture from one's breath and body will condense and make the inside cold and damp.

Made for rapid pitching and striking, these synthetic tents come in many novel designs. Tents with external aluminum or fiberglass poles pop into shape in a minute and require no ropes or stakes. Tents that fold into car-hitched trailers can be erected and collapsed in a few operations. There are tents that pack on the car's roof which can be erected there to provide off-the-ground sleeping. For station-wagon owners, there are tents that fit over the car's open rear end, thereby expanding sleeping and living space. And there are numerous brightly colored synthetic tarps which are pitched from the car roof and offer airy, warm-weather shelter for sleeping and dining.

CHAPTER 10

STOVES FOR TENTS and SHELTERS

FOR CAMPS WHERE wood is available, we both ordinarily prefer the open blaze in conjunction with some sort of a lean-to shelter.

Such a campfire takes a part of anyone back to when our earliest ancestor cooked his meat for the first time and, rolled in furs, spent his initial night in a shallow cave warmed by the newly harnessed flicker of flame. It is the atavistic memory of this discovery, that lifted men above the animals, which is one of the chief urges that draws a lot of us back again and again into the wilderness. A camp without a wood fire, in fact, seems to be no camp at all.

Senses neglected in the humdrum of city life expand to an exquisite sensitivity under the influences of an honest campfire. The friendly deliciousness of smoke, some of which probably still perfumes your outdoor clothing, seeks you out as you get the camp in order. Then there's the special allure not available in the costliest restaurants that hardwood embers—with maybe a slight seasoning of pine—impart to food roasted, broiled, or baked over them.

The campfire cheerfully shows its superiority, too, when it comes to toasting yourself or drying your wet clothes. Such a fire costs nothing, and the wood that you have the satisfaction of gathering for it enjoys the added virtue of warming you twice.

But in spite of all that can be said for an open fire, there are times when a stove either is necessary or is at least indicated by common sense. You can not heat a closed tent adequately with a campfire. To accomplish that, you require a shelter of the open type. Yet with such a bivouac in temperatures well below zero, you would be chopping wood a lot too much. At many public and roadside campgrounds, furthermore, no firewood is available. If women are in the party, privacy may make a closed tent desirable, anyway.

THE MOST POPULAR CAMP STOVE

Cooking over an open fire in a heavy rain can be an awful chore and sometimes practically impossible unless a disproportionate amount of preparations are taken. Furthermore, cooks whose whole experience has been with kitchens take much more naturally to some sort of stove. So let us explore the problems and the advantages of the camp stove.

The most popular camp stove today is one that uses gasoline for fuel under its one, two, or three burners. In many cases the gasoline stove solves the cooking problem admirably, especially when it comes to boiling and frying. A separate oven can be had for baking.

This type of stove is ideal, and often a must for many public camping grounds. It is good for the places where firewood is no longer to be had and where even space may be limited. It is excellent for those automobile tourists who like to cook their own meals beside the road, both for the pleasure of eating outdoors and because of the very real economies thus afforded.

Gasoline stoves are inexpensive, easily and compactly packed, and durable. They can be used atop a handy metal stand that supports them at normal stove height and, when not in use, folds into a small bundle that is easily stowed in the car or boat.

A recent development in camp stoves is the use of propane in disposable, sealed containers. Pumping, priming and pouring of fuel is eliminated; just attach the tank and light the burner. A single-burner stove will cook three meals a day for a single camper for five days. The double-burner model will last two campers twice that time. Ideal for roadside camping, the propane stove is also good for wilderness trips where carrying fuel is a problem.

PUFFERS

The one-burner primus stove has a unique record among explorers, campers, and outdoorsmen. For the past sixty years it has been used by all Arctic and Antarctic exploring expeditions, as well as by at least ninety per cent of all Alpine climbers. If you are contemplating a trip into some such area as the rich Barren Lands—before which the tree line abruptly ends, not dwindling away gradually as might be expected—a compact and light primus stove weighing little more than a pound will be a good thing to take along.

These efficient little heaters may be obtained in units burning alcohol, kerosene, gasoline, naptha, benzine, and other liquid fuels.

A two-and-one-half-pound outfit with less than six inches of height and diameter may be secured that in addition to the small brass stove includes two nesting pots and two frypans as well as a shield against the winds that blow across treeless terrain. There is also a twenty-four-ounce outfit, nesting three and one-half inches and seven inches in diameter, that includes stove, two pots, potholder, windshields, and a combination lid and pan.

WOOD-BURNING STOVES

Whenever a stove is to be packed into territory where firewood is available, a sheet-metal model burning this fuel has decided advantages. You'll seldom see one today in city stores, and they're unfamiliar to campers with little experience. But along the receding frontiers in whose forests you still encounter oldtimers, these woodburning models usually are the only portable stoves ever considered.

Such a stove usually weighs a little more than the gasoline stove and, although available in folding types, is generally bulkier. But there is no fuel to transport, and the sheet-metal stove is not difficult to carry even over a portage or on a pack horse.

You can cook on it in the rain. With a little care, it will safely warm closed tents as well as log shacks. Many sourdoughs we know, as a matter of fact, have no other stove even in their home cabins. It is easy to dry clothing around it. Broiling and toasting over an open pot hole can be a comparative pleasure.

It is particularly handy for river trips in the large kicker-propelled boats that travel the broad and often sluggish streams at the roof of this continent. There odds and ends of dry driftwood quickly afford concentrated heat, protected from the ravenous winds often howling along such shores. By providing a shallow box filled with sand or some other such base, you can even cook enroute.

If the stove you select has an oven, and there is usually no good reason why it should not, baking and roasting will be possible. If it is without an oven, a folding reflector baker can be used.

Some sourdoughs, particularly in cabins, utilize a drum oven. This is a small metal compartment which is set in the stovepipe. There it utilizes for cooking and heating purposes warmth that would otherwise escape unhindered up the smoke outlet.

STOVES FOR TENTS

The standard A-Wall tent is best adapted to a wood-burning stove. Such a tent seven by nine feet is about the smallest that is suitable for this. A nine-by-twelve size is better for two men because the beds will then not be too near the heat.

The stove should not be closer than eighteen inches to any part of the fabric. The tent should not have a sewed-in floor, although you can get around this by using insulation such as an asbestos mat or a container filled with sand or loam. Rocks by themselves are not so good, for dangerous sparks can slip unnoticed among them.

If the stove has no legs and you would like to raise it to a more convenient height, just drive four stout stakes into the ground and cap each with an old tin can. It can be set on flat rocks, too, of course. In cabins a pole enclosure about a foot wider all around than the stove, and generally about a foot high, is often built and filled with rock and loam to provide a base. You see them, too, propped up on four tin cans.

Such stoves are provided with adjustable drafts. If necessary, an additional damper can easily be inserted in the pipe. You can thereby regulate the heat to a large extent. But you should never fill a stove of this sort full of wood and then go away and leave it with the drafts open. If you do, it is apt to become red hot in a hurry, and then you may have the stage set for a conflagration.

With carefully selected wood, it is often possible to build a fire that will last for four or five hours. If an all-night fire is desired, someone generally has to get up during the small hours to stoke up. A lot of hunters and trappers live comfortably the whole winter in the frigid north in A-Wall tents with small sheet-metal stoves.

STOVEPIPE HOLE

The telescoping stovepipe had best go straight up through the roof. Less effective and more hazardous is the practice of angling the pipe through the back wall by the use of two elbows. The outlet should, in any event, extend at least six inches above the peak of the tent. This will not only insure better draft, but it will also reduce the danger of sparks being blown directly against the canvas. It is often a good idea to top this pipe with an inexpensive spark arrester, particularly if you may be using softwoods or if you may be camping in thick dry woods.

There should be a fire guard where the pipe goes through the tent cloth. Consisting of an opening centered in some fireproof material which replaces a small section cut from the fabric, this may be obtained from large outfitters as well as from most tent makers. A wire-reinforced asbestos guard is better than a metal one because, in addition to being reasonably flexible and more durable, it will not set up a disconcerting rattle on breezy days.

This collar may be obtained with flaps that will cover the open-

ing when a stovepipe is not angling up through it. You can also leave
the original tent fabric attached at the top so that it can be rolled
up out of the way and tied or snapped across the opening.

SHEEPHERDER AND OTHER STOVES

The most famous as well as one of the better stoves for tents and
other small shelters is the Sheepherder Stove of the West. This is a
rather large article of the box type, with sufficient capacity for cooking a meal for five or six campers. It is about twenty-seven inches
long, a foot high and wide, and it has a rapidly heating oven five
by eight by eleven inches. It weighs twenty-seven pounds.

Any stove of sheet iron or sheet steel will burn out in time, but
the Sheepherder has the reputation of lasting longer than any other
stove made of such materials. The one used on my last winter trip
had been providing almost continuous service for four years.

The only place I know of where you can get the Sheepherder Stove
is the Smilie Outfits, 536 Mission Street, San Francisco 5, California. These large camp outfitters also have a smaller and lighter
stove, twenty by twelve by twelve inches. Including a small oven,
this weighs only a dozen pounds. Less expensive, it is adequate for
two or three campers. It does not have the longevity of the Sheepherder, however. Both varieties come with telescoping pipe.

Many of the small stores and trading posts near hunting and trapping country in the continental west and throughout Canada stock

Sheep Herder's Stove

stoves of the box type. Many of these are without ovens and, measuring about twenty by twelve by twelve inches, incorporate a door to the firebox and also an adjustable draft. These stoves are also very satisfactory and for those without ovens you can pack along a folding reflector baker.

Four or five joints of stovepipe, usually not telescopic, come with them. As a matter of fact, the interlocking black pipe sold in light flat rectangles is easier to pack. Each snaps together to make a single section, narrow at one end and flaring at the other.

There used to be a number of folding box stoves on the market, but in this country all but one seem to have disappeared. This still available model is made by Sims Stoves, Lovell, Wyoming. It folds flat to a thickness of three inches, and it has a stovepipe. This is a splendid, well-made little stove. Because it is so easy to pack, I believe I would prefer it to the Sheepherder for use with a reflector baker if I had to carry it on a horse.

One drawback to the stoves we've been talking about is that, bulky and heavy, they can not always be sent by parcel post. So if you live far from a source of procurement, you may have an express or freight bill which added to their cost will make them a bit expensive.

A little midget of a stove sold by Herter's, Inc., of Waseca, Minnesota, is remarkable in several ways. This small contraption, which George Herter calls the French Canadian Ice Fish House and Duck Blind Stove, is well made of heavy sheet iron and yet is light in weight. Because of this compactness and lightness, Herter's is able to sell it at slightly less than five dollars postpaid, partly because they do not include a stovepipe with it.

This will warm a small tent or other shelter very nicely, and there is room on top for using both a kettle and a frypan at the same time. The Knapsacker folding reflecting baker furnished by the Smilie Company is a natural for baking and roasting with this functionally diminutive stove with the long name.

THE YUKON STOVE

We read a lot in fiction about the "Yukon Stove" that, stories say, warms tents and small cabins throughout the whitened wilderness. You'd hunt a long way trying to buy one, for the so-called Yukon Stove is a heating contraption made from whatever materials may be at hand. These may be anything from old tomato cans to a gasoline drum.

One such stove that we've seen in a prospector's cabin in the Canadian Rockies consists of an old wash tub turned upside down on a dirt floor. Wood is inserted through an otherwise pot-covered

Sims Folding Stove.

Herter's "French Canadian Ice House
and duck Blind Stove.

hole in the top. Behind this, a second and smaller opening accom-
modates a rusty pipe. Scooping away a little dirt from the lower
front rim of the galvanized tub feeds air to the fire, making it roar
more assertively. Banking this dirt back in place quells the blaze by
cutting off oxygen. Where materials are scarce and packs heavy,
inventiveness thrives.

As one of us suggests in the recently published book, *How to
Build Your Home in the Woods:* A trapper's favorite, because
of the inexpensive ease with which a string of overnight cabins
can be provided with warmth, is the heater made of stovepipe. Join
two sections of knock-down seven-inch pipe so as to make a single
fourteen-inch cylinder. Unless the cabin already has a dirt floor,
set this in a large box of sand or loam. Brace it with several rocks.

Four-inch pipe may be elbowed out of the top rear of the cylinder.
Wire supports are generally improvised to steady this smoke vent.
In a tent, for example, two stakes are sometimes driven into the
ground about eighteen inches from either side of the outlet pipe,
and wire stretched between them to brace this.

A flattened section of pipe, bent at the edges so as to fit the top
of the stove more snugly, forms a lid that may be lifted for fueling.
This is sometimes loosely hinged with wire or with metal clips cut
on the spot. An air hole is generally punched in the top. Variations
throughout, of course, are many.

Make four or more cuts with a can opener or ax, apple pie fashion,
in the lower front of the cylinder. Push these flaps outward to
accommodate, for instance, a small baking-powder tin open at both
ends. Care should be taken to clinch this can securely in place. The
lid of the small container can then control the draft.

Some bushwackers use a cover punctured with nail holes for
medius draft, proving that one may revel in every comfort of home
by merely exercising the little grey cells.

CHAPTER 11

THE CAMPFIRE

WHAT REMAIN MOST fondly in our minds after a wilderness trip, I suppose, are the campfires. The warm blaze that takes the kinks out of you in the misty morning. The handful of crackling twigs that boils the kettle at noon. The cooking coals at the end of the day's sport when the odors build up in such a way that you can hardly bear to wait for that fresh liver or those flaky rainbows. The cheerful flames behind whose sanctuary you sit while the darkening forest comes to life.

There is also the long night fire beside which you lie secure, obedient to no needs but those imposed by darkness and cold and vagrant wind and to no mortal's laws but your own. The campfire then seems little more than a pinprick in a vast and vacant infinity, man's single buffer against an earlier and simpler age when there were no weapons but stones, then clubs, and later spears and winging arrows.

Much of the success of a camping trip, as well as a great deal of pleasure, is going to depend on your having the right kinds of fires. This does not mean, certainly, that campfires should be built in just one way. It all depends upon where you are, what you have, and whether your most pressing needs at the moment are for warmth, light, or nourishment.

The principles governing outdoor fires do not change, however. In the realm of camping there is probably no one set of essentials so often mismanaged. A poor fire can cause a multitude of troubles. A good one is a joy to all around it.

SAFETY

First, let me speak of safety. Never start a fire where it will spread dangerously. Wind may carry a glowing particle an unbelievable distance. Once in a high wind a mere spark ignited dry grass a hundred yards from my own fire, although I had thoroughly cleared the ground for seventy-five feet to windward. If I had not extinguished that conflagration promptly, 20,000 acres of virgin timber would have crowned into ashes, ugly deadfall, and stark black stumps.

On another occasion a very dear friend, a fine and competent woodsman, was camping alone in remote mountains. One morning after washing his hands and face, he stood for a few minutes before the campfire with his bath towel spread in his hands to dry. Then he flung it back onto his sleeping bag, took up his rifle and pack, and departed for a day's hunt. When he returned in the evening there was no camp. Tent, sleeping bag, grub, clothes, everything had been consumed. Nothing remained but a pile of ashes. There had been a small spark in that towel when he had tossed it on his bed.

It does not pay to take chances with fire. Never kindle one on inflammable ground such as that made up largely of decomposed and living vegetation. Fire will sometimes eat down deep in such footing. An individual may think he has put it out but often it may still not be entirely extinct. Unseen and unsuspected, it may smolder for days and weeks underground. It may lie nearly dormant during an entire winter. With the warmth and increasing dryness of spring, it may regain new vigor until one hot day a strong wind may cause it to bloom into a growling, exploding, devastating forest fire.

When you leave a camp or bivouac in a potentially dangerous area for more than a few minutes, put out that fire. Saturate it with water. Stir up the ground beneath and around it, working and soaking ashes and dust into mud. Dig around it until you are certain no root or humus will lead the blaze away like a fuse. Feel with your hands to make sure that all heat has been safely diminished. Examine the vicinity for any activity resulting from sparks and flying embers.

Particular precaution must be taken in some country when a Dutch oven is used. In a few areas, especially during dry seasons, this shallow kettle with its rimmed cover should not be used at all except when you remain on the spot. Make sure, in any event, wherever fire can be a menace, that the oven is buried in mineral soil and that no combustible material of any sort, be it roots or decaying forest litter, is near enough to be started smoldering.

TEST OF A WOODSMAN

A woodsman is known by the time it takes him to build his fire with whatever wilderness materials there may be at hand. If birch grows in your locality, the very best kindling is birch bark. Enough shreds of this can be pulled off by hand so that ordinarily there is no need, even deep in the bush, to disfigure the tree.

In evergreen country you need never have difficulty in starting a blaze in any kind of weather. A fairly tight handful of the dead resinous twigs that abound in the lower parts of all conifers will burst readily into flame at the touch of a match. The only exception you'll occasionally run across occurs in damp cold weather. Then freezing moisture sometimes forms light sheaths of ice over the forest. When this happens, the solution still remains simple. You have only to expose the dry oily interiors of the dead branches.

Shavings from pitch pine light very easily. So do shavings from any dead wood you find adhering to standing evergreens. If no softwood is about, look for dead wood on other trees. If you do have to use fallen litter for kindling, be sure that what you choose is firm and dry.

Fuzzsticks, when you need to bother with them, start a fire quickly. They are made by shaving down on a piece of wood again and again, not detaching the curls. These are commonly employed instead of paper, incidently, to start stove fires in the backwoods. Light these fuzzsticks, and all other kindling, so that the flames will be able to eat upward into fresh fuel.

Ordinarily, you will use dry materials to get the fire going. The job can also be done with live birch and live white ash, however, by splitting out kindling and making fuzzsticks.

HOW FIRES BURN

Although campfires can be made in numerous ways, the principles of conflagration remain the same. An understanding of these renders fire making under every practical circumstance a lot more easy. Firewood, for one thing, does not itself actually burn. A gas driven from the wood by heat is what actually flames. To be capable of this, the gas must first combine with the oxygen in the air.

What we need for a campfire is, therefore, fuel that is sufficiently inflammable, to give off combustible gases in sufficient quantity, to be lit by the heat we are able to concentrate on it. This initial fire, in turn, must be hot enough and lasting enough to release and ignite more and more gas from progressively larger fuel.

STARTING THE CAMPFIRE

An easy way to go about building a campfire throughout much of this continent is first to get a few scraps of something exceedingly flammable. This may be a few wisps of birch bark. Pile loosely over the shreds of bark something a trifle less combustible such as small, dry evergreen twigs.

Above this nucleus lean a few larger seasoned conifer stubs. Also in wigwam fashion, so that ample oxygen will reach all parts of the heap, lay up some dead hardwood. Then ignite the birch bark so that the flames will eat into the heart of the pile.

The lighting should almost always be accomplished with a single match. Even on those occasions when plenty of matches are at hand, the thus slowly acquired skill may on some later day mean the difference between a warmly comfortable camp and a chilly and miserably damp one.

The ordinary, long wooden matches are best. These must be held so that any draft reaching them will feed the fire down the wooden stem where it will be able to keep burning. This you will accomplish in whatever way seems best at the moment. You may face the wind with your two hands cupped in front of the flaming match. You may stretch out between the breeze and the carefully heaped flammables so that your body will act as a shield. You may use your jacket or any other handy articles, such as large sheets of bark, to protect the first feeble flames.

There is no time in any wooded area when a campfire can not be thus built from materials at hand. You can always either find or make a sheltered nook. Even when a cold rain is freezing as it falls, shavings and kindling can be provided with a knife. If you don't have a knife, you can still shatter and splinter enough dead wood with which to kindle a blaze. If preferably birch bark is available, one sheet will form a dry base on which to arrange campfire makings, while other bark angled about and above these will keep off moisture until the fire is crackling.

MATCHES

You will want a waterproof container kept filled with wooden matches whenever you are in the bush. This should be unbreakable so that even should you happen to slip in a stream, the matches will remain intact. This match case, which may well include some provision whereby it can be attached to the person or clothing, should be stowed where it will not be lost. In the North, we figure it is inexpensive insurance to carry a second filled container. Other

B'iling the Kittle

matches may be conveniently distributed among the pockets where they will be readily available for ordinary uses.

B'ILING THE KITTLE

The northern woodsman, particularly the Canadian, must sip his steaming cup of tea at noon and contemplate its rapidly changing surface colors even if he has nothing to eat. This is almost a religion up under the Aurora Borealis and is called "b'iling the kittle." For the temporary fire required, nothing elaborate is needed. Sufficient is a handful of dry wood that will flare up briefly and as quickly disintergrate to ashes, a few grey feathers of which invariably swirl up to float almost unnoticed in the dark brew.

The Campfire Club for more than forty years has sponsored an annual competition in boiling a kettle of water, with prizes and with time limits for qualification. The participant is given a billet of dry wood about five by twelve inches, a sharp hand ax, a kettle holding about two quarts of water, and one match. That is all.

The best technique is first to split the wood to include three full length pieces about three-fourths of an inch thick. These three sticks are driven into the ground to form a triangle about six inches high upon which the kettle is set. The remainder of the wood is reduced to shavings and split kindling which are placed under the kettle and ignited. If the competitor is experienced, he has picked up a small dry pebble on which to strike his match, and he kneels facing the wind. I know of no quicker way to boil tea water than this.

Your woodsman is not so elaborate. He builds a fire in the easiest way he can, depending on what fuel there is at hand. He cuts a green pole several feet long. This tea stick he shoves into the ground so that one end extends over the center of the heat. He may adjust its height by propping it up with a rock or chunk of wood.

The kettle he hangs by its bale at the end of the tea stick. This container, incidently, is very often a large enough tin can near whose rim opposite holes have been punched and a handle, perhaps a foot of light copper or snare wire, inserted.

COOKING FIRE

If in addition to heating water for tea you want to fry some steaks and maybe boil up some nearby wild onions, one handy method that will do away with a lot of teetering and tipping is to dig or stamp a trench in the ground. This may be about six inches across, six inches deep, and eighteen inches long. Place this trench lengthwise with the wind to assure a good draft, and in it build your fire. Kettle, skillet, and other utensils can then be steadied across it.

The fire must have oxygen with which to burn, of course. If the kindling and other wood is packed too compactly, the result will be a smudge that will soon smoke out. You can sometimes help the blaze along by blowing on the flames or by fanning them. If the day is unusually quiet and the fuel none too ardent, however, you will do better to build the ordinary sort of cooking fire above the ground.

THE LONG COOKING FIRE

We like to have all the makings of our meals served at once—hot meat, vegetables, biscuits, and beverage. This means that for dinner several receptacles and perhaps a reflector baker will be functioning all at once, with probably one cook to manage everything. A job of this sort is hard to control if you are using the ordinary round fire. More functional is a fire about eight inches wide and four or five feet long.

A cooking fire of this sort can be built between two fairly dry logs some four to six inches in diameter. Let these be about five feet long. If they are raised an inch or so by stones or billets of wood, air will be able to circulate freely beneath them. Build your fire of long wood placed between these two logs. Keep adding fuel, preferably split hardwood, and let it burn down until you have either a bed of coals or an enduring fire that does not blaze up over a foot high. It will then be ready for the vittles.

In the meantime, cut two posts of green wood about two inches in diameter, each with a fork at the top. Drive these into the ground at either end of your two logs so that a green crosspiece laid between the crotches will extend above the center of the fire. Make pothooks for each kettle as shown in the sketch.

If you are using a reflector baker, set it on the ground about a foot from the fire. While baking, encourage a high blaze in front of it with split kindling.

GRATES AND IRONS

A substantial wire grid, available from dealers in camp equipment, will provide a convenient base on which to set pots and pans above a wood fire and over which to broil meat. Some of these have folding legs which, stuck into the forest floor, will hold kettles and frypan the desirable eight inches or so above the ground.

Our own experience deep in the bush, however, has been that these sharp extremities are somewhat of a menace when one is constantly on the move. We have removed them, partly also to save weight. The grids can as handily be laid across rocks or billets of wood. In a stony spot, this has to be done anyway.

A similar arrangement, less bulky to pack, is two iron rods about one-half inch in diameter and four feet long, or flats or angleirons of similar stiffness. Support them above your fire with rocks or logs at each end, and have them just far enough apart so the smallest kettle will not slip down between.

FIRE MAKINGS

Before you turn in at night and certainly before you leave camp even for the day, provide a plentiful supply of fuel with which the next fire can be built. These makings may include birch bark, three or four good fuzzsticks, some split kindling, and a few pieces of larger wood. Place all these under cover where they will be sure to keep dry.

Fire for
a simple
meal.

This arrangement of the wood fire for cooking a full meal is quite general throughout all the wilderness of North America. See also cut titled "A study in camp comfort."

You may arrive back in camp dog-tired, cold, and wet, with numb hands that will scarcely grasp a knife for whittling. Or when your turn comes to build the morning fire, it may be raining or snowing. It won't take many such experiences to make you remember to have the makings always ready.

One of the unforgivable sins of the north woods is to quit a camp or cabin without leaving both kindling and a plentiful supply of dry firewood by the stove or fireplace.

WOOD FOR BURNING

The difference between softwoods and hardwoods is botanical. The evergreens are called softwoods. Hardwoods come from trees that have various types of flat leaves instead of needles or scales.

Generally speaking, the resinous softwoods when dry make the quickest kindling. They flare up rapidly. They are smoky, however, quick to throw sparks, and not very long-lived. The seasoned hardwoods, as well as a few green hardwoods such as birch and ash, burn longer and more steadily. It is these that break up into the bright hot coals that furnish the even heat desirable for broiling and other such forms of cookery.

The woods that spark most, roughly in the order of their doing so, are: white cedar, red cedar, alder, hemlock, balsam, the spruces, the soft pines, basswood, box elder, chestnut, tulip, sassafras, and willow. Often you have to use wood that sparks because no other is conveniently available. Don't put fresh wood on the fire in front of your shelter and go away and leave it even for a minute under such

Where poles for suspending kettles are not available, as on plains or desert, build up two walls of rock or logs, making trench about 9 inches square and as long as desired. Build your fire in it, and place a wire grill over it on which kettles and pans rest, or on which you can broil. A magnesium griddle is also excellent over such a fire.

circumstances. Sparks don't often burn through heavy canvas, so if you have a pack cover or tarp lay it over your sleeping bag.

NIGHT FIRE

Suppose you have a cooking fire built in front of your lean-to tent, and the weather is either nippy or downright cold. When the evening meal is over, take away the pot hooks and poles. Drive a couple of stout posts about ten inches behind the backlog of your present fire, slanting them a little backwards. Pile up a wall of good stout logs, dry or green, against these. Over your cooking fire lay some smaller logs. Pretty soon you'll have quite a blaze, with the log wall in the rear reflecting the heat back into your tent—a cheerful fire to spend a frosty night before.

If you will build up this fire just before turning in, you may be able to keep it going all night. It will then provide warmth while you sleep and, in the morning, a bed of coals that will do for cooking breakfast. There is no sure formula, however, for keeping a campfire alive all night without attention. Sometimes it will hold, but if the heat is necessary for comfortable sleeping, more often someone has to pile out around two a.m. to freshen it.

This is not much of a chore to an old woodsman. He lays on some logs that have already been cut, and perhaps he lights a stub of a pipe from a coal. Never does smoke smell so sweet. An owl hoots. The sparks and the smoke go straight up to heaven where gleams Orion's belted brightness. It's good to be awake at such a time.

CHAPTER 12

THE BEDTIME STORY

NO SLEEPING BAG or blanket of itself produces any warmth. In the absence of a fire, the human body is ordinarily the only heat-generating machine in a wilderness camp.

The normal man, sleeping or lounging relaxed beside a campfire. liberates somewhat less than a hundred calories of heat every hour. This output can be increased in two ways. Rigorous exertion can, over the day, multiply the yield as much as six times. Even shivering, a form of muscular exercise and one of nature's safeguards against freezing, will build up the release of body warmth several times. Eating, too, stimulates the caloric output. The increase is quicker although of shorter duration with carbohydrates, greater and more lasting with proteins.

The skin automatically begins to shut off surface blood circulation when exposed to cold. It can thus decrease the heat loss from the skin as much as a fourth of normal. Alcohol, it so happens, prevents this natural thermostat from functioning properly; bringing on rapid and sometimes dangerous heat losses at the same time that the individual may be deluded into believing himself warmed and stimulated. Wind, as well as low temperature, produces chilling and accelerated dissipation of bodily warmth.

All that a sleeping bag or any other bedding can do, therefore, is to delay the loss of body warmth by insulating the individual both against undue waste of that heat and against encroachments of cold and wind.

The most effective insulation known for this purpose is dry, still air. Thus the effectiveness of bed materials in keeping one warm is in direct proportion not to their weight but to the number of dead

air cells they contain. The thicker a sleeping robe or blanket is and
the fluffier its nature, the more inert air it affords.

BLANKETS

Fifty years ago sleeping bags consisted of several thicknesses of
wool blankets sewed into bag form inside an outer sack of canvas.
They were little else, in fact, than a more or less convenient and
controversial way of preventing the kicking off of blankets during
sleep. Horace Kephart, calling them unpleasant traps, did not dis-
agree that on the whole sleeping bags were an accursed invention
of a misguided soul.

For nearly three centuries the most famous blankets on this continent have been the Hudson's Bay Company Point Blankets, spun
and woven of virgin wool and still distributed throughout the
farthest regions of North America by the Governor and Company
of Adventurers of England trading into Hudson's Bay. One sees these
everywhere in the northern wilderness, in use under the severest
conditions for every conceivable outdoor purpose, from trapping gold
at the bottom of a sluice box to providing temporary sails for a
canoe.

During the years more closely following the H. B. C.'s incorpora-
tion on 2nd of May, 1670, the short stripes or "points" on these
blankets signified the number of large prime beaver skins it took
to barter for them. The present 3½ and 4 points now indicate difference in blanket areas. The material is of standard quality and weight.

Army blankets are closely woven for durability and are not nearly
as warm as Hudson's Bay Blankets. However, in my youth I got
along fairly well with army blankets, five pounds each, pinned into
bag form with six horse-blanket safety pins. This arrangement, incidently, was also used by the other half of this writing team when
on the verge of his teens he was making his first weekend and
summer camps in New England. Like him, I customarily spread
this improvised sleeping sack on top of a poncho and a browse
mattress.

Protection from wind and rain was necessary, for the insulating
value of a blanket is in ratio to its functional bulk when sheltered
from these. One blanket sufficed for summer. Four were a lot more
comfortable during fall hunting trips.

Then it froze most nights, and you sometimes could hardly sleep
because of the scraping of snow overhead. This insomnia was not
the result of any discomfort, for ordinarily such a storm is soothing,
while snow piling up lightly against a shelter has an insulating effect.
Rather it was because of the exciting realization that the most stir-

ring of all hunting conditions might be awaiting us the next morning—a fresh white tracking snow.

The combination was heavy and bulky, and it took more than
half an hour to make the bed including the browse mattress. But
we had plenty of time those days.

SLEEPING-BAG MATERIALS

The better modern sleeping bags utilize more effective insulating
materials which are at once thicker and lighter than blankets, affording therefore much more dead air space pound for pound. The best
insulating filler, providing maximum warmth with minimum weight,
is genuine waterfowl down.

This pure down is expensive, and some makers mix in a few
feathers, reducing both the cost as well as the insulating properties.
But you still have a pretty good bag. Feathers themselves are bulkier
and not so resilient, therefore still less warm, although such fillers
are sometimes improved by the removal of the quills.

Next in thermal value probably come some of the new synthetic
materials such as Dacron, which are light and durable as well as impervious to mold, moths, and mildew. Dacron, one of the synthetic
fibres developed by DuPont, has a heat-retaining value about mid-
way between goose down and wool. If weight and bulk are not
primary considerations, Dacron, a material that by now has been
thoroughly tried in the field, seems desirable as a filler for ordinary
summer and fall use because of its low cost as compared to down.
It is not as superb as pure waterfowl down for back packing or for
extreme cold.

Wool batting and kapok bags attract many buyers. The latter is a
vegetable fiber that is reasonably effective for a while but which
eventually mats and finally powders with use. Speaking very generally, the inexpensive bags filled with these materials, when con-
scientiously made and honestly advertised by reputable outfitters,
are satisfactory enough for warm weather camping when night temperatures do not go below 40° Fahrenheit and when easy transportation is assured.

Not very much money should be spent for a bag with a questionable or mediocre filler. It would be more prudent to add a few more
dollars and purchase one of the less expensive down or feather bags,
getting along with blankets in the meantime, if necessary.

Too, you can emulate some trappers and prospectors we know
and make your own bag. Materials including shells, liners, covers,
fasteners, and pure new down in bulk can be purchased from some
of the outfitters for this purpose.

SLEEPING-BAG FABRICS

The down, feathers, batting, or other filler for sleeping-bag use must be enclosed in a light and very tightly woven fabric from which it can not escape. This container should be sewed into tubes or other restricted compartments so that any shifting of the stuffing will be held to a minimum, maintaining as nearly as possible a uniform thickness throughout.

Outside of this insulating layer is a strong, light, and high-count cover which should be water resistant and fairly impervious to wind but not waterproof. If the cover were waterproof, it would, unless kept partly open, confine the vapor that the body constantly throws off. This would soon make the bag clammy and cold. In frigid weather, such a condition could mean freezing to death.

In many bags there is no inside lining, the sleeper being in contact with the shell that contains the filler. Some of the better bags intended for use in cold climates have a thin woolen liner that, adding but little to bulk and weight, is particularly appreciated on subzero nights when one first crawls into the sack. There is no especial objection to pinning light cotton, linen, or woolen sheets inside a bag if care is taken not to puncture tubes holding such an escape-prone filler as down.

AWNINGS AND POCKETS

A number of sleeping bags are provided with an awning that,

Woods 3-Star Robe, used by most experienced outdoorsmen through Canada and the Northwest, and by both authors for many years. Good for forty below zero for most rugged men.

attached to the cover, may be erected as a shelter over the head. Advertising agencies delight in picturing sleeping bags with this awning raised and the camper sleeping blissfully in the rain. It is a provocative selling point, certainly.

The difficulty in real life is that any such sleeping bag would have to be waterproof. This, as we have already considered, would be an impractical arrangement. In warm weather no matter how dry, it would be like sleeping in a steam bath. In cold temperatures, the imprisoned body moisture would soon negate all insulating qualities and freeze us. You need to sleep under a tarp, tent, or some other shelter in stormy weather.

Such an awning can have its uses, however, although you may care to trim it down some so as to conserve space and weight. The flap can be used, for instance, to roll the bag in for carrying and may thus eliminate the need for a special container. You may also find it convenient as a mat on which to store a few odds and ends where they will be instantly available if you should want any during the night. Otherwise, cut the appendage off and lay it on the ground alongside your robe, so that when you get up to dress you'll have a flat clean area on which you can stand until you get into your socks and boots.

The pockets provided by some manufacturers for air mattresses are neither necessary nor advisable. They add both weight and expense. They are just something else to wear out. Employing them means that you will not be able to use the bag equally on both sides. Alternating the top and bottom as is possible with sleeping robes opening down one side will add both to the article's longevity and to your comfort.

There is absolutely no need for a mattress pocket. The reason some individuals are troubled for awhile by a bed's slipping off its pneumatic softener is almost invariably a result of the latter's being blown up too hard.

AIR MATTRESSES

Maximum comfort is attained when one has an air mattress under a good and adequate sleeping robe. One of these requires only several minutes to inflate. A browse mattress takes about half an hour for proper making, and then it mats down enough to be uncomfortably hard after the second if not the first night.

The natural tendency among individuals accustomed to sleeping on the rather solid conventional bed is to pump their air mattress too full. It will be just about right if you will inflate it until you can just barely touch the ground when pressing down on the center with your fist. Another way to accomplish the same result is to pump in more air than you'll need and then lie on it on your side and open the valve until your hipbone just touches the hard surface beneath. One of the small light rubber pumps is convenient for inflating. This bulb attachment can be worked by either hand or foot.

If weight and space are important considerations, a good air mattress to secure is one about four feet long by half as wide. This should be located just beneath the shoulders and hips. Browse, leaves, brush, or anything else suitable, such as a horse blanket, may then be used to level off under the head and legs.

The stability afforded by this last evening-off of the sleeping surface generally eliminates any tendency there may be to roll off the mattress during the night. Poles or even a couple of large rocks can always be placed at either side of the bed to keep everything in position. Once the average individual has slept out on such an arrangement for several nights, however, he won't have any trouble in making his bed stay put. Most never do experience any difficulty.

If a little additional bulk and weight will pose no problem and if the amount of use you plan to put the bed softener to throughout the years will justify the added expense, by all means secure the best available full length air mattress. These are particularly excellent for cabin use.

All air mattresses are by themselves admittedly cold in frosty weather. The shortcoming can be entirely overcome by spreading some insulation such as a fur robe or spare woolens between the mattress and the robe. This disadvantage is more than offset by the unexcelled coolness afforded by having nothing more substantial than a mass of air beneath you during the hot months.

An air mattress should be laid on a hard, flat, rigid surface. There is no need to bother removing minor irregularities. The mattress will automatically adjust to them, although some of the more fragile models need something such as a tarp between them and rough ground for protection against puncturing.

One occasionally sees these mattresses being used on sagging bunks and cots, to the discomfort of the occupant. Sleeping on the floor under such conditions is far more relaxing. Such a bed can be adapted for air mattress use, however, by providing it with a solid surface of boards or poles.

WHAT ABOUT WARMTH?

Sleeping robes containing three to four pounds of mixed down and feathers are usually satisfactory when temperatures are above zero. For fall hunting in the north and at high altitudes, four to five pounds of down will provide comfortable repose in cold as low as ten to twenty degrees below zero.

We've both put in good nights in our eiderdowns when the colored alcohol in the thermometer has contracted more than one hundred degrees below freezing. When it's that icy, you appreciate five to six pounds of down in addition to a shaggy woolen lining that doesn't let you shiver too long when you pile in and draw the top up over your head. Inside the bag is the place for your head to be when the sap in the trees starts freezing, and the banging and snapping of tearing, bursting fibers joins the heavier cannonade of expanding ice. Your nose, however, must be outside, both for fresh air and to avoid filling the bag with moist vapor.

On the frostiest nights with too light a bag, you may have to turn in with your clothes on. These should be absolutely dry. Loosen all tight areas beforehand and empty your pockets, placing the contents where none will be lost. If you have a flashlight which you may have cause to use during the darkness, take it in the bag with you. Extreme cold may otherwise immobilize the batteries.

It will be better when possible to figure on carrying a heavier bag and sleeping raw in it. Flannel pajamas are ordinarily appreciated, but in very cold weather you'll actually be more comfortable without even them because of the way they will retain a certain amount of body moisture.

Except for something to protect the feet, you won't need to don anything if you have to haul out for any reason. The body will retain its own aura of warmth for a couple of minutes or so. When the cold does strike, pajamas aren't going to keep it out. Such exposure will not be harmful in any respect or even unpleasant. You'll probably be shivering when you crawl back into the sack, but warmth will soon take over and almost at once you'll be drowsing again.

ADJUSTING WARMTH

It is best when possible to choose a sleeping robe suitable for the lowest temperatures you expect to encounter. A good down robe that will keep you warm on nights when twinkling ice crystals form a scintillating ceiling close above the throbbing earth, to which campfire smoke ascends in unwavering pillars, will still be pleasant during the warmth of summer.

By that time you will be using it nearly open and you will probably be sleeping with at least your head, arms, and chest uncovered. A robe with snaps, preferable anyway to the vulnerable zipper for wilderness use, can be adjusted most satisfactorily to changing temperatures.

The warmth of a down bag, and to a lesser extent that of all bags, can be regulated to a very large degree by the frequency with which it is aired. In very cold weather, daily airings will keep the down fluffed out and heat-conducting moisture expelled. In hot weather you'll find it more comfortable if aired only as it lies on the bed.

Care should be taken when the robe is hung across a line to suspend it parallel to the tubes that contain the insulation.

REDISTRIBUTING THE DOWN

One difficulty experienced with sleeping robes in which down and similar fillers are used is that this insulation has a tendency to shift toward the bottom. This leaves the upper area of the robe vulnerable to low temperatures. In many instances it results in the expense and nuisance of returning the article to the factory for renovation.

You can redistribute the filler yourself on the spot, as a matter of fact. The process is very simple. Open the robe Lay it on a hard surface, such as the ground or floor, with the inside upward. Procure a supple stick about a yard long. Then start beating the robe lightly from the foot up toward the center. You will be able to feel when a reasonably uniform thickness has been returned. If necessary, turn the robe over and go through the same process on the other side.

MUMMY BAGS

Several outfitters supply small, body fitting, mummy bags which contain from two to three pounds of down and which roll into very small bundles weighing about twice the weight of the filler. Such bags are intended chiefly for hikers and climbers who have to pack all their equipment on their backs. They offer wonderful possibilities in putting together a go-light outfit. One of us has ridden many wilderness miles with a little bag of this sort, still as good as new after ten years of rough usage, rolled in a small tarpaulin along with some grub and other essentials and tied behind his saddle.

Our experienced mountain climbers have found these are satisfactory down to about ten degrees above freezing provided they are used in a small Alpine tent with some sort of soft insulation under them. If it gets too cold for a night or so, you can turn in fully clad, except for boots, in dry and preferably fresh clothing.

These mountain bags, which can be bought to fit your height, are made about eighteen inches at the bottom and up to some thirty-six inches wide at the top. The user is thus encased like a mummy. When he turns over during sleep the entire bag is apt to turn over with him. This is not objectionable after one becomes accustomed to it. As a matter of fact, after a few nights you can get in the habit of holding the top down with your two hands and maneuvering sufficiently with the hips and feet to keep the bag in place when you move. This soon comes to be second nature. My collaborator's wife, for example, prefers this model of eiderdown.

Some, however, never do feel fully relaxed in the mummy bag, particularly if they have slept many months in the large ninety-by-ninety-inch titans of the tall timbers. Such individuals, when they want a lighter bag, may prefer the more conventional rectangular sacks which run on up from thirty inches wide when closed, and in some excellent, all-waterfowl-down models weigh less than four pounds. A large man, six feet or over, will find a bag forty inches wide or more a lot more comfortable. You may also have to hunch up on the hands to turn in these, too, but a few nights of this makes the process as natural as stepping over a log.

PILLOW

You may find that some sort of a pillow will add greatly to your comfort. This may be a folded shirt. It may be a pillow case that you stuff with dry pine needles or wild marsh hay. It may be an air pillow that you can blow up by mouth in a few seconds. One of these weighs but an ounce or so and can be carried in a game pocket during wet weather to double as a dry seat.

TWO WAYS TO MAKE A FUR BLANKET

The more remote Indians of the North often made blankets of rabbit skins and similar furs. They still do, for that matter, although the squaws' activities along these lines have decreased considerably since tribes have found it easier to get money by other means and with this to buy commercial blankets and sleeping bags. The job is not a difficult one, however. Anyone on hand during a rabbit year can fashion such a robe. There are two general methods.

One way is to stretch and dry the skins of varying hares, snowshoe rabbits, marmots, or similar small creatures whose light and fragile pelts are not particularly valuable. Each skin is then cut in a long ribbon about three-fourths of an inch wide. This is done by starting outside and cutting around the circumference. A ribbon several yards long is thus obtained from the larger pelts.

The ribbon is then spiraled around a rawhide cord, often known locally as babiche, whose simple manufacture is described elsewhere in this book. The resulting fur ropes are sewed together at the ends, making a single long line. A pole frame the size of the desired blanket is lashed or otherwise fastened together. The fur rope is woven into it to form the blanket which is finally bound on the edges with cloth or buckskin.

The weave customarily is very loose. You can poke a finger through it anywhere. A blanket about five by seven feet, therefore, weighs in this stage little more than a pound. These fur robes have never been very durable, and the hair keeps coming out. To offset both these faults to some extent, they're often quilted between two thicknesses of some fabric such as light wool blanket.

The second method consists of shingling a blanket or other fabric, occasionally the fine burlap in which the Hudson's Bay Company sews and seals its furs, with tanned whole hides lapped an inch or so. The so basted pelts are then sandwiched protectively by sewing over them another piece of jute, canvas, blanket, or any other hardy fabric.

BROWSE BEDS

The real browse bed is not made by lopping off a half dozen spruce boughs and dropping them beneath the tree where the sleeping bag is to be spread. A really functional browse bed is thatched. Movies often accomplish the task in a minute or two, despite diversions that may include turning just in time to club an oncreeping wolf or two. In real life, even without interruptions, the process requires more like half an hour.

As old outdoorsmen sometimes remark, they go into the woods to have a good time, and a third of that time is spent in bed. You won't have an enjoyable or even a refreshing vacation unless you get a reasonably relaxing sleep most nights, and it is in the bed of the beginner that most discomfort starts. When an experienced woodsman makes camp, he gives attention to his bed first of all.

He wants it soft, dry, smooth, and warm. He therefore selects a level, clean, dry piece of ground about three feet by seven feet. First pulling up any shrubs, dislodging a stone or two with a heel, and perhaps knocking out a root with the back of his ax, he cuts four poles and stakes them in place to form a rectangle in which to confine his bedding. He can, as we've often done, fill this with pine needles and let it go at that. However, the best mattress that can be extemporized from forest materials, if this is to be a special sort of camp and he can spare the time, is one built of evergreen boughs.

The springiest evergreen branches obtainable are needed for this. Best, for example, are the small boughs of the heavily needled balsam. All such branches can be most easily carried to the bed if they are dropped one by one over the handle of an ax. The needles will then interlock, holding the entire mass in place. If you are using a knife, a stick with an up-pointing stub at the end will serve.

You start a browse bed by placing a deep layer of boughs at the head. The branches are placed upside down, opposite to how they grow. The butts point toward the foot of the bed and are well covered by succeeding layers. Row after row is laid in this manner. The final mattress should be at least one foot thick. It should be leveled off and given additional resiliency by shoving in young evergreen tips wherever a space can be found.

The first night on such a bed is something that everyone should experience at least once. The second night will be a bit lumpy. After the third night, you will probably bring in an ax-load of fresh boughs and, fluffing up and rearranging the aromatic greenness, essay to renovate it by interposing new materials as sagaciously as possible.

CHAPTER 13

TOOLS FOR OUTDOORSMEN

THE MOST INDISPENSABLE TOOL for a hunter or fisherman or camper, and in fact for any outdoor man and boy anywhere, is the knife—a businesslike knife, sharp and keen. Mrs. Whelen's aunt, who taught high school Latin for thirty years in Nebraska, had the right idea. She asked every class, "Which boys have a jackknife in their pocket?" The ones who had none did not rate very high with her.

Her philosophy was that if a boy did not have a knife and know how to use it, he was not likely to grow up able to do many things for himself. And an outdoorsman has to be capable of doing everything for himself unless he everlastingly ties himself to the apron strings of a guide—and then he is not an outdoorsman.

COOK'S KNIFE CAN BE TOO SHARP

You need a knife constantly afield, and for many purposes. For example, the camp cook will require one for slicing bread and meat, paring vegetables, and for a dozen other chores. Any fair-sized knife will do for such duties. It is better to have a special one for kitchen work, however, as this blade is almost sure to get such rough treatment that it would take a lot of labor to keep it sharp enough for other jobs.

Furthermore, such a knife both performs and holds up better when not given the fine edge desirable for pocket and hunting knives. One reason for this is that breadstuffs are sliced and meat is carved more easily with what is actually a sawing action. A coarse edge made by sweeping the blade forward a few times against a carborun-

116

dum diagonally from heel to tip, first on one side and then on the other, actually resembles the teeth of a saw when viewed under a strong magnifying lens. This edge can be quickly renewed by the same process.

An ordinary, small butcher knife goes well with most outfits. Have a sheath for it, and keep it in the bundle with the knives, forks, and spoons.

THE POCKETKNIFE

In the open spaces, particularly the woods, you will need a knife for whittling as much as for anything else. All boys should learn to whittle when they are young. You can't do it for shucks with a little vest-pocket penknife, so named because such a small pocket-knife was used back in pioneer days to make and mend pens fashioned from feather quills. The best all-around type is the so-called trapper's knife, made by most large cutlery concerns, with one blade for rough usage and another for finer work in closer quarters.

The first blade, with a rounded point, is excellent for general skinning. The second blade, with a point sharp enough to lift a splinter from your hand if need be, can be kept for the more delicate skinning around eyes and ears and also for small animals. Whatever other knife you have, you'd better have one of these that you can keep in your pocket always. I have had a knife like this in my back pants pocket ever since I was knee-high to a chopping block.

SHEATH KNIVES

While the trapper's claspknife will do everything necessary for the outdoor sportsman, many of us, particularly if we hunt big game, find it handy to carry a sheath knife. Almost all interest in outdoor knives revolves around this type. There are some who think it is a sort of Billy the Kid weapon, and that one on the belt marks its owner as a tenderfoot. But there is no law against carrying it in the rucksack, if you prefer, or tying it safely out of the way on a saddle. If, for some reason, you want to wear it in the wilderness where you can get at it most easily, there's no proviso against that, either, and under certain conditions this practice just could come in plenty useful.

The trouble is that most sheath knives one sees are entirely too large, long, and thick bladed to be entirely practical. The sheath knife with which we are here concerned is primarily for the hunter's use. It should be designed chiefly for skinning and butchering animals. At the same time, it should also be good for all reasonable outdoor purposes. One can be invaluable for a lot of different jobs: blazing, cutting browse, repairing leather goods, and making fuzz-sticks for starting a fire.

If you spend much time in remote regions, you'll also want one that you can depend on in any number of possible emergencies, such as cutting a fallen horse loose from a tangled picket rope or driving it into solid ice for a handgrip after you've broken through into a wilderness lake.

It is true enough that you can skin out the biggest moose and bear with nothing more than a tiny penknife. You can do it better with a sharp and thin small blade, as a matter of fact, than with a dull and thick large blade. But a fine sheath knife makes such jobs a lot easier. Many old-time hunters, for that reason, prefer to keep their sheath knives for hunting alone and really sharp. They usually prefer a blade not more than from four to six inches long, with the edge straight until it curves to the point.

A rounded point, rather than a sharp spear end, makes for easier skinning. A thin blade that tapers all the way from the back to the cutting edge will take a much keener edge, and you can work faster and easier with it than with a blade that is thick from back to middle and which then tapers sharply to a wedge like a cold chisel.

The illustration shows several good types, in our estimation. Number two is my own knife that I have always carried since 1916 when hunting. It was made by hand from a Green River butcher knife, and it has served my every need well. The mountain men of a century ago used Green River knives, and I call mine Seeds-ke-dee which is the old Indian name for the Green River of Wyoming.

Number three is excellent in every way, and anyone wishing a knife of moderate cost would make no mistake in selecting this type. It is made by many cutlery firms.

Number four is a custom knife, made to order by hand. I think it is the finest knife I have ever seen, although it is rather costly. The size and shape of bone handle and blade are just about right, to my way of thinking. If I were getting a new knife, this is the one I would choose. But I guess I will stick to Seeds-ke-dee to the end for sentiment's sake and because of all the good it has done me.

THE SHEATH

You will want a substantial leather sheath to protect both the knife and yourself. Safely strapped in such a container, the tool may then be carried on your belt, in rucksack, duffle bag, saddle pocket, or wherever you wish. In any event, it will be advisable to make sure

Good types of knives for the wilderness.

that the sheath is well made and if necessary reinforced, perhaps with copper rivets that you can add easily enough yourself.

Points have a way of cutting themselves loose, particularly after a sheath has been accidently cut at the top with the result that the blade sets in deeper than intended. When points are so exposed, they may drive into your leg or hip should you fall, and there is even more constant danger that they may slash a hand. Some of us find it advisable, in addition to adding rivets, to stitch the lower part of the sheath with copper wire, making sure that the ends of this are worked off in such a way that they will not scratch.

Oiling sheaths is commonplace. It is not a desirable practice, however, because of the way it softens the leather. Not only is the knife then difficult to sheathe, but the point has a tendency to catch and to puncture the flexible and often curling leather. Saddle soap is preferable for preventing the leather from becoming too dry. Ordinary shoe polish is good, too, and is also the application to use if you desire a darker and less conspicuous case.

KNIFE STEEL

The first question most anyone asks about a knife is, "Is it of good steel?" When I was a boy everyone swore by the Sheffield steel knives made in England, although some thought that certain German knives had good steel, particularly those manufactured in Solingen. But times have changed, and for many years United States has led the world in the metallurgy of steel. Practically all our knives made by reputable companies have excellent steel in them.

Anyone who has used and sharpened knives for some time will recognize good steel the moment he touches the blade to a whetstone. There is something indefinable in the way a good blade takes hold and slides on a whetstone, and this is soon detected after you have tried to sharpen a few good knives and some poor ones.

For a general purpose knife, and particularly for a hunting knife, avoid those with stainless steel blades. They may be all right for fish and table knives, but ordinarily they won't take a keen edge. When they are dull it takes forever and a day to bring them to even half decent sharpness on a whetstone.

Stainless steel knives made by hand are harder than mass manufactured products, for a tougher metal can be used than can be handled by die stamping. But usually if you are going to put out the money for a handmade knife, you may as well have the very finest high carbon steel.

It is true that all carbon steel blades are stained by the acids in meat. This discoloration does not injure the metal, however. It can be polished off with crocus cloth if that seems desirable.

SHARPENING STONES

A knife, ax, and any other edged tool should be kept sharp for best and safest results. Knives, when they come from the makers, do not usually have a keen edge, and these should be honed before use. It does not suffice merely to sharpen your knife before you start on your trip. It will continue to dull whenever used, the dreams of advertising writers to the contrary, and it will require sharpening a proportionate number of times afield.

Skinning an animal takes the edge off a blade very quickly. When dressing out a bear, for example, you probably will need to sharpen the knife three or four times. In fact, one of the first things we do when coming up on a kill is to lay our carborundum in some handy spot so that we won't have to start digging gingerly for it in a few minutes with slippery fingers.

The carborundum stone is the best for outdoor use. Models can be secured that are coarse on one side for the quick initial work and fine on the other for putting on the keen edge. Carborundums have the added advantage of being usable with water only. The finest Arkansas whetstones are perhaps better for producing a fine edge, but they are slow cutting and require oil.

SHARPENING

The best carborundum stones for general use by the outdoorsman are the round ones. These can be held in the hand and do not require a bench or a wood base. In sharpening, hold the blade in the left hand and the round stone in the right. Use stone with a circular grinding method. It's best to have two stones, one for your camp kit and the other for your person, so that one will be at hand whenever you have need for it.

For the latter, the familiar small rectangular stone is more convenient to carry. Put a few drops of moisture on this stone. Lay the blade flat on it. If it is a pocketknife, raise the back of the blade about one-eighth of an inch off the stone. If you are sharpening a broad sheath knife, raise it about one-quarter of an inch. In either event, keep the blade at the same angle throughout while sharpening.

Pressing with medium weight on the blade, grind the edge with a circular movement for about thirty seconds on one side. Then turn and grind the other side. Tilt the blade a little to grind the curve up toward the point. After a few minutes of this work, it will be quite sharp but will have a featheredge.

To get rid of this, push the edge of the blade straight forward across the stone several times. Turn it over and press the other side forward, and the featheredge will double and come off. The knife is then sharp enough for most purposes. If you want to shave with it, finish by stropping it on the soft leather of your boot top.

AXES

The ax is an almost indispensable tool for the woodsman, many of whom rate it even above matches as the most valuable item to have along in the bush. It may be, nevertheless, a very dangerous instrument in the hands of a novice.

The ax is not really needed in the average warm weather camp. It is not necessary, either, on summer back-packing trips where at most the lighter short-handled hand ax will serve every purpose. It is rather the tool for heavy work, for getting in large wood for fires, for building big shelters, and for cutting out timber that may fall across trails and canoe streams.

The ax with a two-and-one-half or perhaps a three-pound head is big enough for most sportsmen. Heavier axes bite deeper and there-fore, in the hands of an expert, do faster work. This is why lumber-jacks, frontiersmen, and others who grow up in ax country and use these mobile wedges regularly throughout the years pick a heavy model. These, besides being tiring in the hands of a tyro, re-quire a lot of skill and are therefore more potentially dangerous.

Double-bitted axes are very tricky tools in the hands of all but experienced and careful men. In addition, they can not be used as hammers, for which purpose (although it is not to be recommended) the camper is sometimes apt to find himself employing it a dozen times a day.

The handiest ax for packing, although not for any great amount of work, is the Hudson Bay model with a narrow butt and a face of normal width. You see an occasional craftsman using one of these painstakingly on a log cabin, but such an individual is usually a perfectionist who has more of the qualities of the cabinet maker than of the carpenter. This model, because of its narrow poll through which the handle is attached, does not hold up too well in all cases.

But for ordinary camping requirements, where weight is a factor and you still want an ax, a Hudson Bay with a one-and-one-half-pound head and a twenty-four-inch handle will do a lot of work. A metal-riveted leather sheath should ordinarily be added. The Hudson Bay ax, incidentally, is a convenient one to tie behind your saddle.

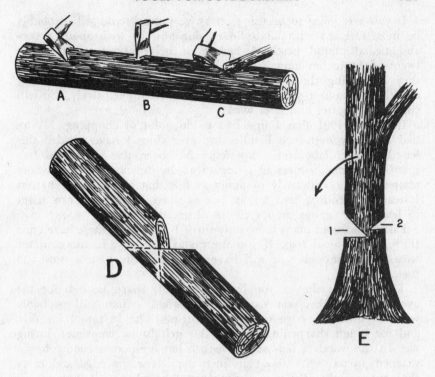

AXMANSHIP

A. Chop at an acute angle to the grain.

B. The ax, hitting at a right angle to the grain, will hardly bite at all.

C. The way to chop limbs off a trunk.

D. Start each of the pair of notches needed to chop a fallen log in two as wide as the log itself. Two such Vs, joining at the stick's center, will sever it most economically.

E. To fell a tree in the direction of the arrow, begin notch 2 as a safety measure. On the opposite side, cut notch 1 about three-fifths through the trunk. Deepen notch 2 until the tree begins to fall, and then stand aside at an already chosen point of safety.

Keep your ax sharp. A dull ax makes slow and hard work and is liable to glance.

If you are going to be using an ax very much, you will probably be most satisfied with an ordinary single-bit ax with about a two-and-one-half-pound head. A handle or helve about twenty-six to twenty-eight inches long is generally enough, though some may find they can swing the thirty-six-inch handle more naturally. In any event, if you adopt one length handle and use it exclusively, you will come to do better and safer work.

It was in 1901 that I first had to do a lot of chopping. My ax had a twenty-seven-inch handle, and ever since I have wielded this length. My collaborator's experience has been the same, and he's spent numerous winters in a log cabin in the north woods where temperatures occasionally plummet so low that a saw blade shatters instead of bending and an ax not warmed beforehand can sliver to fragments against an icy chunk of green wood.

I have not used many axes, only three I think, but these have gone through a pile of logs. If you use an ax decently, it almost never wears out, although you will have to replace the handle now and then.

The edge on the ax you buy is probably sharp enough for the average two-weeks-a-year camper. The good axman will probably want to thin this edge for keener cutting. The best tool for this, and for rough sharpening as well, is a grindstone, kept wet during use. In the woods a ten- or twelve-inch flat file does a good job. To sharpen an ax, start about an inch back from its edge and carry that out straight. Taper very slightly to the edge itself, but do not overdo this or the ax will bind. Finish the job with a carborundum stone.

AXMANSHIP

A whole volume could be written on the subject of axmanship. Our best axmen almost all picked up the art as boys on the farm or in the woods, but with practice and care anyone can learn well enough for all the usual camp chores. Incidently, if you've played much golf, you'll find the desirable free and easy swing to an exact point almost second nature.

The main thing is to be careful. You can ruin a hunting or fishing trip mighty easily with just one stroke that lands a fraction of an inch from where you want it to go. The best general precaution is to anticipate the worst and to be so placed that even if it does occur no one will be hurt. Too, a sharp ax is safer than a dull one in that it is not so prone to bound off the wood.

Be prepared to have the ax glance off a knot and have your feet and legs where they will not be hit. Take the time to clear away any shrubs or branches that might catch the blade, instead of relying on a perfect swing. Don't take the risk of steadying a billet with hand or foot.

Avoid, too, the common practice of leaning a stick against a log and half chopping and half breaking it in two. A lot of head injuries from flying wood have resulted from that all-too-prevalent habit. When you're felling a dead tree for firewood, watch out that another tree doesn't break off the top and send it crashing back toward you. In other words, there are a great many possible misadventures. The more of these you can foresee and protect yourself against, the less will be the possibility of an injury.

When you stop to think of it, axes are far less dangerous than such a very common substance as glass. Any shortcomings do not lie in the ax but, rather, in the individual. Use this wedge with a nice easy swing. Let the gravity fall of the ax do most of the work, and you'll be able to cut all morning without pressing. Keep your eye on the exact spot where you want the edge to strike, and practice until it does always strike there.

FELLING TREES

Even the most inexperienced cheechako can drop his first trees almost exactly where he wants them to fall if he will follow the few very simple principles set forth here. He will, of course, have to take into consideration such external factors as wind, tilt, weight, and nearby objects. He will do well, too, to start on trees small enough that their fall can be guided to some extent, if need be, by hand.

You cut, first of all, a small safety notch as insurance against the tree's splitting or the butt's kicking backwards. Slightly below this safety notch, on the opposite side of the tree, on the side where you want the timber to fall, you chop a wide notch. When this cut is about three-fifths through the trunk, a few cuts at the first nick should be enough to send the tree toppling.

These two notches are so located, as can be seen by illustration, that they provide a hinge. This hinge not only directs the way in which the weight of the tree will cause it to fall, but it also lessens the possibility that the butt may slide perilously backward on the stump. It is advisable, however, to have a safe place already picked out and to hasten there when the fibers start their final cracking.

It is even easier to drop a tree by using a saw. The principles remain the same. You make the same brief initial cut. You follow it with a deep slit opposite and below. You then deepen the first incision. An ax, or perhaps a wooden wedge cut on the spot, may have to be driven into one gash or the other to free the saw. Too, you can often topple a heavy tree that is pretty much on balance and come closer to pinpointing its fall by using a wedge in the higher cut.

HAND AXES

The light one-pound ax with a twelve-inch handle will do about all the work necessary in the summer or auto camp and on backpacking trails. The average camper will use it with more effectiveness and greater safety than he will a long-handled ax. As a matter of fact, some of the more skillful backwoods axmen often turn to such a hatchet. Up in the Peace River country, Charlie Ohland, the best axman we know of, can smooth off a pole or log so skillfully with a light hatchet that you'd suppose it planed.

Such a hand ax can come in useful when you're butchering, although you'll have to touch up the blade afterward. It works well enough in securing wood for a small campfire. It's a lot more useful than a knife for blazing a trail. Secure a substantial sheath for it, but don't carry it on your belt. This is both inconvenient and uncomfortable. Stow it instead in a rucksack or saddle pocket.

THE CROOKED KNIFE

The famous crooked knife is one with a thin, curved blade about six inches long. It is the Indian's and occasionally the backwoodsman's substitute for a plane, drawknife, or spokeshave.

The crooked knife is used in making snowshoe frames, paddles, and thin planks for toboggans. The worker holds it in his hand and, drawing it toward him, can easily shave wood to most any curved or flat surface.

Crooked knives could once be had from many of the Hudson's Bay trading posts in Canada. Now often unheard of in a lot of these, they can, however, be secured from Hudson's Bay Company headquarters at Winnipeg, Manitoba. They are made in both right-hand and left-hand models, usually without a handle. You put on your own handle.

SAWS

It is usually much easier and faster to saw all but small logs than it is to chop them. If you are using a wood-burning stove, such a tool will be invaluable for working available fuel into the right lengths to fit the firebox. Even when you're bivouacking in weather nippy enough to argue the companionship of an overnight blaze, a saw will make the task of accumulating enough fodder for that campfire a comparatively easy one.

The long slender blade of the swede saw is a favorite of campers, bivouackers, and sourdoughs in the cold climates. It is so thin that it speeds through logs with a minimum of effort. It is so light that it can be handled easily in any position. The long narrow blade is so flexible that, except during extreme cold, it can be coiled to the circumference of a saucer, held together by a cord wound and tied among its teeth, and wrapped with a piece of canvas for carrying.

The two-piece, light, tubular handle is easily slid apart and packed. If you want, you can even dispense with this and bend a husky green sapling into place for a frame when necessary. Make a small hole through each end of the sapling, at right angles to the wood, with a knife or nail. Then split each end. The improvised handle can then be attached by inserting the blade in the slits and securing it, through each hole, by wire or whatever else is handy. Carrying along two butterfly bolts for this purpose will be worthwhile.

Whatever saw you take with you into the bush, don't make the mistake that some tenderfeet do and carry a blade with the ordinary crosscut or rip teeth of the carpenter's tools. See to it that your saw is designed for cutting rough timber.

REPAIR KITS

Some kind of repair kit should be included in every camp outfit except perhaps that of a back packer who has to pare everything down to the last ounce. Don't attempt to carry a whole shop with you, but include only those small articles that you think will be needed and for which nothing else will serve.

Everyone has his own occasionally changing opinions about what such a kit should include. After years of adding and discarding, here is what the two of us find in our own repair outfits: A small set of fine screw drivers, all nested within the handle of the largest. A small flat-nosed pliers with wire cutter, something of this sort being especially advisable wherever a dog accompanies you in porcupine country. A small flat file for sharpening the ax. A tiny can of assorted small nails, tacks, copper rivets, and buttons. Thin copper wire, shoe thread, rawhide lace, a bit of wax, and a coil of light snare wire. Various needles. A tube of all-purpose adhesive. Some nylon fish line.

We both carry very small saws that will whir through metal as well as bone. Once in a hardware store I found a light, metal, pistol grip handle that would hold a short hacksaw blade. I bought it and a dozen blades. It has gone along on every trip since and has come in mighty handy a hundred times.

CHAPTER 14

FOOTWEAR FOR WILDERNESS TRAILS

MUCH ADVICE has been offered about the selection of footwear for extensive use in rough and difficult country. A great deal of this counsel, unfortunately, has come from those whose backgrounds have been more theoretical than practical. Many important considerations have been both misinterpreted and incorrectly emphasized if not omitted entirely.

Additionally confusing is the understandable fact that not all the popular shoes offered and advertised are by any means desirable under many outdoor conditions. Salesmen, not always experienced and conscientious, are likely to urge the makes and incidentally the sizes that are in stock.

The matter is a very serious one. The sportsman taking to the woods for perhaps the •first time, on a trip that requires long and difficult foot travel, is apt to discover when it's too late that he is irrevocably committed to footwear that will handicap or badly cripple him, thus ruining the grand outing he has maybe been planning for years.

Perhaps this writer had better qualify as to experience. To a certain extent, I might be called a professional walker. I served twenty-two of my forty years of military service in the Infantry. There we certainly hiked ten times as much over rugged terrain as the average hunter and fisherman. There, too, I had to attend not only to my own footwear and foot care: I also had to supervise that of large numbers of men under my command.

In this latter duty, I didn't feel I was in a position where I could afford to make any mistakes. Staring at me over the years was this statement included*by Horace Kephart in what has long been the best and the most widely read and accepted of outdoor manuals.

What Kephart wrote was: "Lieutenant Whelen, so well known to us as a sportsman and military authority, says of it (the Munson army last): 'In the light of what the army now knows, sore feet are absolutely inexcusable. The presence of sore feet in an officer's command is a cause for investigation as to the efficiency of that officer.' "

During the eighteen years since my retirement from active service I have, you might say, been a professional outdoorsman with a very large mileage of rough hiking in all kinds of country and climates.

'TIS A FEAT TO FIT THE FEET

The shoe size you wear in the city, and the one that the ordinary salesman there will measure you for, will perhaps do well enough for the not more than three or four miles of walking which is all many an individual covers on an outing. But beware of this size of shoe for a daily tramp of eight to twenty miles over wild country, even through fairly open bird cover if it is a bit hilly.

One such excursion in city-size footwear will almost certainly lay you up with blisters and abrasions. After three or four miles of tramping over rugged terrain, your feet swell considerably because of the repeated and varying pressure of walking and because of the increased blood supply that is pumped into them because of the stimulation of exercise. The shoes you select must be large enough to remain comfortable when your feet are in this enlarged condition.

THE RIGHT SORT OF SOCKS

The simple but all-important formula for wilderness walking is: heavy socks and big shoes. Regardless of heat or cold, dryness or wet, only wool socks are suitable for long hikes. These may vary from thin to medium during the summer and from medium to heavy during the frosty months. Throughout the year, however, you want only genuine, top quality, finely processed, and well-made woolens. Don't have anything to do with shoddy if you can possibly avoid it. Poor woolens mat. They contain impurities that irritate the feet. They wear poorly. As for loosely and skimpily knit socks, these are an abomination from the first day you put them on.

A few people's skin seems to be allergic to wool. Such individuals can often wear thin socks of some other material under the wool with advantage. These may be made of cotton. Some individuals select nylon which is certainly long wearing but which, for a lot of us, is a lot too slippery unless either worn too tightly or unless gartered up in some manner, neither of which is compatable with the outdoor routine.

Taking the thickness of your socks into consideration, here is a general rule you can apply in selecting the ideal size of footwear for hard outdoor wear. With one pair of thin or medium wool socks, have your shoes one full size longer and one full size wider than your proper fit in city shoes. For heavy socks, have them one-and-one-half sizes longer and wider. If half sizes are not available, increase to the next full size. For the additional socks they may be desirable in extremely cold weather, experiment to get the same comparative freedom of fit as above.

BREAKING IN FOOTWEAR

It is highly important that you break in new outdoor footwear to fit your feet well in advance of a trip. Some of us have feet that are differently shaped from normal, such deformities being more or less caused by past improper if stylish fittings of city shoes. The lasts on which good outdoor shoes are made are designed for normal extremities. When the resulting shoes are new, even when correctly fitted, they may bring undue pressure on parts of your foot. The new footwear will gradually stretch at these points, however, if broken in slowly and easily.

There are two functional ways of breaking in new leather shoes. You can do it gradually by hiking two miles the first day, three miles the second, and so on up to five miles, by which time the process should be completed. The second method consists of standing in four inches of water for fifteen minutes and then hiking until the shoes dry on your feet.

HIGH-TOP BOOTS

Did you ever notice the shoes of the professional walker, the Alpinist, or the marching apparel of our infantry? You will find no high tops here. You'll see, rather, a height of not more than seven inches as measured in the rear from the bottom of the heel to the top.

High tops almost always sag and wrinkle more or less at the ankles. This can bring pressure to bear on the Achilles tendon at the back of your ankle. It is true that this becomes negligible in the case of gradually softened and well broken-in leather tops, and that in any boot it can be offset to a large extent by inserting some stiffener such as folded heavy paper or a piece of birch bark.

Unless there is a definite and valid reason for high tops, however, the fact remains that this pressure, if not relieved, will set up a painful inflammation of the sheath through which this greatest tendon of our body runs. The only cure for this is ten days off your feet.

My regiment was issued a then new type of shoe with nine-inch tops, back in 1911, when the Army was experimenting with shoes. These were almost exactly like the majority of sportsmen's boots now advertised and illustrated. Shortly thereafter, my regiment was ordered on a 300-mile practice march to test this footwear. Thirty per cent of the command suffered from this inflammation, medically known as synovitis. That ended the experiment.

There is also the weight factor. A boot with a ten-inch top will weigh about eight ounces more than one which is six inches high. That is an additional half pound to be lifted three inches high and to be carried twenty-eight inches ahead about 2500 times every mile. Such additional expenditure of energy tells like the dickens on a long, all-day tramp.

Get your hiking shoes six inches, or not over seven inches, high. Leave the high top boots for horsemen, for exceptionally wet and muddy country, and for bad snake regions. Paratroopers wear high boots for other reasons, and they have little walking to do.

CARE OF THE FEET

Three precautions will usually suffice. Wear only well-fitting and fairly new socks with no rough seams nor unduly harsh darned spots. If your feet are tender, dust both them and your socks the first week with foot powder.

Wash your feet at least every night, and change your socks daily. When the going is rough, as a matter of fact, it is refreshing to stop, when possible during the day, and bathe the feet. A lot of us carry an extra pair of socks to switch to at that time.

Good woolen socks are easily washed, without shrinking, with soap and barely warm water. They should be rinsed, gently squeezed reasonably free of moisture without wringing, and stretched back into shape to dry slowly, preferably in the open breeze but in any event well back from the campfire.

CANVAS SNEAKERS

Ordinary rubber-soled sneakers and basketball shoes are popular along fairly smooth wilderness ways, such as the Appalachian Trail, and in comparatively dry country. For rugged use do not buy the low ones, however. Select, rather, those with canvas tops about six inches high. The rubber soles should be roughly corrugated or substantially cleated as a safeguard against slipping.

The chief advantage afforded by such footwear is that of lightness which is a joy. They are best worn with one pair of medium-weight woolen socks. They are not very durable. A hundred miles over rough terrain is about the limit of most. But they are comparatively cheap.

They soon wet through in rain and even in morning dew. This makes no particular difference, however, for they dry out quickly and without becoming stiff. They are painful and almost impossible in rough scree, slide rock, and along stony shores. They're fine for still hunting in crisp country.

Both of us have even used them successfully for hunting sheep and goat during the early fall in the dry belt of British Columbia where their negligible weight has been very much appreciated. They are also pre-eminently the shoes for boys on summer hiking trips.

BIRD-SHOOTER SHOES

These are oiled leather shoes, usually of mock as well as true moccasin types with composition soles and heels. The true moccasin shoe, of course, is built about a single piece of leather which extends all the way under the foot. Beneath this entity is attached the sole. To make sure that a shoe is a true moccasin, look and feel inside the toe to ascertain if a single area of leather forms both bottom and sides.

This footwear is made by a dozen manufacturers of sporting shoes under many different names. Worn with thin or medium woolen socks, such shoes are very satisfactory for bird shooting and in general for long hikes over trails. In fairly steep country, however, they should have soft crepe or heavily cleated rubber soles.

Being fairly light, they make quite satisfactory footwear for hunting mountain game in the higher western mountains when they are provided with suitable soles, which we will discuss in a moment.

ARMY MARCHING SHOES

The old type marching shoes used by our Infantry are of leather with the smooth side turned functionally in and the rough side forming the exterior. There is no lining. The soles are usually composition. The shoes are only six inches high and are made on the Munson army last.

This last is, in my estimation, the best that has even been devised for the normal American man's undeformed foot. These shoes can usually be obtained from any of the many dealers in army surplus goods and at what are usually very reasonable prices. All the remarks about bird-shooter shoes apply to these, also.

RUBBER BOTTOMS AND LEATHER TOPS

Shoes with rubber bottoms and leather tops are made by many manufacturers. For practically all wear, unless there is a definite reason to the contrary, they should be purchased with tops only six or seven inches high. For extremely wet country, like Newfoundland where in many areas you sink almost every step in several inches of water, the tops had better be eight inches. In muskeg areas of the continental Northwest, where even in winter, the periodical chinooks and the almost constant overflow make for slushy going, you may have a real need the year around for tops as much as ten inches high.

These boots should be worn with insoles and one or more pairs of wool socks. It's not a bad idea to get an extra pair of insoles so that a dry pair will be available each day. Felt is a favorite. For those who do not care for the flatfooted sensation that is characteristic of most such rubbers, leather insoles with arch support steel shanks if you want them are available. For very cold weather, these may be secured with clipped lambskin next to the feet. L. L. Bean, Inc., of Freeport, Maine, is one supplier.

The better boots of this sort are ideal for deer and other big-game hunting in the fall, except in the steepest country, because they are almost noiseless and because they can be kept water repellant clear to the top. They can also be used in winter, although rubber gets pretty cold around twenty degrees below zero and a steel stirrup feels mighty frosty against them when the thermometer drops much below that range.

One of us, however, has consistently found them preferable when afoot during such temperatures. Often hidden overflow from brooks and rivers can then be a serious problem, for regular channels freeze in the intense cold and water is forced to the surface where many times it spreads concealed under thin ice and snow. With lambskin insoles and two pairs of heavy socks, such boots are not too cold.

The low-topped ones are not uncomfortable or clammy like rubber boots. If worn with adequate insoles and not laced too tightly, the insoles and socks compress with each step and pump air in and out, ventilating the feet. These boots are by no means out for warm weather. I have worn them all day and every day all summer for sixteen years at my New England summer home, where the grass is soaked with dew until noon, and there are many bog-swamps.

Throughout eastern Canada they are donned practically universally, and even the Indians are coming to prefer them to moccasins during summer and fall. More and more trappers and prospectors in the north are shifting to them. When the rubber bottoms wear out, you can have new shells attached to the leather tops at a considerable saving.

They're not good for wear in the very steep mountains of the West, particularly not on abrupt snow-covered slopes. I darn near broke my fool neck, and did sprain my ankle, on such a precipitous incline in Montana some years ago when wearing them. They are treacherous on smooth ice, too, although for traversing occasional short stretches encountered during a trip, creepers or light crampons can be used to offset this hazard. For deer and moose country and for northern canoe routes, they are the most satisfactory of all footwear.

MOUNTAIN BOOTS

Mountain boots are for use in the steep mountains of our continental West and Northwest; for the rougher country off the usual hiking trails; for climbers; and for the hunting of sheep and goat and grizzly in the taller ranges. Boots for such terrain were not obtainable readymade in the United States until very recently. Mountain climbers usually imported their footwear from Europe and from two Canadian makers. It is tempting providence to attempt to negotiate extremely steep and uneven mountain country with the soles that are standard on almost all sporting footwear in the United States market.

For climbing in the higher peaks where precipitous rock, snow, and ice conditions must be bested, the shoe should be of the heavy Alpine type. The Alpinist does not usually hike for miles. His daily efforts, rather, are short if severe. He needs a shoe that can be planted, pounded down hard, and that will stick right there.

The hunter of big game in tall mountains needs a slightly lighter shoe. His day's hunt may take him many miles. Almost certainly, however, he will come on dangerously perpendicular country, particularly in the final stalk for mountain game. There he must not slip. The soles of his mountain hunting shoes should be similar to those of the Alpinist, or he will run great risks of a crippling fall if not death itself.

To that both of us can strongly testify. I've already mentioned my experience in Montana. The first Stone Mountain sheep the other of us shot, he stalked while wearing rubber bottom boots. The only way he could work his way across some icy slants that dropped off in nothing more substantial than ozone was by driving his hunting knife into the crust and using it for a handgrip until he could set himself sufficiently to repeat the procedure.

If you will examine the hoofs of mountain sheep and goat, you will see that the outer rim of each hoof consists of a hard shell with a sharp edge where it contacts the ground. The interior of the hoof has a comparatively soft pad not greatly unlike crepe rubber. The entire foot is a fine example of how the sole of a safe mountain shoe should be constructed.

HOBNAILS OR RUBBER CLEATS

Two types of soles are preferred, each having its advocates. There are the hobnailed varieties. Hobnails can be applied to any of the bird-shooter or army marching shoes providing these have leather soles. Nails and calks will not, of course, stick in either composition or rubber bottoms. Hobnailed boots are excellent for Alpine climbing, particularly on ice and glaciers, although they are a little noisy for hunting.

My own experience in hunting and climbing throughout British Columbia and Alberta has indicated that the hobnails are best ar-

SKETCH No. 172

Pattern for hobnailing shoes.
■—Square Swiss edging nails.
●—Ordinary cone-headed nails.

ranged as shown in the accompanying sketch. The square Swiss edging nails are placed an inch apart around the edge of the sole and heel. The sharp square edges of these heavy nails insure against front, back, and side slipping on any surface except hard, smooth rock.

These Swiss edging nails you may obtain from at least four of our leading sporting goods outfitters who cater to mountain climbers. Your bootmaker or cobbler will be able to install them. They should be cleated all the way through the edge of the sole outside the uppers.

The round interior nails shown are ordinary cone-headed hobnails which are procurable anywhere. They prevent slipping to some extent. Their principle function, however, is to keep the inside of the sole from wearing too fast. They should be cleated through the outer leather sole only, never through the inner sole, or they will eventually dig into your feet prohibitively.

This means an extra job for the shoemaker. Regardless of this, make certain that he does not cleat these through the inner sole. Such soles are very safe, satisfactory, and durable. The only objections to them are that they are sometimes noisy for hunting and that you should remove them before entering a house, for they literally "play hob" with floors.

Many experienced mountain men are coming to prefer heavily cleated or lugged rubber soles which can be applied to any suitable leather sole by practically any shoemaker. These have square cleats or lugs about one-half to one inch square that project at least half an inch below the rubber sole proper. These are usually quite satisfactory. They stick well on all steep pitches and in snow. They are superior to hobnails on smooth rock although not on ice. Furthermore, they can be almost noiseless.

There are several domestic soles of this type which are readily procurable. At this writing, however, all seem to be made of too soft a rubber. They wear and round off at the extreme outer edge where sharpness is highly desirable. Still, they will probably not wear dangerously on even a hard two-week trip, and then they are not too expensive to replace. But their makers should take a hint from the European manufacturers who have been supplying such soles to Swiss and Himalayan climbers for many years and who fabricate them of much harder and considerably more durable rubber. Several American suppliers stock these lug soles which include the Vibram and the Bramani. (See Appendix.)

THE QUICKEST WAY TO RUIN SHOES

Wet leather footwear can be very quickly ruined if dried out near a campfire or stove. The best treatment is to wash off any dirt and mud, wipe away any free moisture, and then allow the gear to dry slowly in the air. If the bottoms are of leather, shape will be better retained if the boots are first straightened and then stuffed with something such as dry cloths or moss. If any artificial warmth at all is used, it should be extremely mild. Even the natural enough procedure of hanging footwear at the far end of a hot cabin can very easily stiffen, shrink, and crack and ruin the leather.

After they are dried, they should be rubbed with neat's-foot oil or any good boot conditioner. Black bear grease and grizzly oil are, for example, favorites where they are available. These will go on easier and penetrate better if the leather is slightly warmed.

Leather shoes can not be made entirely waterproof, nor would this be desirable. They would then defeat their own purpose by trapping perspiration and soon making the feet more uncomfortably wet than, under ordinary conditions, would be the case in leather that could breathe.

They may be fairly waterproof when new. After a few miles of hiking they will leak more or less at the seams, however, while under continued immersion some water will work through the leather. If dubbing is then worked thoroughly into the seams, they will again be fairly waterproof for a little while until the preparation works out. This is one reason why leather footwear should be greased well once a week when in use. So treating them too often, of course, can make them too soft.

When boots are to be put away until the next hunting or fishing season, it is a good idea to keep them in shape either with boot trees or by stuffing them with crumpled newspapers. Then grease them and store them, away from pests, in a reasonably cool and dry place.

MOOSEHIDE MOCCASINS

Genuine Indian moosehide moccasins are not made commercially

In the glorious mountain wilderness of our Northwest you need footwear that will not slip.

nor, for that matter, in quantity anywhere. Not only are there too few smoke-tanned moosehides but, particularly these days not enough squaws are willing to do the work. Money is easier come by in other ways.

It has been our experience that the only places these usually can be obtained, a pair or two of them, are at little trading posts and occasional trailside stores away back in the sticks in western Canada and Alaska. Nearby squaws make a few for sale at the post, and a few white women with time on their hands also turn out an occasional set.

We both have often secured moosehide moccasins of our own from such sources, occasionally leaving an outline of a stockinged foot before heading into the bush and picking up the finished products upon our return. Fit is not all critical, however, and we've also done well enough from stock numerous other times. If you go north, you will probably also find it possible to secure a pair by one of these two methods.

Imitation moosehide moccasins are merely tourist junk. On the other hand, moccasins made of oil-tanned leather by our better bootmakers are far more practical for most purposes than the moosehide varieties. They wear longer. There is no comparison in the way they retain their shape. They are not ruined by repeated wettings. They are less expensive.

In fact, you see a lot of the manufactured types these days at even the remoter trading posts. More and more, the Indians don't want to be bothered with the work. The high price of red squirrel fur in much of the moccasins country is one reason. It's considerably easier to snare or shoot, then process, two or three of these, than to eke out a pair of moccasins worth the same amount.

In the sub-Arctic, however, many Indians are still partial to their own moccasins when they can get the skins, because the footwear is then practically at hand except for necessary tanning and sewing. When the weather is at all moist, they invariably wear a husky pair of the white man's rubbers over them. These rubbers are identical with the heavier rubbers seen on city pavements during rainy weather.

Moosehide moccasins wet through as soon as you start to walk over even slightly damp ground. They become, at the same time, almost unbelievably slippery. It is, for example, considerable of a task to get up a dew-glistening slope aromatic with pine needles.

The moccasin plus the rubber is similar, in principle, to our leather-topped lumbermen's rubber. As a matter of fact, numerous aborigines these days wear the latter article much of the time.

A good type of mountain shoe with vibram sole. The Trailwise "Packer" Boot.

DRY SUBZERO COLD

But it is another matter entirely, in the dry snow and the subzero cold of the Far North. There the basic footwear of hunters and trappers, both white and native, is the locally made moccasin. This is usually large enough to be worn with several pairs of thick woolen socks.

The way one of us customarily travels when temperatures drop thirty degrees or more below freezing, is with two heavy pairs of woolen stockings, moosehide moccasins, a third long and heavy pair of woolen stockings, and finally low heavy rubbers. The feet not only keep warm, this way, but they remain dry. When it is time to go into a cabin, the customary procedure is to remove the outer socks and the rubbers, shaking and beating them free of snow and leaving them outside. Sometimes, depending on snow conditions, a second pair of moccasins is worn directly beneath the rubbers, and then these are treated as outdoor wear.

A variation of this practice, witnessed among both whites and natives, is the use of ordinary fabric overshoes for the outer clothing. The third pair of socks is then ordinarily worn directly beneath the overshoes and is still removed and left outdoors before one enters a warm cabin. If the individual is going to remain inside for any considerable length of time, of course, the outer wear is brought inside and warmed.

HOMEMADE SOLES

When I was a youngster and hunted that full year and one additional summer and fall in the dry belt of British Columbia, living and traveling with several old mountain men and in touch now and then with bunches of Indians, we all wore buckskin moccasins. These always had a buckskin sole which we sewed to their bottoms with sinew or buckskin thongs. Whenever the sole wore through, we put on a new one. The sole lasted from three days to a week, depending on the weather and on how much traveling we did. One pair of moccasins would thus last over a month.

One of the old mountain men had a klooch, a squaw, and I used to trade her two deerskins for one tanned skin and then do my own resoling. This ratio of exchange is still common today, incidentally. We wore the moccasins with two pairs of socks. Your feet had to be tough and then some, but they were the most perfect footwear imaginable for high dry country.

When the snows came, however, one could break his fool neck wearing them in such terrain, although rough soles with cleats helped a little. But only a very sure-footed individual can cover steep snow country in moccasins with any safety. The old plains Indians all wore soles on moccasins. See the exhibits in any large museum. Even so, the squaws were tanning skins and making moccasins all the time.

Native moccasins, in any event, are most delightful to change to when you come back to camp after a day afield. Even in the biggest city, their unforgettable woodsy odor imparted by hours of tanning over smoky conflagrations takes one back to the sort of campfires you get going in the wilderness at dusk.

CHAPTER 15

MOSQUITOES, FLIES, ET AL

SUPREME COURT JUSTICE William O. Douglas once remarked that horsemanship consists of the ability to remain unconcerned, comfortable, and on a horse—all at once. We likewise asert that a part of wildcraft consists of knowing how to remain unconcerned, comfortable, and at the same time in a country plagued with accursed bugs.

CAMP SANITATION

Before the Spanish-American War, we knew little about camp sanitation. At Chickamauga where I served for three months with my regiment, a fifth of the command, myself included, got typhoid fever. We called it "The Battle of the Sinks." The latrines were close to the kitchens and were unscreened, so flies carried the germs to the food on their feet.

By 1916 we had learned most of the important facts. That year my command, encamped most of the time on tropical service, had practically no sickness.

You go camping not to prove you can survive but to enjoy yourself. You should come back healthier than you were when you left. The matter of sanitation may sound like a tough part of your journey afield. As a matter of fact, keeping the camp healthy is simple once you've learned a few of the tricks. Besides food and water, which are considered elsewhere, these mostly concern mosquitoes, flies, and other such pests.

Here's the whole story. It can make or break your vacation.

MOSQUITOES

Mosquito protection these days is easier than it ever has been before. This is fortunate, for the confounded buzzers are still the most common pests with which outdoorsmen are cursed.

They are more or less prevalent from late May and early June until September in all country close to nonflowing waters in which they breed. They may be only slightly annoying along the trout streams in New England or in the high open country where animals seek relief, but we've also seen unbelievable millions actually blackening the sky in other regions. Our northlands and low coastal belts are usually the worst infested areas.

Ernest Thompson Seton, the naturalist, kept a record of their numbers on a journey he made to the Barren Lands of Canada. On July 9, he counted four hundred mosquitoes on the back of a companion's coat. He then began to establish a standard by which to gauge their numbers as he proceeded North.

He would hold up his bare hand for five seconds and count the number of mosquitoes on its back. At first there were five to ten. Every day added to their number. In Mid-July on Great Slave Lake, where the waters of the Peace River pause before continuing down the Mackenzie to the Arctic Ocean, there were fifty to sixty. Several weeks later on the wet and treeless tundra, the figure rose from one hundred to one hundred and twenty-five. There the insects settled on his tent in such numbers when the wind was not blowing hard that he estimated 24,000 were darkening the outside of the canvas while as many more hovered exasperatingly about the door.

Yet local conditions, such as dryness and cold and occasionally a forest fire, sometimes operate to reduce or eliminate the mosquitos in a particular locality. I spent one June and July in the well-watered Cascade Range in British Columbia, at elevations over four thousand feet, and never saw a skeeter. The Athabasca River has always been noted as being one of the very worst mosquito rivers of the North, but a friend of mine canoeing from Jasper Park to Waterways in July of 1949 reported "no mosquitos."

Last summer at Hudson Hope, the severest mosquito season in the memory of the oldest trappers and gravel punchers got so rough that one of the few and incidentally perhaps the toughest of the prospectors who still took to the bush ditched even his pack-board and rifle to get away from them. Yet this segment of British Columbia is usually so free of the hummers that some years my collaborator has camped around from spring to fall with only a tarpaulin and not even a mosquito bar.

Around the first snowfall he commiserated with a then returning neighbor of his, who has a cabin a dozen miles away beside the

Butler Range and who'd been cooking with a survey party in notoriously bad mosquito lands above Jasper to the south. But instead of the perverse little beasts being proportionately thicker there as everyone around Hudson Hope had assumed they would be, his friend, Joe Barkley, reported almost none.

WHAT TO EXPECT FROM MODERN REPELLENTS

The Culex, one of the three general species of mosquitoes on this continent, is the common brute we know better than we want throughout far too much of the United States and Canada. It is not regarded as playing an important role in human diseases, but it can be a blasted nuisance. In fact, this little varmint can completely spoil a camping trip if one is not prepared for it.

Take along plenty of mosquito repellent. The old pinetar products, many of which also contained citronella and maybe a little creosote to lend them at least an aspect of authority, used to get all over everything and were not particularly efficacious to boot. Many individuals, furthermore, used to object to their odors more than insects did.

The better of the modern products are colorless, non-irritating, and nearly odorless. They really work, too, under ordinary conditions discouraging insects from alighting and deterring most of them from biting for from one to five or six hours, in ratio usually to how much you perspire.

They're even effective some inches away from the skin, under mild conditions keeping the majority of mosquitoes from hovering annoyingly near your ears. When skeeters are thick, though, you're going to have to rub the dope on exposed parts every half-hour or so, always keeping it away from where it'll run into the eyes and mouth. You're also going to want to douse some on your clothing as well, especially around the neck and ankles. The one that between us we've found most effective in really rugged testing grounds in the Yukon, British Columbia, and Alaska is *Off!*

Any repellent should be used according to the particular instructions accompanying it, especially as some can damage plastics and synthetic fabrics. Whenever an individual happens to be allergic to one of these, as many others of preferably different compositions should be tried as may be necessary.

SPRAYS

The time that mosquitoes annoy campers most is at night. Then it is very often their sing even more than their sting. For a quiet sleep, a good idea is to give the quarters a complete going over with one of the sprays containing DDT just before turning in, using the particular product according to accompanying directions.

Even this precaution did not amount to much with the repellents that were available before the building of the Alaska Highway and the other military construction in that corner of the continent showed a few individuals who could do something about it that the humming multitudes were tougher threats to the dignity of man than mud, dust, muskegs, snow, or congealing cold so intense that the hardening graphite in a pencil made only a colorless groove on paper and paraffin melted so slowly that a candle would scarcely burn.

Present insectifuges even when they do not kill immediately—and DDT does not—make the mosquito so sluggish that he stays pretty much dormant until you can find and dispatch him the next morning. The stupified insects should in any event be cleared out periodically, or some will revive to buzz again.

The effectiveness of these preparations, and you'll usually find local stores stocking the best for their particular region, lasts for several weeks in that they will sicken and eventually slay certain pests that come in contact with them, as by walking over a sprayed wall. To some extent, they discourage the presence of mosquitoes, flies, and their ilk, especially for the first hour or so. This does not mean, however, that during the height of the season in troublesome areas you will not have to spray several times daily. During the worst of the time, keeping the dispenser by the bed will enable you to deal with any new annoyers with scarcely an interruption in your snoozing.

The better of these sprays are useful, too, in ridding an individual's clothing of mosquitoes before he enters sleeping or living quarters and for assuring him a certain brief amount of protection when he is about to leave camp. They should in general be kept away from skin, food, animals, and open flame. Any repeated, prolonged, or excessive inhalation of the fumes is also inadvisable.

OTHER MEASURES

Smudges of damp and green wood and vegetation will discourage mosquitoes and flies around camp, making it possible to cook and eat meals without having bugs in everything. If you travel with horses, they will find much comfort when standing in such smoke which they soon learn to seek. A smudge may be very irritating to eyes and nose, but often it is far preferable to continual skeeter and fly attacks.

If an individual happens to get caught out without matches or dope in bad country, perhaps as the result of a plane crash, plastering his exposed skin with mud can even save his life.

LOCATING CAMP

In mosquito country do not camp on the edge of a brook, or along a lake shore, or in thick woods. Get higher up, as far from non-running water as is convenient, and in the open where wind will carry mosquitoes and flies away. Often you will be immune on small islands or on points of land extending well into open water. A high cut bank above a mountain river is usually good. So is an open ridge or high meadow near a small clear spring.

INSECTPROOF TENTS

For spring and summer camping where insects are bothersome, and for all seasons in the tropics, tents with screened doors and windows will help to retain a lot of the joys of camping in the open. The door net commonly is made to open and close with a zipper, or there may be a hole in its center that is controlled with a puckering string. Either arrangement is an exasperation, slow to get in and out through and an invitation for swarms of mosquitoes.

A much better technique is to have a very full net sewed to the junctions of the front and the walls, so that it will fall in a loose drape long enough for at least a foot of it to lie along the floor cloth. You simply lift the net, walk in or out, and let it drop after you. If skeeters are thick, you go in and out on your knees. It becomes the accepted etiquette in many backwoods localities for an individual to rid himself of any mosquitoes, either by spraying or by standing in a smoke, before coming into the living quarters.

When the net is not needed, tie tapes can be used to hold it up out of the way. If the tent does not have a sewed-in floor, a sod cloth should be weighted down all around during fly season. You may want, also, to put down a separate ground cloth that will lap over the sod cloth on all sides.

A BAR FOR MOSQUITOES

With lean-to and other open shelters, a mosquito bar may be erected over the sleeping bag and its bottom edges tucked under the mattress. One way to put it up is atop stakes driven in at the four corners of the bed. Another method is to suspend it from the roof.

Thin flexible poles, too, may be bent and thrust into the ground on either side of the sleeping bag in such a way that they will curve over the upper half of it in an arc reminiscent of the roofs of the old covered wagons. This framework may be covered with a large piece of cheesecloth, large enough to drape on the ground for at least a foot all around, protecting the exposed upper part of the body.

CLOTHING IN FLY SEASON

Clothing in mosquito country should be such that mosquitoes will not be able to bite through it. You may even need garments that can be tied or otherwise fastened tightly around neck, wrists, and ankles. You'll want to avoid, at the same time, fabrics that don't breathe. Some of the new synthetics are particular offenders in this respect, making you feel after a mile or so as if you'd been immersed in a steam bath. A loose shirt made from one's own deerskins is, we've found, especially pleasant to put on along toward evening. It is not too warm if you wear nothing beneath it.

Mosquito head nets may be purchased which droop from the broad brim of the hat down over the face and head and either tuck in at the neck or, preferably, extend over the shoulders to tie under the arms. Easiest to see through is black. Amber is practical, too. Incidentally, blue is the color most attractive to skeeters.

Gauntlet gloves, either leather or canvas, may be necessary. Both these and nets are abominably warm in summer, but where mosquitoes are notably savage and aggressive, as in parts of the Arctic, they can be far preferable to the incursions of the winged pests. Even in the worst country, however, it is very often possible to stay comfortable by keeping to open ridges and along broad streams where there is usually a breeze.

PREVENTING MALARIA

Malaria, yellow fever, and occasionally other diseases are transmitted to human beings by mosquitoes. Anyone going into the southernmost portions of the United States, to Mexico, or the tropics should know what mosquitoes carry these diseases, how they transmit them, and the precautions to be taken.

There are three general species of mosquitoes in America. The *Culex* is the common tormentor of the northern United States, Canada, and Alaska. When at rest or biting, its body is nearly parallel to the surface to which it inclines the rear tip of its abdomen. It is a very annoying pest, and its bite is irritating, but it does not play an important role in human maladies.

The malaria mosquito belongs to the genus Anopheles. A night flyer not ordinarily about in the daytime, it is found in large numbers in the southern United States and the tropics. When it rests on a surface such as your skin, it carries the rear of its abdomen elevated. That is, it assumes such a tilted position that it more or less appears to stand on its head to bite.

Only the female of the species sucks blood, the males being vegetarians. In order to infect you with malaria, the female must first feed on some human being (or in extremely rare instance, a monkey) suffering with malaria. It must then, within ten days or so, bite you.

As they are night flying, and as they seldom go over a mile from where they are born unless carried by a heavy wind, it is possible under certain conditions to avoid infection. When exploring in Panama where the rain forest is full of anopheles mosquitoes, I invariably camped at least a mile from any human habitation. Furthermore, none of us ever approached a settled area after nightfall. As a result, neither I nor any of my men ever got malaria, for the only mosquitoes we encountered were not infected. I did once get malaria myself on another occasion when I was bitten by an infected mosquito while marching through a native village at night during a maneuver.

The garrisons in the Canal Zone, as well as the large modern cities and popular tourist resorts in South America, are practically free from mosquitoes. But a large majority of the inhabitants of the smaller towns and villages in our tropics have malaria in their blood, and most of the mosquitoes there are carriers of malaria.

It is difficult if not impossible for a sportsman visiting our tropics to avoid being in or near such settlements at some time or other at night. Unless he takes particular precautions, he is therefore apt to become infected with the malaria parasite which multiplies in the red blood cells, destroying more and more of them and causing progressive anemia and recurrent chills followed by high fever.

When there is danger or probability of malaria infection, there are certain preventive or precautionary drugs that you can take. The old prophylactic was five to twenty grains of quinine, taken daily after the evening meal. Atebrin, known commercially as Atabrine, was later largely substituted for this bitter extraction from cinchona bark, partly because many individuals are allergic to quinine which for a time was in short supply. The atebrin dose is from one-half to two-and-a-half grains taken six days a week just before dinner.

The trouble with both quinine and atebrin is that neither will protect you from becoming infected with malaria. Both anti-malarial drugs merely prevent the disease from reaching an active stage while you are taking either. When you stop the dosages you are almost sure to come down with a full fledged case, provided, of course, that you have become infected in the meantime. Of course, when this happens you are probably out of the woods and within reach of medical treatment.

The most effective preventative for malaria at this writing, a very recent medical development, is 5/10 grain of Camoquin Hydrochloride, followed by 15 millegrams of Primaquine Diphosphate taken in a single dose daily for fourteen days by members of the white race. Deeply pigmented patients may take similar dosages under close medical supervision for possible toxicity, at which they should be discontinued. This is now in use in our Army and apparently kills the malaria parasite so that there is no after development of the disease and no recurrence. Ask your physician about those of these drugs which, under various trade names, are now on the market in tablet form. Parke, Davis & Co. is the supplier for the Army.

FREE VACCINATIONS AGAINST YELLOW FEVER

Yellow fever, a most dangerous and often fatal disease, is carried in much the same manner as malaria by mosquitoes of the genus Aedes, formerly called Stegomyia. These are also southern and tropical insects. In the Americas, happily, yellow fever has been pretty well stamped out. Where it does not exist, these mosquitoes have no chance to become infected and hence do not become carriers. Now, too, there is a successful inoculation against yellow fever. But if you have not been inoculated and get in a region where there is an epidemic, the best thing to do is to hitail out of there pronto!

In these days of ever quickening transportation, mosquitoes of various genera, some of them potential carriers of these diseases and of others such as dengue and filariasis, are liable to reach our shores. There have been rare instances of disease occuring in the United States from such sources of infection. However, while such mosquitoes may be brought here, most of them, particularly the aedes, can not establish themselves where frost occurs.

Vaccination against yellow fever is recommended as a health precaution for travelers to infected localities, especially if these journeyers are sportsmen who expect to go into the wilderness. Yellow fever exists in the Americas as far north as Honduras and Trinidad, and as far in the other direction as the southern extremity of Brazil, although many areas free of yellow fever lie within these limits.

International travelers who within six days of their arrival in a receptive area have come from or passed through an area which is considered infected with yellow fever are required to present a valid certificate of vaccination against yellow fever. One of these remains in effect for six years, beginning in this hemisphere ten days after the date of the standard single inoculation.

Immunization against this disease can not usually be obtained from private physicians. The U. S. Public Health Service, Washington 25, D. C., will furnish without charge a list of the usually free yellow fever vaccination stations in the United States, their hours, fees in the few instances there are any, and other pertinent information. Ask for the free pamphlet, Immunization Information for International Travel. If the supply of these happens to be exhausted, this same publication may also be secured from the Superintendent of Documents, Government Printing Office, Washington 25, D. C., at twenty cents per copy.

Sportsmen and tourists visiting almost all foreign countries except Canada, including even the interior of Mexico, must be immunized against certain diseases before they are allowed to return from such countries. Immunization is also often a requirement for foreign entry. Some of the recommended inoculations require more than two months for completion, so measures should be taken in plenty of time before you plan to leave the United States or Canada.

CHIGGERS

Chiggers, jiggers, chigoes, and red bugs—which are all the same pestiferous little biting mites—annoy us chiefly in the southern half of the United States, particularly along the lower coastal belt of the southern Atlantic states, and in the tropics.

So small they are difficult to see with the naked eye, they penetrate inside the clothing. Their bite is bright red and the size of the head of a pin. It is not painful. It is only slightly irritating if left alone and if a daily bath with soap is taken. Some individuals find, too, that Calamine and Benadryl Hydrochloride Lotion afford them relief from bothersome itching. In any event, the main thing is not to scratch the bites, which may then become infected.

I found they did not trouble me except right at the top of my shoes where the continual friction of walking irritated them. Anointing my ankles and socks with repellent did some good in stopping them from nipping there. Dusting the skin and underclothing with powdered sulphur or dimethyl phthalate will also afford some immunity.

I came up from Panama to the United States in 1916 on a

short leave, and while here I was ordered up for examination for promotion. When the medical officer who was to go over me physically got a look at my hide, he exclaimed, "What's the matter with you? What disease have you got?"

I responded that so far as I knew, I was physically fit. Well, what were those red spots over every inch of my body?

"Oh, those," I replied, "Those are just red bug bites. I've been in the field in Panama for a year." Best thing to do about chiggers is to forget them and don't scratch.

TICKS

Ticks are usually found where chiggers are. They are also troublesome in cattle country and in the mountains as far north as New York, Idaho, and Montana. Some are carriers of a dangerous tick fever, particularly those found on the west side of Bitterroot Valley in Idaho, from where they are occasionally carried on cattle to other localities. One of my best friends died in three days from the bite of a tick he received in the Blue Ridge mountains of Virginia. Vaccination with spotted fever serum is sometimes used as a preventive. Chloromycetin has dramatically controlled this fever within twenty-four hours.

Ticks in the United States are bothersome only in spring and summer, but in some tropical areas they are all-year pests. They cling to the tops of tall grass and weeds. When you brush by, they attach themselves to you and prowl around until they find a favorable spot to dig their heads into and suck blood.

What can be especially dangerous, according to Dr. Thomas J. Gray, is the penetration of a gravid female at the base of the skull. There the egg-laden tick, concealed by the hair, can remain unsuspected until perhaps a disturbing stiffness of the neck motivates a close inspection. Respiratory paralysis and even death are grave possibilities if the tick is not discovered and all parts removed.

They usually do not fasten in for some hours, however, and when I was exploring in Panama we always took a bath late each afternoon and deticked each other. In this way almost never did we have a tick burrow in. Before they fasten themselves, you can easily remove them by passing a sharp knife between them and your skin.

If they have taken a firm hold, the heat from a lighted match or cigarette will cause them to back out. So, usually, will daubing them with kerosene, gasoline, alcohol, or the tarry substance from a pipe stem. Attempts to pull or unscrew them from their holds are not so good, sometimes leaving parts of the head behind to cause irritation if not serious infection. They should never be crushed to remove them. Even after they have been taken off intact, the common practice of squeezing or mashing them with the fingers is to be discouraged because of the danger of infectious organisms being absorbed by the body. Heat from a match or ember will explode them in an instant.

A troublesome bite can be lanced one-eighth of an inch deep and suction applied for twenty minutes. A hot epsom salt poulice, if not too irritating to the particular individual, may help if left on about half to three-quarters of an hour. An antihistamine ointment affords relief to some. You can also apply some antiseptic such as an aqueous solution of merthiolate, cover with a sterile pad, and bandage.

BLACK FLIES

In the northeastern United States and in wooded eastern and central Canada, black flies can be equally annoying as mosquitoes from Spring until about late August. They are about one-third the size of houseflies, and they bite chiefly at the back of the neck, ears, and face. With me their bites cause more pain and inflammation than those of mosquitoes.

Punkies, midges, no-see-ums—so diminutive you can scarcely see them—are also often prevalent, especially at dawn and dusk, where there is no wind to blow them away. These microscopic menaces, capable of going through all but the finest netting, will have you scratching before you even realize what is the matter. Although they are extremely annoying when about, their bites are rather insignificant.

The measures you take to avoid mosquitoes will also be effective with these other venomous legions. With the old dopes, flies used to be almost implausible nuisances along the salmon streams of the northeast. We've looked up while casting in one and another woodland pool and seen hatch after hatch of them moving upriver in narrow black streaks all day. Then at night came the mosquitoes. The new repellants have given today's fishermen a brighter outlook.

HOUSEFLIES

The ordinary housefly is the common carrier of many disease germs, particularly typhoid. In the old familiar pattern, it lights on human or animal excreta and other refuse such as garbage. Then, carrying the germs on its feet, it investigates what is going on in the dining department. All food, as well as all cooking and eating utensils, should be protected from flies in camp, either by keeping them in flyproof containers or by covering them with cheesecloth. Fly sprays are also effective, but they should be kept away from food, dishes, and, incidentally, from open flame.

Special precautions should be taken in camps around civilization and in those that are maintained in one spot for more than a few days. Latrines and garbage pits should be provided, and these screened or darkened against flies. Deposits should be covered at once with dirt or ashes. The use of disinfectants is also effective. Garbage, including cans which should first be burned and flattened, should be placed in such a pit and covered with dirt, not just dumped on the ground. Bottles should be broken and then deeply buried.

It is highly desirable that the wild places remaining on this battered globe be kept unspoiled and clean, so that they will not lose too soon their attractiveness and their spiritual and aesthetic values. At home, some people have been accustomed to paying garbage men and caretakers to keep their surroundings clean and sanitary. Some others scatter their litter in neighbors' gardens and along streets and country roads, where it may be also eventually removed.

Entirely too many forget that in wild terrain there is no one to clean up after them. As a consequence, castoff clothing, scattered papers, rotting food, and other debris of every sort imaginable are sometimes seen. Along dry stream beds and across trackless deserts you can always tell these days where an automobile can penetrate, by a trail of rusting beer cans and slowly disintegrating facial tissues.

Any camper can do worse than copy the woodchuck who is one of our cleanest animals, although most unjustly called a groundhog. His burrow never smells of anything but clover, grass, and clean earth. In it he has a blind alley, at the end of which he deposits all refuse and covers it with earth.

Remember that you are camping in God's clean country. Leave it as pure and unspoiled as you found it, and do not make it look like Hell. Take good care of yourself, and take good care of the places where you pitch your shelter. You'll return home healthier, and you and those who follow you will always have fine places in which to kindle your campfires.

TAKING CARE OF YOURSELF

CHAPTER 16

THE CHANCE OF an accident or serious physical trouble in the wilderness, remote from medical care, is exceedingly small. It is much less than in a city, certainly, where accidents and infections are so often due to the carelessness or ignorance of others and not to any lapse on our part. In God's unspoiled country there is comparatively little probability of infection. If you take sensible precautions, mishaps and misadventures on trips back of beyond are like most other worries; they almost never happen.

Anyone would be foolish to absent himself from quick medical aid if he had any serious organic weakness. Someone with a weak heart, for example, should not plan a strenuous mountain or backpacking trip. But for the usual healthy individual, the chances of infection, except from insects or reptiles which we cover elsewhere, are so remote that you may discount them nearly a hundred per cent. This leaves just accidents to consider, and the larger proportions of these in the wilderness are the result of, in that order, either falls or the ax. You can not afford to take chances. Literally, watch your step.

CHANCE OF TROUBLE REMOTE

To indicate to you how extremely unlikely it is that you will have any trouble at all in wilderness camps and travel, during a lifetime of wandering in the wildest and roughest places in North America neither I nor anyone with me has ever incurred any disease, I have had but one personal accident of any consequence, and but one has occurred to a companion.

Once when a hundred miles from nowhere in the northern Rockies, I fell in jumping across a creek and broke my arm. I was four miles from my camp where I had a horse wrangler and cook. We bandaged the arm and put a splint on it, and I took a dose of aspirin and rum. We were delayed by a blizzard, and it took us six days of walking and riding to reach civilization and a doctor. The experience was not so rough as you might think, but it completely spoiled a trip for which I had planned and saved for ten years. The mishap was due entirely to my own thoughtlessness. I took a chance on a jump which I could have easily avoided by a climb of a few feet over a steep bank.

Another time, also a long way back among the peaks and high meadows, the old mountain man with whom I was hunting cut through the front bone of his leg above the ankle with his ax. We had no first-aid material at all. So I charred some underwear over the fire to sterilize it, bound up the wound, and put his leg in a splint.

Then I drove in our horses, saddled them, lifted him into his saddle, and for three days we rode toward a cabin. Each night I put him to bed with his leg higher than his body, but nevertheless the limb swelled badly and was very painful. At the cabin I made him as comfortable as possible. Then I rode twenty-four miles to the little town and sent a doctor out to him. After that I went to bed and slept around the clock. Willis Allen's leg healed eventually, but I shudder to think of what the poor fellow went through, and what might have happened, all because he neglected for an instant one of the rules of safe axmanship.

FIRST AID KITS

The soldier constantly wears a first-aid kit attached to his belt. This is for bullet wounds only. We think that it is entirely unnecessary and inadvisable for you to burden yourself with any such kit merely for a one-day trip away from your camp. You could not possibly carry one that would help with any of the dozen remote things that might but almost certainly won't occur. Anyhow, you are at the most usually only a few hours away from the medical kit back at your camp.

SNAKE-BITE KIT

There is one exception to this. In a country where there are poisonous snakes you should always have an adequate snake-bite kit in your pocket, because in the very remote possibility that you might be bitten, immediate first aid would be highly essential. There is a

Cutter Compak Suction Snake Bite Kit which takes up little more room than a 12-gauge shot shell and which answers excellently the demands of emergency treatment. Simply pocket the kit, which contains complete instructions, and don't worry. The mortality from bites treated with such a kit is less than one per cent.

SPORTSMAN'S MEDICINE KIT

Whenever you go into the bush it is wise to take along a small but reasonably comprehensive kit, to deal chiefly with such common accidents as might occur and with the minor ills liable to upset us mortals. Generally, this outfit should take care of most emergencies until the patient can be taken to a doctor. Based on our experience, or rather on the things we have known to happen to other campers, we would suggest the following articles:

1 triangular bandage for exterior bandaging and slings.
1 gauze bandage, 2″ wide in sterile package.
6 gauze compresses, 3″ square, each in sterile package.
1 package assorted bandages.
1 roll adhesive tape, 2″ wide.
1 bottle antiseptic such as 2 oz. aqueous solution of merthiolate and, if you wish, 6 small iodine applicators or merthiolate bottlettes.
1 tube sterile vaseline ointment for burns. Butter, lard, or saliva can cause very severe infections.
1 bottle aspirin compound.
1 jar boric acid powder for eyewash, etc. A teaspoon to a pint of clear water made sterile by boiling.
1 bottle water purification tablets.
1 cathartic, the kind you prefer.
1 snake-bite kit. Except for personal pocket use, we suggest the Saunders from the Medical Supply Co., Rockford, Illinois.
1 scissors, small and strong.
1 tweezers, for splinters.
2 razor blades.
1 eye dropper.
Some large safety pins.
American Red Cross First Aid Textbook, from any bookstore.

Add anything else that your experience or that of members of your party indicates that it might be wise to take. Antibiotics and powerful sedatives have been omitted because it is thought they should not be used except on explicit directions given by a physician. By all means consult a physician if you do not understand the use of any of the above.

We suggest that the articles of this kit, with which each member of your party should be familiar, be packed in friction top cans such as pipe tobacco is sold in, so as to keep them dry, clean, sterile, and unbroken. You might also paint a prominent red cross on each can. Fill in with a few small, plain adhesive bandages such as Band-Aids, etc.

SUBSTITUTES

Plain ordinary table salt, a rounded teaspoon to a quart of warm water taken preferably before breakfast, will serve as a purge. This also makes a fair antiseptic. Baking soda is an excellent dentifrice. Balsam gum may be applied to small cuts. A tourniquet can be extemporized from any piece of clothing, or you might include for this purpose a long strip of rubber cut two inches wide from an inner tube.

CARBON MONOXIDE AND THE OUTDOORS

Carbon monoxide is more of a threat to outdoorsmen than is generally realized. It is a colorless gas. It has no oder. Being cumulative, it often so weakens a victim that by the time he is aware that something is wrong, he no longer has the strength to do anything about it. There is not even any prior difficulty with breathing to warn him.

Carbon monoxide is a potential danger in any closed area where heating or cooking is being done with wood, gasoline and any of the other oil products, alcohol, fat, coal, and in fact anything that contains carbon. It kills by combining with the red blood corpuscles which are thus prevented from taking necessary oxygen from the air that is breathed. Fatal results can occur from inhaling small amounts of the unsuspected poison day after day, for these will remain combined with more and more hemoglobin until one more perhaps otherwise inconsequential dose is disastrous.

The best precaution against carbon monoxide poisoning is good ventilation. You'd think that a tent, certainly, would therefore be a safe place. But when, for example, tent fabrics have been closed by waterproofing in some instances and by frost or rain in others, small heaters have sometimes killed all occupants.

The fact that log cabins are seldom tight affords a certain intrinsic insurance, which is fortunate, for even a fire in a tight new stove with sufficient drafts can be perilous, inasmuch as the heat-glowing metal itself is able to release dangerous amounts of carbon monoxide. The hazard is heightened, of course, as cold becomes more intense. Fires are not only increased at these times, but it is only natural to seek to restrain ventilation.

A particular danger lies in wait for sportsmen whose automobiles and trucks are held up in cold weather by storm. The tendency is to keep the cab tightly closed and the motor purring so as to operate the heater. The peril, especially if snow is drifting around the car, is that carbon monoxide can and too often does collect inside the unventilated vehicle in fatal quantities. Even when one is traveling down the road, it is a good idea to maintain positive ventilation.

The treatment for carbon monoxide poisoning is to provide plenty of fresh air with the least possible delay. Get the victim out of the enclosure if you can. At any rate, smash or slash away for fresh air to enter a closed space if that is the best you can do at the moment. Keep him warm. Have him relax as much as possible, perhaps by lying quietly in a sleeping bag. Breathing deeply will help rid the blood of the effects of the gas. Stimulants such as coffee, tea, or chocolate are good.

As soon as it can be done safely, the cause should be eliminated. The best way to protect yourself from the gas is to hold the breath while in its presence. Breathing through a handkerchief is no protection. Incidently, smoke such as that from a forest fire often carries dangerous amounts of carbon monoxide. If a victim has stopped breathing, or is having difficulty in breathing, artificial respiration may be necessary. When oxygen inhalators are available, they should be sent for without delay.

WHEN IT'S COLD

A great many false notions surround the subject of cold weather, running on up in potential seriousness from the often-repeated assumption that during extremely frigid spells saliva will freeze between the lip and the ground. It gives no sign of doing so at better than 100° below freezing, certainly. Inasmuch as such freezing would require a drop in the saliva's temperature of sixty odd degrees in a rather brief period of time, the fact that it doesn't is not particularly surprising once you stop to think about it. The fallacy may have grown from the fact that if for instance when filling your water pails during an intensely cold spell you splash a bit on previously wet and now frozen ground, a crackling like that of firecrackers will result.

Another common but more dangerous error in reasoning is the basis of the widely proffered warning that when caught outdoors in very cold weather you shouldn't let yourself fall asleep or, freezing to death, you'll never awaken. The exact opposite is true. To put it briefly, passing over the obvious effects to be expected from excessive perspiring and from exhaustion, the only way the human system can manufacture the warmth needed to offset cold is by burning calories. The reserve of these energy units readily available for this need will be greatly lessened if, as many advise, we're also consuming them by aimlessly walking around a tree all night.

The ideal, of course, is to get a good fire going and then lie up in its reflected warmth. The next best procedure is to hole up while you're dry and fresh in as sheltered a spot as you can find, curl or hunch as comfortably as possible on something dry such as bark or boughs, and relax as much as possible. If you fall asleep, the increasing coldness will finally awaken you just as it does in your own bed. You stir around just enough to get warm, which is often all you do at home, and then you relax again and maybe grab another nap. From a perspiration-chilled sleep of exhaustion that is too often the result of trying to keep going, there is often no awakening.

The same sort of good judgment can be applied to the widely reiterated nonsense that the way to thaw a frozen cheek, for example, is to rub it with snow. First of all, thawing frozen flesh by friction is at best an extremely slow process and one that is apt to compound the damage by tearing the sensitivized area. Second, rubbing the skin with snow under such conditions is like reaching around right now and scrubbing your face with gravel. Third, how can applying frozen snow to the frozen cheek be expected to accomplish anything except perhaps to extend the freezing?

Warmth is, of course, what is needed. To thaw a frozen cheek on the trail, pass a warm hand over it. To thaw a frostbitten finger, shove it under the warm armpit. To thaw a foot that has started to freeze, build a fire if you can do so quickly. Otherwise, keeping as well covered as you can, hold it against a warm part of the body such as directly against the bare thigh. If a companion is with you, the thing to do if he'll agree is to thrust it against his bare abdomen. A horse, dog, or freshly killed trophy may also afford a solution.

Don't ever make the terrible error of trying to thaw a part of the body by immersing it, as has been done, in some liquid such as oil or gasoline which has been stored at subzero outdoor temperatures. Although far colder than 32° F., these and other fluids have sometimes been so used in the disasterous belief that because they themselves were not frozen, they were just the things with which painlessly to thaw something else.

Freezing, like every potential danger in the wilderness, isn't actually much of a threat to an experienced outdoorsman except as it may result from accidents. Against these, you habitually take simple but ample precautions. Your own inbred ingenuity and resourcefulness, stimulated by the racial instinct for survival, takes care of the rest. Besides, it has been said that a man sits as many risks as he runs.

CHAPTER 17

ALWAYS KNOWING WHERE YOU ARE

IT IS ALL VERY NICE, if you have the wherewithal, to employ a professional guide on your hunting and fishing trip into back country. He will make camp for you, and do the cooking and many other chores, permitting you to devote the maximum time to hunting, fishing, photography, or just plain loafing. He will even guide you to the best hunting and fishing grounds, point out the game or bait your hook, and smilingly have the lunch out of his packsack at midday. When it's time to return to camp, he'll show you the way.

The owner of a big sporting camp once told me that none of his patrons ever went home without a deer. "How many sportsmen shoot their own deer?" I ask him. "You ought to know," he replied. "About one third are babes-in-the-woods, and the guides shoot a deer for them."

But I guess we're both rather old-fashioned. Harking back to our pioneer ancestors, we have always thought that the charm of life in the open lies in the complete liberty of action that it affords. The intrinsic allure of outdoor living, it has always seemed to us, is caught up in the soul-satisfying independence of being your own master and in the deep-down pride that comes from being able to look out for yourself under any circumstances and in any country or climate.

NEVER GETTING LOST

No one is going to feel confident, relaxed, and utterly at home in the bush until he understands the few very simple principles of finding his way anywhere and, alone or not, of always knowing for sure where he is.

There is nothing at all difficult about finding your way through strange wilderness, of always knowing the direction back to camp, and of never getting lost. It is downright easy, in fact, for staying found is just a matter of plain common sense and of keeping your wits about you.

But, first, let's disabuse ourselves of the commonest of the several utterly false notions that have been formed about this all-important part of wildcraft. No man is born with the innate ability to find his way out and back through country entirely strange to him. This prowess is acquirable. It is not instinctive.

Neither does any human being carry a compass in his head. Even the most intuitive native, who has spent all his years in wild places, can find his way without outside help only through regions with which he is thoroughly familiar.

ONE WAY OF GETTING BACK

Probably an Eskimo by the name of Natkusiak, the companion of Vilhjalmur Stefansson during the dozen years the latter explored the unknown Arctic, was one of the most celebrated native hunters known. You may already have discovered by personal experience that it is difficult at best to get natives to accompany white explorers into strange wilds. They talk of being afraid of people they might meet there, who "kill all strangers." But most of all, although they seldom say so, they fear becoming lost. Natkusiak was an exception. He had apparently learned the knack of finding his way anywhere at any time.

One day the camp was out of meat. There was even fear of starving. Natkusiak started out to hunt. Eighteen hours later he returned, carrying the heart and liver of a caribou he had killed "far off."

The next day he started out with his sled to bring in the remainder of the kill, saying he would not be back for almost a day as it was a great distance away. That afternoon Stefansson went up on a hill about a mile from camp. From that eminence, to his surprise, he saw Natkusiak hauling a sled load of meat and heading away from camp.

It seems that the Eskimo's wonderful secret for never getting lost consisted of always following his trail back. He had wandered about on his hunt, paying no attention to where he was going. He had actually killed the caribou within two miles of the encampment. But, unaware of this, he had trudged back along the same twenty miles of curving and twisting footprints. He had returned to the kill by the same circuitous route through the snow, and he was once more following the now well broken trail when Stefansson intercepted him. Any tenderfoot could do that on fresh snow, but no one would have much success at it on the bare ground of North America.

THE FORMULA

The educated man, although he may have been born in the city and lived there most of his life, makes a far better explorer than any native, as has been proved innumerable times.

One reason for this is the fact that knowing where you're going, being sure of where you are, and of always having the certain knowledge of how to get back is no mysterious and negative matter of instinct and mumbo jumbo. It is, on the other hand, a positive and ever intriguing problem of distances and angles.

The formula for all this is not hard to understand. It is not difficult to learn. Everything you need to know is contained in these next few pages. As a matter of fact, most of it is in the next paragraph.

We stay found by always knowing just about where we are. This is not as complicated, nor as contradictory, as it may at first glance seem. Even the most inexperienced greenhorn can keep track of his position by the use of a map, a compass, and a pencil. Every ten minutes, or every time he changes direction, will not at first be too often to bring that map up to date. What if you have no map? Then, using the camp or road from which you leave as the starting point, you draw one as you go.

The wisest old woodsman uses exactly the same technique, whether he is aware of it or not. His map is in his head, that's all, Sun, moon, stars, vegetation, and any number of other natural factors may be his compass—under, it should be thoroughly realized, favorable conditions.

COMPASS

The sun and the moon have always risen in the east and set in the west. Everyone knows that at midday in the United States and Canada the sun is in the south, and that at midnight so is the full moon. The new moon (concavity to the left) is in the west in early morning. The old moon is in the east. The full moon rises in the east and sets in the west. The two outer stars that form the bowl of the Big Dipper point to the North Star, which has the appearance of being about seven times as far from them as they are from each other.

The only difficulty with these primitive ways of reckoning comes in cloudy, stormy, foggy, and otherwise obscure weather. Then everyone in strange country needs a magnetic compass. Moss does not grow on the north side of trees often enough to be a reliable indicator, and a prevailing wind is apt to change direction without being noticed. Even in familiar wilderness, a compass will often save a lot of time that would otherwise be expended on trial and error.

There are many questions asked about a compass. Some people think a compass will point the way back to camp. It will do no such thing. All a compass can tell you is where is north—and where, reading clockwise, east, south, and west are located. But if you use your bean along with your compass, you can keep from ever being turned around or bewildered.

Set any man at all down in country that is strange to him, on a day when he can't see sky or previously identified landmarks, and he will quickly get hopelessly turned around unless he has a magnetic compass. What he'll then probably do, if he's an experienced outdoorsman, is camp until the weather clears. If any man tells you he never uses a compass, put it down that he never gets beyond country that is thoroughly familiar to him.

However, many woodsmen are so used to navigating in the way we're going to describe, they think they have an infallible sense of direction. If this were true, you could put them out from the south shore of Great Bear Lake in a canoe on a misty black night and they'd instinctively know exactly in which direction to paddle.

WHAT IS NORTH?

Using a compass is a very simple matter if you approach it with an open mind. If in the United States and Canada you place a magnetic compass away from metal on a flat surface and let the needle settle down, it will point north.

That is, it will point to the magnetic north. This is a shifting point up above Hudson Bay in extreme northeastern Canada, almost due north of the center of Ohio. In the state of Washington the needle points east of true north about twenty degrees. In Maine, the declination runs about twenty degrees west.

Although this is not technically exact, it is in general accurate enough for everyday travel. Actually, the entire earth is a magnet, causing the declination to vary at different spots. In some localities, this may be as much as fifteen degrees away from the magnetic shift indicated on ordinary maps.

To determine the declination from true North with fair accuracy, find the North Star. This lies almost exactly over the North Pole, being only slightly more than one degree away from precise north. You can then either note immediately the variation between almost exact north and where your compass needle is pointing. Or you can scratch a line pointing to this Pole Star, or indicate it by two stakes, and in daylight compare your compass to the thus established north-south mark.

The declination must be taken into consideration when you're reading a map. As a matter of fact, it is marked on many maps. If no compass directions are shown on the particular chart you are using, north may be assumed to be at the top, this being the way most are laid out.

WHAT COMPASS TO BUY

Your compass need not be an expensive model. Choose one, however, in which the north end of the needle is unmistakably marked, perhaps by being shaped like an arrow. Some varieties simply have one end of the pointer white and the other end black. When someone is mixed up, he often can't always remember which is which, particularly as some imports we have seen reverse the usual procedure of letting the more prominent end indicate north. You may prefer a compass whose entire dial moves.

Compasses are inexpensive. You may as well get a good one, although there is no need, nor it is advisable, to burden yourself with one of elaborate surplus devices designed more for military use or for surveying. Get a good small compass, and one that is rugged and preferably waterproof. Keep it where you will be sure not to lose it. It's not a bad idea to carry a tiny spare in real wilderness. There seems to be no good reason to buy a compass that does not have a luminous indicator.

THE SECRET OF STAYING FOUND

There are two kinds of maps. One is the mind map which you keep in your head as you go along. The other is the more or less accurate published map.

Your mind map, plus plain ordinary common sense, will keep you from getting turned around or lost. If for any reason whatsoever you have the slightest doubt of being able to retain this map accurately in your head, then sketch it on a piece of paper as you go along. Let us illustrate exactly how you use it.

Suppose you have camped the night before in a country utterly strange to you. It is now morning, and you elect to go hunting or

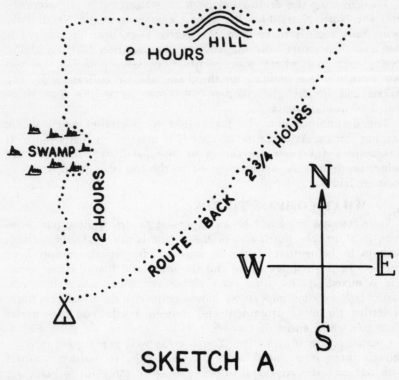

SKETCH A

trapping alone. You grab a lunch and, as shown in sketch A, you head north for two hours. Time in the wilderness is, as you will no doubt agree, a far more reliable indicator of distance than trying to estimate it in miles.

Then for some reason best known to yourself, you turn to the right and hike east for another two hours. On the first course, you detour around a swamp. On the second, you curve around the base of a steep and rocky hill. You make allowance for both these detours in your time-distance record.

At this point, it will therefore be perfectly plain that if you travel a little less than three hours southwest over the same type of country, you will arrive right back at the camp from where you started.

THE ENTIRE SECRET

The entire secret of finding your way and not getting lost lies in this little example. You must always know where you have gone and, by this knowledge, always approximately where you are. If you can not rely on your memory, then it is only reasonable to sketch a map showing these two essentials.

Whenever you know where you have been and where you now are, you will always know the way back. This is not nearly as complex as it may sound. In fact, it is not complicated at all. You merely keep oriented and, using a watch if you want, you keep count of how far you go in each direction. The map, if you elect to draw one, can be as simple as Sketch A.

As you gain experience, following this procedure becomes more and more easy. But it is really foolproof from the start. That old woodsman, whose ability to find his way anywhere under all conditions you so admire, has used this system for so many years that it has become second nature to him. In all likelihood, he now follows it with scarcely a conscious thought.

Most of us have come across old bushmen who tell us that they find their way naturally and that they never get confused. Many of them insist on this until we pin them down with direct and pertinent questions. Then we always find that stored in their noodles are detailed and accurate mind maps.

Now there are certain complications to this technique, as there are to every simple example. But as we come to each of these, you will see that the solution is in every instance merely a matter of sound judgment.

WHEN CAMPED ON RIVER, ETC.

Suppose your camp is located beside a river, tote road, or some similar boundary. For purposes of illustration, let us assume if we may that this landmark runs east and west, as indicated in Sketch B.

Someone who has never tried this in unfamiliar country may think that he could hunt all day north of this line, and then in late afternoon merely head south with the assurance that he would surely come back to it and then be able to follow it to camp. But which way should he turn upon reaching it? If he headed in the wrong direction, he might hike for miles and get nowhere.

The most professional solution to this basic problem, which in one form or another confronts every outdoorsman innumerable times, is to aim deliberately at one side or another of the goal.

The best technique, in other words, is never in strange country to attempt to hit a blind objective of this sort on the nose. If you miss it, you'll have no better than a fifty-fifty chance of turning in the correct direction. For all practical purposes, the gamble is not

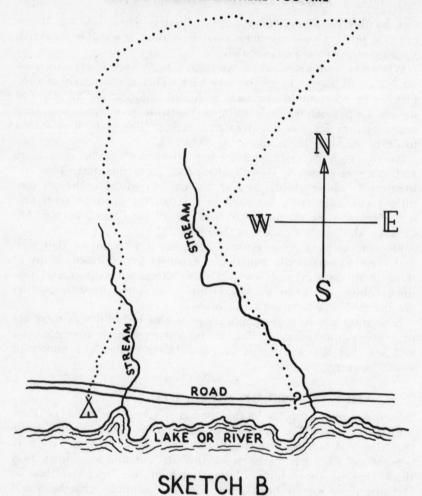

SKETCH B

even half and half. The human tendency if you're not sure you've chosen the right way is to give up too soon and turn back, only to have to come back over the same ground later.

If you bear positively to one side or the other of a long boundary, upon reaching it you will know for certain which way to turn.

BE SURE OF YOUR LANDMARK

There is one basic precaution to follow in this regard. Be sure of your road, river, lake, or other such boundary. Rivers cut back on themselves. Roads, particularly in the woods, sometimes come to abrupt ends in the midst of nowhere. Lake country, as you appreciate, can be particularly deceptive.

You may, of course, have a reliable map of the country, preferably checked by a dependable local inhabitant, that will resolve any such doubt. In any event, use only facts of which you are sure on which to base your procedure. If you have reached camp along that strange road, aim for the particular side of it of which you have personal knowledge.

KEEPING ORIENTED

When you start out in the morning, suppose you follow the little brook shown in Sketch B up into the hills. You hunt there all day, keeping a careful record of your directions and distances. Toward evening, on your way back, you come to a little brook.

You think to yourself, let us assume for purposes of illustration, "Why, here's that brook again. I may as well follow it down to camp." You start off along its bank. You go along beside it a long way and get nowhere. You realize that somewhere along the way you've miscalculated.

The trouble is that when you went up that brook in the morning, you did not note its various twists, formations, shores, bars, pools, chutes, and other peculiarities. If you had, when you came to that second brook in the afternoon you would have soon realized it was not the same one. You would have oriented yourself and made a beeline for where you knew camp to be. You can still do that by, at worst, retracing your steps to where you went wrong.

This same general error can be made in relation to tote roads, game trails, watersheds, and other such features. It is best never to rely too positively on such landmarks but, instead, to stay oriented all the time and to keep track of your distances. Then you will always know just about where you are.

DENSE FLAT COUNTRY

Suppose your camp is in dense level country where there are no landmarks. Suppose, for example, you are in thick jungle as were many of my camps when I was exploring in Central America. How are you going to leave camp in the morning, travel all day in trackless wilderness so thick that often you can not see the flaming sun, and return surely and silently to your outfit at night?

The most practical procedure is to prepare for your return while still in contact with camp. You and your companions can do this by running blazed lines for a half mile or so north, east, south, and west from camp. This will give you an objective, for all practical purposes a mile or so in diameter, at which to aim.

In this situation, you will keep very close track of your whereabouts. You will increase your margin for error by trying to hit this particular target plumb center. Once you have struck one of these four radii, you will be able to follow it right into camp. Two blazes on the side of each tree *towards* camp will show you which way to turn. One blaze will do on the outgoing sides.

The usual blaze in the woods, as you know, is made by chipping a piece of bark from a tree trunk so as to expose a conspicuous white patch of wood beneath. These are commonly at about eye level. You sometimes come across a very high line of blazes in the North Woods; puzzling until you realize they were made by a trapper on snowshoes. Each succeeding spot, in any event, should be clearly visible from the one preceding. Changes of direction in particular should be clearly indicated.

For a temporary mark, you can break occasional small branches, taking care to leave the back route plainly evident. There is an understandable objection in National Parks and National Forests to all varieties of marking which damage natural growth. The Appalachian Trail, for example, uses a dab of paint on trees and rocks to indicate trails.

OPEN COUNTRY

The variations already considered, although they hold true everywhere, pertain mostly to wooded terrain where you can not get much of an extended view and where each swamp and glade and green-bedecked hill looks pretty much like every other.

In the much more open milieu that characterizes much of the continental West, it is generally far easier to keep track of your whereabouts. This is offset to a considerable degree, however, by the fact that uninhabited distances are often so tremendous and the country many times so stark and rough that one can not afford to take chances. In some of the rugged mountains where we've camped, our objective has been in sight and yet more than a week away if we'd tried to walk straight to it. Under such circumstances, the important question often becomes less one of where camp is than of how to get there.

Generally speaking, however, finding your way about is often so easy that it hardly requires a thought—with one important exception. In case of storm or suddenly obscure weather, you should always be able to get to where you are going by compass.

Otherwise, for example, let's assume that two miles due west of your camp there is a hill with a peculiarly shaped rocky prominence atop it. You can see this conspicuous eminence for miles. It will change its outline slightly as you travel. By keeping track of this, you can gauge just exactly where your camp lies in relationship to it. If you keep looking back and noting the appearance of things, you'll easily be able to journey back over the same route.

WHAT TO DO IF LOST

If during your ordinary wanderings you suddenly discover you are not sure of your whereabouts, keep your shirt on and don't get excited. You are in no danger at all. You needn't even undergo any particular discomfort, especially if you have a knife and some matches that are safe from dampness. At the very worst, all you are in for is perhaps missing a couple of meals, and that is nothing.

The very real perils that can beset someone who is, or who believes himself, lost commonly arise from mental attitudes rather than from any physical circumstances. It is a disturbing comment on civilization that apparently stable city men, particularly those who for the first time are in what is actually the human race's natural habitat, will sometimes lose all rationality when they discover they are not sure of exactly where they are. Many, when they are rescued, are completely unbalanced and in a pitiable state.

There is nothing unusual about going astray. If such a situation is new to you, the best thing to do is to sit down, let your muscles go as comfortably slack as possible, and begin thinking things over calmly. It will usually help if you go about your reasoning logically. A simple way to start is by asking yourself what's the trouble. That's easy. You don't know where you are in relation to where you want to go. In the vernacular, you're lost.

Once you've accepted that fact, ask yourself another question. So what is the worst that can happen to you? Well, you can starve. Yes, but on the other hand if a man doesn't unnecessarily exhaust himself, he can go for weeks without food. Besides, in a pinch, even the inner bark of such very common trees as birch, poplar, and the numerous evergreens will furnish nourishment. All cacti are good to eat. In the Arctic all vegetation is edible except for one species of mushroom, although you'll want to soak the bitterness out of some of the lichens. All freshwater fish on this continent are edible, and so are all birds and all animals.

You probably won't starve then, but what about wild beasts? As a matter of fact, there is no wild animal in all North America that's dangerous to a man who does not provoke it.

What next? Well, you're expected back by nightfall, and you don't want to worry anyone. Of course, you don't want to worry anyone. That's one reason you're not going to blunder along inanely and maybe get into real trouble. If worst comes to worst, you can build a fire and sleep safely right here. It'll be a lot better to take care of yourself and let those who are waiting for you be a little anxious for a few hours, than to give them something really to worry about.

So that much is settled. If there is a real woodsman in your camp, you can take it easy right where you are. He will find you without any particular difficulty by at least the next morning. But if you start moving around, that can be another matter entirely. You may roam right out of the area of search. So why not select a cheerful spot nearby? Collect a lot of dry firewood, and go about preparing yourself an overnight bivouac? When viewed from retrospect, as a matter of fact, it'll probably be the high point of your trip.

AGREE BEFOREHAND

If you are in the wilderness with a party, the sensible thing to do is to agree among yourselves beforehand exactly how you all are going to proceed in any such emergencies. This is no more than a fundamental precaution. Even the most experienced woodsman can have an accident that will immobilize him and make help necessary. Just to mention one possibility, a branch from a dead tree might fall and break a leg.

Such an understanding may include the agreement that anyone lost or otherwise in distress shall fire, on the hour, three shots that are evenly spaced about ten seconds apart. Fired at appreciable intervals in this way, and on the hour, these would patently be distress shots and not merely casual shooting at an animal. Furthermore, anyone alerted by hearing the first shot or the second would have a good chance to determine the direction. Besides if your companions suspect you may be lost, they will be listening for you on the hour.

They may answer you and they may not, depending upon your arrangements and on a number of other factors. It may be that for one reason or another, such as wind direction, they may not hear those particular shots at all. In any case, sit tight. If you move and your friends hearing the shots come to where they sounded from, they would not find you there.

Above all, do not try to travel during the night. That's plumb dangerous. Not only are you apt to go really astray, but there is great danger of sticking a limb into your eye or falling over a bank in the dark.

You'll do a lot better to stay where you are, to repeat your shots each hour up to pitch dark if you can, and in the meantime to get enough dry wood together to keep up a hearty and warming fire during the night. If you are short on ammunition, the most auspicious time to signal is at dusk when the wind usually quiets and when, if you are not already back in camp, your companions will be most likely to be listening for it.

There are numerous other ways of signaling, too, with fire or smoke, by flashing with a mirror or any other bright surface, by thumping a hollow log or dead tree, and by innumerable other procedures that'll suggest themselves if the situation demands.

GETTING OUT BY YOURSELF

If there's no woodsman back in camp, then it may be advisable for you to try to find your own way out. You should travel only during the daylight hours, however, unless there are grave reasons for you to do otherwise. On the desert, to cite one exception, you'd

GETTING MIXED UP

Despite high water and the other place, you will occasionally get mixed up for a time. A little thought and common sense, however, will usually straighten you out. I can recall a dozen instances where I got messed up, all due to my own carelessness. Here is one of those instances.

It was in heavily wooded lake country. The day was clouded over. I had a fair map of the region. I arrived at the point marked "1" intending to go to the lake at the top of the map along the route shown by the dotted line.

It was obvious that all I had to do was to fight my way for a hundred yards through the alder swamps, and then around Hill A with the slope dropping off to my right, until I struck the lake. It was all so obvious that I paid on attention to my compass, intending to be guided by the contour of the hill. Except for the slope, the place was so wooded you could not see for any distance.

I crossed the thick alder swamp, but there was where I made my mistake. Without realizing it, I got turned too much to my left in the swamp. When I came out onto firm ground, there was the gentle slope slanting off to my right. I followed on around as shown by the dash line still not looking at my compass. I reached the first question mark. No lake! So I climbed up on top of Hill B to the second question mark. Still no lake!

Where was I, and what had I done? So for the first time I got out my compass, and then it was obvious that I had circled around to the left. It was also perfectly obvious that if I steered south I would strike the little river and be able to follow it up to the lake. Which I did.—T.W.

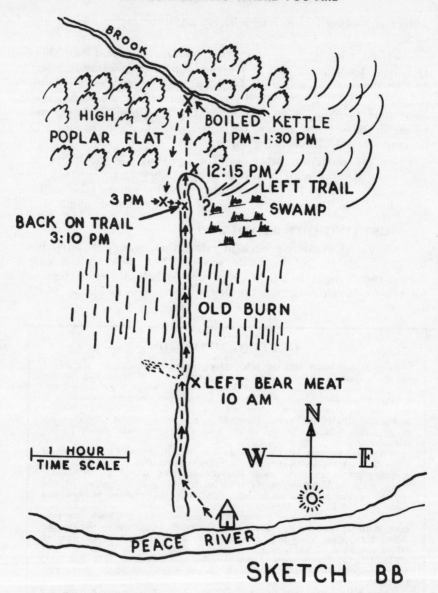

SKETCH BB

do better in hot weather to lie up during the day in shade, digging a narrow east-west slit for this purpose if necessary.

Whatever you do, you should proceed systematically. One way to commence is to sit down and smooth off a piece of ground on which you can scratch a map with a stick. In what direction did you start off from camp in the morning? That information, incidentally, should be exchanged daily between all members of the party. It is not a bad idea either if you start out alone, either from a solitary camp or from a parked automobile, to leave a message in some prominent place stating your probable whereabouts and the expected time of your return.

Now that you are making a map, put in every detail that you can remember. It's remarkable how many times a seemingly unanswerable situation will clear up completely once you start applying concrete logic to it. How long ago was it when you knew just where you were? If this was only an hour before, then you probably have not traveled more than a mile or so since that time. You therefore know within that distance just where your camp is.

Draw whatever you are sure of on the map. Is the camp on a river? If so, you will have a long boundary to shoot at. The river runs from west to east and your outfit is on the north shore? So you head south. Are you, by any chance, in a wooded area crisscrossed by country roads? Then traveling in any direction in a straight line will bring you out.

Is there a hill nearby from where you may be able to see a telltale lake or mountain range? Perhaps an easily climbed pine will put you in a position to locate where you are. What about sounds? Automobile horns indicate roads; locomotive whistles, probable miles of track. Sounds of chopping carry far, and so does the bark of a dog. Perhaps you can see or smell smoke from a stove or campfire. Possibly you can glimpse some sort of light at night. If you spot the latter, watch and find out all you can about it, in most cases staying safely where you are and marking the direction so that you will be sure of it in the morning.

When you realize you are lost, you are not apt to be very far out of the way. So in attempting to get back, be sure you keep oriented. You can head in a straight line. This you can do without sun or compass by keeping two objects such as trees always lined up ahead of you. Before you reach the nearer of these, select another that maintains the direction. Or you can travel in a generally straight course, picking the easiest route and averaging the changes of direction. The latter technique, although usually preferable and in some terrain absolutely necessary, requires much closer attention.

If you have the slightest doubt about what you are doing, carefully blaze or otherwise spot your way as you proceed. You will then be able to get back to where you started and from that center to try another route. Furthermore, such markings may very well help your friends to find you. If someone may be searching for you, don't ever quit a camp without leaving information about where you're heading.

WHAT ABOUT FOLLOWING STREAMS?

The advice is often repeated that when anyone seems hopelessly turned around, all he has to do is follow a brook or river downhill. This, it has been said many times, will lead one to civilization sooner or later.

The theory sometimes even takes swamps into consideration and recommends that one should skirt these on their higher sides. Less prudently, it occasionally adds that if you can't find running water to follow, you have a good chance of locating it by climbing down into a canyon or ravine.

The whole idea of the advisability of lost men heading along streams, however, reasonable it may sound to someone who has never been in real wilderness, is actually impractical in the extreme. You might travel down some rivers for as many days and weeks as you could keep going, and you would end up even farther from human habitation.

Such a route, furthermore, would almost surely lead you through the roughest and thickest sort of going if not into valleys and muskegs dangerously impassible, or you might very well come to a tributary river you could not ford.

WALKING OUT

If you know of a well-defined road or a large lake with settlements on it that lies in a certain direction, even though it is a couple of days away, you might head for this as a last resort. For instance, if you are about twenty-five miles west of the Alaska Highway, you could travel generally east with the assurance that if you keep going you'll surely come to it.

But any time you are really lost and happen upon something such as a power line or a telephone wire strung through the woods, do not pass it by because you may have some other sign of habitation in your mind. If you come to a road, do not cross it and continue on into more wilderness just because it does not seem to be the one you're looking for.

Such a precaution would seem, at first glance, so elementary as not to merit mentioning. But even in Alaska Highway country—

where if one passes this 1600-mile thoroughfare, he will in some cases not encounter another though he proceed to the Pacific Ocean, or to Hudson Bay, or to the Arctic Ocean—the tracks of some lost men have showed that they crossed this unmistakeable wilderness turnpike two and three times and yet plunged right back into the bush.

COMMON SENSE

Whenever you go into strange country, be sure to keep a mind map of your whereabouts. This is a great deal easier than it sounds. It gets to be second nature with just a little practice.

But suppose, in the excitement of the chase, you forget to keep such a map up to date? There is still nothing to worry about. Again you simply use common sense. Sit down and draw a rough map from your memory up to the point where, half an hour ago, you wounded that buck and started after him. You are now not more than a mile and a half from that point.

MESSED UP WORSE

When big wet flakes began tumbling thick among the lodgepole pines the first winter I was lucky enough to stay in the sub-Arctic forest, I still needed a well larded bear. Fifteen minutes from the gleaming newness of my log cabin, I picked up a trapper's trail heading true north along an old survey line.

Although this trail hadn't been cut out for a couple of years, travel over it was far easier than in the bush. Besides, it slanted up a series of benches where bears had been working on bushes to which a few saskatoons still clung. Sure enough, I picked up a fresh track and had a packload of plump young bruin back on the trail by 10:00 a. m.

The snow had stopped by then. The sun was bright on its thinness, and a dry warm chinook wind was feathering flakes from the trees. It was too fine a day to head back so soon. So I kept following the trail which continued north, for the first hour and a half through a jackpot left by fire. At 12:15, it doubled back downhill somewhere toward a swamp.

I decided to keep up on what was now a high poplar flat. This I did, continuing north at the same pace, with my shadow generally straight ahead of me but a trifle to the left, until I cut a brook at 1:00 p. m. Here I boiled the kettle for half an hour. The chinook was really whipping through the open country by then.

I'd been figuring on following my tracks easily back to the trail, ambling leisurely along the fast and easy going to my loaded pack, and being at the cabin by dark. No snow!

Now what? Should I head back due south and try to hit the north-south trail on the nose? Pretty slim chance! Should I travel south one hour at the same pace and then start zigzagging southeast and southwest, extending these lines until I crossed the trail? Too long!

What I finally did was head south-southwest, where the walking seemed better than on the other slant, for an hour and a half at the speed I'd been traveling all day. I was then sure that the trapper's trail lay a few minutes east of me. Which it did.—B.A.

Take a course, say north, for a mile and a half. You won't be able to use time in this instance, for you are going to mark your route. Then if you do not come to the place where the buck was shot, return to the point of confusion. From there, set off on another line which you also blaze. Pretty soon, one of these radii will take you near enough to where you wounded your deer that you'll recognize just where you are. Never thereafter need you fear that you will get lost in any country.

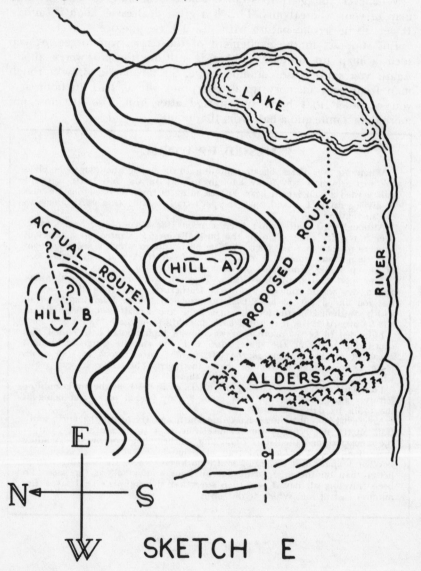

SKETCH E

CHAPTER 18

MAPS
and
MAPPING

A GOOD MAP OF THE wilderness you visit can be of enormous help. It may well save you a lot of time and unnecessary work, enable you to plan your vacation better, and keep you from getting mixed up. In the faint forest flavor of its projections, relief-indicating shades, and intriguing keys lies the power to make any excursion more interesting and more challenging.

There is now scarcely a region in North America above the yellow deserts and the brown waters of the Mexican border that is not competently and accurately mapped. This does not mean that every niche of North America has been thoroughly explored and that no longer are there blank spaces where a man who loves unknown country can not wander. Included among the primitive expanses, where your foot can still make the first human print, are those vast surfaces that have been mapped by aerial photography only, many after the last global conflict pointed up the wide gaps in the United States' and Canada's map systems.

All such charts are extremely accurate insofar as the features depicted are concerned. The intimate details which would not show from the air are lacking, however. Such characteristics as rapids, trails, portages, wooded and open ground, and burns are often missing. Hills, mountains, and ravines many times do not stand out on aerial maps.

READING A MAP

It used to be that we had to start out and tell the uninitiated how to read a map. But with the almost universal use of automobile road maps, that time is past. Nearly everyone now has a certain basic understanding of cartography.

The first thing to do when reading a map in the field is, of course, to orient it. Almost all are drawn so that the true north is at the top. When this is not the case, the map is usually so marked. Very often on those showing comparatively small areas, the magnetic north—where, in that particular tract, your compass needle will point—is also indicated.

When your map is turned so that its north is in line with actual north, it will show the direction from where you are standing to every feature on it. From where you are, for example, a lake appears on the map about five miles away in a northwesterly direction. If you travel northwest for five miles, you will reach that lake. Conversely, if you are at the lake and your camp is at a junction of two streams drawn on the map, orient your map, lay a twig on it between where it shows the lake and the camp location, and that twig will point directly toward your outfit.

WHERE TO GET MAPS

The finest maps of the United States and Alaska are those produced by the U. S. Geological Survey. These are published in quadrangles which, at a scale of one inch to one mile, cover usually fifteen minutes of latitude and longitude. Such a sheet averages seventeen by twenty-one inches. Many of the more recent quads are scaled at one inch to a half mile, embracing seven-and-one-half degrees of latitude and longitude. A degree, of course, is 1/360 of the circumference of the earth or 69.4 miles.

Each quad sheet is designated by the name of some town or prominent object included in it. Maps covering areas in the states east of the Mississippi River are procurable from the U. S. Geological Survey, Washington 25, D. C. For states west of that river, including Louisiana and Minnesota, you will be able to obtain maps from the U. S. Geological Survey, Federal Center, Denver 15, Colorado.

Write first for a free index sheet of the state in which you're interested. These detail the available quadrangles. When you order the individual maps you need, enclose twenty cents for each in cash, or by check or money order payable to the Geological Survey. Stamps are not accepted.

The back of every map shows the conventional signs and how to interpret any contours that indicate height, shape, and slope of hills and mountains. An arrow shows the compass declination. These maps are extremely accurate, but some were made fifty years ago and may not depict recent roads, trails, and new small towns. So you'd better get an ordinary automobile road map, available without charge from gasoline dealers, to use with them.

Colored three-dimensional maps of many of the national parks, monuments, and historical sites are also published and sold by the United States Geological Survey. They are of great value to anyone interested in the natural features, geology, and history of the area and to those planning hiking or pack trips. Prices vary. Write for the free checklist.

The topographic maps—which describe the earth's surface by contour lines and in a few instances by shaded relief—show mountains, hills, valleys, passes, glaciers, trails, lakes, ponds, streams, springs, sand dunes, cliff dwellings, ruins, buildings, and other natural and man-made features. They also indicate the boundaries of the national parks and other areas of the National Park System.

MORE MAP SOURCES

From the U. S. Forest Service, Washington 25, D. C., you can get maps of our national forests. Maps of our parks, showing recent trails and other physical features, may be secured from the National Park Service, Washington 25, D. C.

For Canadian maps write to the Map Distribution Office, Department of Mines and Technical Surveys, Ottawa, Ontario. Give the exact location or the latitude and longitude limits for which you wish maps, and ask for the price of the best ones available. Many of these are based on recent air photographs and are absolutely accurate, although they do not always show features that are not visible from a plane. It's generally a sound idea in wilderness areas everywhere in the world to have a dependable warden, ranger, prospector, trapper, or local sportsman check trails, portages, and the like on your map before you take to the bush.

Canadian maps may also be procured, without charge, from the various tourist bureaus which are located in the capital cities of the various provinces. One central office to contact for free maps and detailed information is the Government Travel Bureau in Ottawa, headed for years by D. Leo Dolan.

As a rule the best maps of other countries are those published by the National Geographic Society, 16th and M Streets NW, Washington 6, D. C. A government source for Mexican maps, which will supply information about these upon your written request, is Direccion de Geografia y Meteorologia, Tacusaya, D. F., Mexico.

MAPPING

You are making a long journey through strange country by knapsack, with a pack train, or in a canoe. You are going to be gone many days, weeks perhaps, and possibly even months. You want to be able to find your way back. Or perhaps you wish a record of where you are going. Or it may be that you are aiming to come out at some particular point at the end of your trip.

You may even be planning to do a little of the occasionally very profitable sort of prospecting we'll consider in a moment. In case a later assay indicates you've turned up something rich, you'll want to know exactly where you located those particular samples.

Over such an extended trip it is obvious that you will not care to rely on a mind map. For one thing, there would be too much of it to remember. So why not draw one as you go along? No matter how unhandy you are with pencil or pen, you will be able to make a map that is plenty good enough to refresh your memory and to keep you straight as to general direction and distance. At the conclusion, you may like to burn a nostalgic copy into leather made from some trophy animal you secure along the way.

MEMORIES IN NOTEBOOKS

You can draw your map on any piece of paper. We have found convenient the inexpensive loose-leaf notebooks small enough to fit neatly somewhere about the person.

One of us has a little bundle of these whose pages recall a stray odor, brush of breeze, animal call, the resiliency of juniper with its pleasantly woodsy blue berries, and many other transient pleasures. A cool cedar swamp where deer can be secured at midday. A railroad bridge in the midst of spruce woods where we unloaded our canoe and outfit at midnight from a stuffy baggage car and were off down an uninhabited wilderness river in the misty dawn. A northern slope where a black bear hibernates. A stream where a grizzly was pouncing on flashing trout. The way a line of moose meadows are strung together like a giant necklace although, because of intervening brush, you'd never suspect it while in them. A desert cave near the brook-sized Rio Grande in the shadow of the Sangre de Cristo Mountains.

Distances on your map should bear as close a relationship to distances on the ground as you can reasonably manage. We suggest that your drawing be scaled at a half inch to every one mile. You can then usually get a day's journey all on one sheet.

Draw, first of all, an arrow on the paper to indicate north, referring either to your compass or to sun and watch. Every time you sketch in any feature or route, you orient your paper; that is, you turn it until the arrow points north. If your journey for the day is to be in a westerly direction, you start your draft at the east or right edge of the paper so as to get it all on the sheet.

MAPPING PACK-TRAIN TRIP

If you are traveling by pack train, the map shown in Sketch C is the type you might draw. You start out from your one-night camp at dawn and travel southwest down a fairly steep hill for half an hour. On such a slope and a fair trail, your horses will not average over 2½ miles per hour. So you draw, toward the southwest, a dotted line 1¼ inch long to indicate that portion of your trip.

At that point you come out into a valley extending westward, with high mountains on each side and a little stream glittering through its middle toward the rising sun. To the south is a high mountain with a peculiar summit. This you estimate to be about two miles from the creek which divides the valley. On the margin of your paper you draw an outline of this mountain, so that when you come to it on your return, you'll know exactly where to swing southeast to catch the hill trail down which you now have just dusted.

You now ride up the broad open valley with your shadow almost straight ahead of you. The slope up the creek is a gentle one, and the animals in your string nip occasionally at clumps of grass. You are following a succession of game trails. On such going, your pack train will probably make about 3½ miles an hour, and so you time yourself accordingly.

At the head of the depression, there appears to be a pass through the snow-coned range you hope to pierce. So about halfway along you pause for a couple of minutes and sketch a rough outline of the way that pass, if such it is, looks from the center of the valley. Pretty soon the creek heads up in a little lake which you draw in to scale. It took you a little less than an hour and a half to reach this lake from where you started up the vale. You have traveled about five miles in this stretch, therefore, and you mark it in with a dotted line 2½ inches long.

After you go around the lake, the way becomes steeper and rougher. Your cayuses are making only a couple of miles an hour now. It takes nearly sixty minutes to reach the summit of the pass, so you note that in a dotted line one inch long. About a mile further along, you drop down into the timber beside a little creek where there is good grazing. You unpack your animals, hobble them, bell your saddle mare who's the leader, and you make your camp for the night. Adding this information on your paper, you conclude your charting for today.

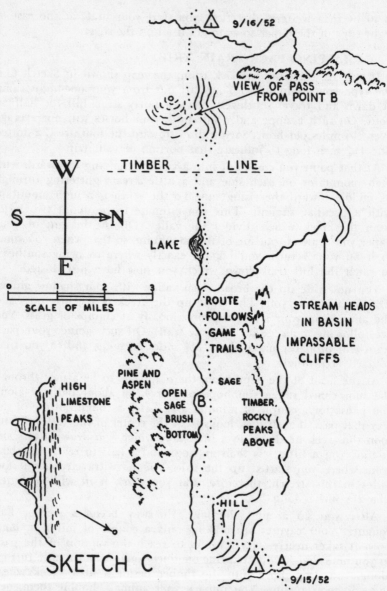

SKETCH C

Now on this sheet you have a pretty good little map. It is not as fine a one as a topographical engineer would make, but it is plenty accurate enough to enable someone else to follow your trail or to make certain that you will be able to return this way next month or next year. If your total journey is to be for twelve days, you will end up with a dozen of these sheets. Joined together with the north arrows all pointing in the same direction, these will make a composite map of a probably unforgettable journey.

PROSPECTING

The urge for certain raw materials being what it is these days, you may like to do a little prospecting along the route. The more you know about this subject, the more you'll enjoy yourself, but it is not necessary even to be able to distinguish between serpentine and schist to have a reasonable chance of making a rich strike.

When you see an unusual ledge or outcrop, knock off a sample. Number it. On the map you are keeping enter. a corresponding number. Don't bother too much with loose rocks. Because of glacial and stream action, these may be thousands of miles from their source. It is sometimes possible to trace drift back up a river, then up a certain stream, and finally along a short tributary to the mother lode. But some of our acquaintances have spent entire lifetimes trying to do just that. So stick mostly to interesting formations that are in situ.

Not far from where you live, there is some governmental or educational group that will give you at least a preliminary report on your perhaps mailed samples without cost. If something does turn out to be promising, you can tell by looking at your map exactly where to relocate it.

PANNING

Unless you are going in for gravel punching in a big way, you can handle all the panning you need to do for samples with a frypan burned free of grease. Fill this with gravel and sand generally from spots where heavy small materials, borne by water, might be expected to accumulate: back of large boulders, on the upstream portions of bars and, especially, down close to bedrock and in any crevices therein.

Panning merely capitalizes on the tendency of heavy particles, such as gold, to concentrate at the bottom. Large stones and such you pick out. Filling the pan with water, you break up any lumps of dirt and such by hand. You rotate the vessel briskly under the water which, in dry desert washes, may be in a big kettle. In this case, the handle of the frypan will have been removed.

Keep shoving the coarser stuff out. When you've sized down pretty well, tilt the receptacle a bit and rotate it easily so as to bunch any heavy minerals on the bottom. Then raise it until the tilted lip is just beneath the surface. Rotate and dip a few times, brushing off the lighter top materials.

Pretty soon you should be down, depending on where you're washing, to maybe a damp patch of black sand that's largely iron oxide. Swirl this about in a little water, looking for colors. These small particles of gold remaining after washing may be little more than specks, but enough of them will add up to the pokes of dust that can rock empires.

Copper or iron pyrites, known as fools' gold, are bright only in light and shatter easily. Muskovite, seen in flakes of brassy looking mica—containing aluminum, silicon, oxygen and either hydrogen or potassium—will break up readily between your fingernails. Gold, often accompanied by platinum and silver, is characteristically although usually dull colored. It gleams yellowly even in dark canyon shadows.

CHARTING A CANOE JOURNEY

Now let's take another kind of country—the lake and river expanses of the northeast through which, as indicated by Sketch D, you and a companion are gliding with a canoe. You will need, first of all, some kind of a time-distance schedule. This you should make yourself by paddling over a measured mile or a longer course, for a great many factors influence the speed you can maintain in a canoe; how strong and skillful you are with the paddle, the physical aspects of your loaded craft, wind direction, type of water, current, and a dozen other factors.

Under some of these conditions, as when your efforts are added to the smooth flowage of a river, you'll find you will make ten miles an hour. When you have to pole and occasionally line the craft up through bad water, it may take you all morning to cover one-fifth that distance. All these aspects you must take into consideration in setting down your distances on the map.

You make this map just as you did the one when your rifle in its saddle scabbard bulged under your knee. If there is any feature about which you are not sure, show it in dashes rather than with a solid line. As you came out of the inlet between Lakes A and B, for example, you saw two points of land against the north shore of the latter. You could not see up into what looked like a bay, however. As a matter of fact, the second mass of land may well have been an island. So you simply show the dashed line extending a little way into the opening between the first and second promontories.

Almost every lake in the canoe country of North America has old Indian portages connecting it with other lakes. Many a river has similar carries around rapids. Some of these are marked by lob-sticks, prominent trees from which a number of upper branches have been conspicuously lopped. The beginnings of others are so obscure that it is difficult for even an experienced bushman to find some of them. There may be an old tea-stick, or grass bent down, or a scraped log or rock. It is important that you note the start and the end of such portages as accurately and definitely as possible on your map, detailing particularly any salient features by which they may be distinguished, as suggested in Sketch E.

Often in strange country you may be able to locate other lakes, and the portages between, by ascending a high hill from which you can get an extended view. Where two such bodies of water come closest together is where you'll usually find a carry, even though this may be an old Indian track that has not been used for fifty years. Evidences still remain of the portage Alexander Mackenzie made past the upper waters of Rocky Mountain Canyon when, in 1793, he led up the Peace the first party ever to cross the North American continent north of Mexico. Others had been trying to accomplish this feat ever since Columbus happened upon the New World 301 years before.

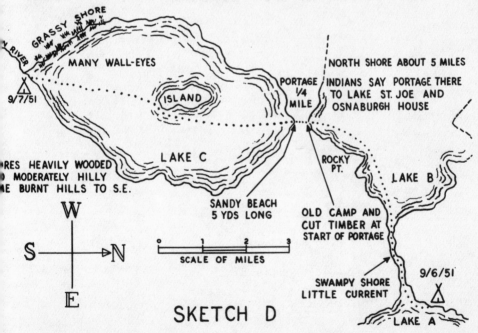

SKETCH D

WILDERNESS LORE

When you are trying to follow a string of lakes, or to make your way along a river which is continually expanding into small and large stillnesses as big streams often do in Canada, it is sometimes exceedingly difficult to find where the outlet of one body of water leads into the next. It may be at the head of any one of a half dozen bays.

Near such an outlet or inlet there is usually a little current which will cause the water grass to bend over in the direction of the flow. You'll sometimes see an old bushman trying to detect such motion by dropping some bannock crumbs overboard and watching their action. There are such telltale matters, too, as gulls on the watch for feed congregating near such passages, while the dip of hills holds for some a significant story.

These and many other wildcraft matters are lore to which an outdoorsman, however experienced, is continually adding, especially when traveling alone in what is to him terra incognita. There is nothing like this lone journeying in the farther places, whether it be by canoe, with a string of horses, with a solitary pack dog who'll curl up close at night, or alone with a rucksack on your back. You learn things of whose existence you'd never dream if you merely followed the shirt tails of even a good guide.

CHAPTER 19

AUTOMOBILE and MOTORBOAT CAMPING

LITTLE DIFFERENCE EXISTS between automobile and motorboat camping when it comes to methods and equipment. Each vehicle has so much capacity that those who want can take along many of what they consider to be the comforts and the laborsaving conveniences of the big town. The route back to the provisioner is usually so short, in time at least, that the camper need not deny himself fresh meat, vegetables, nor his choice of the more perishable fruits. He can even have refrigeration.

Some localities where camping is possible impose certain restraints on both motorists and boatmen. Public campgrounds may not permit wood fires, nor the cutting of boughs for beds or poles for tents. They usually require a type of shelter that affords privacy.

A few hours of travel, on the other hand, will often take you into wilder country where camping on roadside or beach is free for the enjoying. Even five or ten minutes of journeying away from traveled ways will many times bring you to uninhabited places where there are no restrictions other than those having to do with decency and the keeping of unspoiled country inviolate.

With the costs of lodgings and meals being what they are today, camping out can result in a very considerable saving. For food, you need spend little if any more than you would at home. Rent can be nonexistent. You'll require gasoline. but this you would need anyway on such a trip. Furthermore, you will be free to turn wherever fancy lures you instead of being tied to a consideration of restaurant and motel stops.

SHELTER AND SLEEP

Of primary importance is the matter of shelter. You may, it is true, sleep in your automobile or in the cabin of your boat. While these will be available in cases of necessity, there is generally the problem of luggage. Besides, when you halt you usually want to get your feet on the ground and stretch your legs. At some particularly appealing location you may wish to stay for days, using your ready transportation for daily trips to nearby attractions. So we tackle the subject of tents.

Your tent for such vacations should be one that can be easily and quickly pitched. Besides being commodious, it may well be wind-, water-, and bugproof. Certainly, it should insure privacy. Its own clean floor will be appreciated in public places. For family parties and particularly for groups including women, probably the best all-around solution is the previously described Umbrella Tent. Models, including some with extra rooms in the form of side shelters, can be secured to accommodate any reasonably small and congenial unit.

The Umbrella Tent also has the virtue of affording sufficient head room for moving erect anywhere within it, a particular convenience for those unaccustomed to the usual limitations of canvas. It is expensive, yes, but its price tag is smaller then what the tab would be a week's room and board for three at a motel. Given reasonable care, such a tent is good for a decade or more.

In it you may if you wish use folding canvas beds complete with blankets, sheets, and pillows from home. The cost of special bedding will thus be eliminated. Such an arrangement, too, will appeal particularly to the feminine sector. With a cot, however, some form of mattress will be necessary for warmth except in the hottest weather. Least bulky will be a blanket or two folded beneath you. An air mattress adds no warmth to a canvas cot and, furthermore, is uncomfortable when not laid on a firm surface.

In windy country, you may find it prudent to secure your umbrella or similar tent with added guy ropes and perhaps even to collapse it when leaving camp for the day.

MINER'S TENT

Particularly for the seashore, the wind-scoured desert, and the open plains, the small Miner's Tent is a functional choice for a party of not more than three. This simple pyramidal model stands up better than most in the gales and the savagely enveloping storms you often encounter in such terrain.

It is extremely easy to pitch. All you usually need, except when guys may be advisable, is a simple jointed pole and a few stakes. When there is something such as a sufficiently rigid branch from which you can suspend a single line hitched to the peak, not even the pole is necessary. You can also stretch a rope into position for this purpose.

WHELEN LEAN-TO

Many automobilities report that the Whelen Lean-To Tent, already considered in detail, works out well when pitched beside a car. All you have to do is to throw and tie the front hood over the car top and to stake down the rear wall. Enter by lifting either side wall, and you have immediate access to the interior of the vehicle from the tent. If you move the car, the shelter must come down. This involves no particular inconvenience, as the Whelen Lean-To is so easily put up again.

COOKING

Don't count too much on using wood fires. You will likely have to camp in many places where either firewood is not obtainable or where such blazes are in fact prohibited. The two- or three-burner gasoline stove is usually the favorite solution. With it you will require a safe container in which to carry fuel.

Kitchen and eating utensils can take up a lot of room unless you adopt one of the previously discussed sets of nesting pans, pots, cups, bowls, plates, and other such necessities. You are sure to need a lot of water at your campsite, and the source may be some distance away. Collapsible canvas buckets are procurable. For your particular use, two galvanized pails will be cleaner and more convenient, however. These can nest inside one another, and you will be able to pack safely within them items particularly susceptible to leakage or breakage. A large pan for washing dishes as well as clothes, and a wash basin for personal use, will also be desirable.

A small refrigerator chest may be what you want for keeping meat and other perishables fresh in warm weather. Regular ice will work better in this than will dry ice. The latter not only will freeze anything that comes too close to it, but it will not last as long as the regular ice. A good idea, by the way, is to get this small refrigerator as cold as possible before you leave home.

Food may to some extent be packed in small waterproof bags and in cans, and these carried in a compact grub box. Or you can devise and build a kitchen cabinet of your own which, when you're motoring, will fit in the baggage compartment of your car. This may be comprised of drawers, compartments, racks, and the like; all made secure by a door that will let down for use as both a kitchen and serving table.

Another item you will particularly appreciate in camps of this sort is the thermos bottle. With it, you can enjoy steaming hot coffee even before breakfast is ready.

OUTFIT

An ax, enclosed in a safe sheath during travel, will be needed for driving tent stakes and for clearing ground. If you travel very far back of beyond, it may be required for removing trees and other obstructions from secondary roads and small water courses. You can never tell when one of these is going to be invaluable. A light Hudson Bay model that one of us always keeps in his station wagon recently saved a man's life on a major highway by cutting him free of a wrecked truck.

A rugged folding shovel will also frequently pay its own way. Naturally, you will include a kit of tools for maintenance and repair of car or boat.

FURNITURE AND LIGHTS

When transportation offers little problem, there is no reason why you should sit on the ground and eat your meals from your lap. By all means, take a folding table and camp chairs if you have the room. Let the latter have arms and backs so that everyone can lounge and relax.

The turning on of the lights in your car may, especially in public campgrounds, disturb nearby vacationists. A universal solution to this problem is the carrying of a pressure lantern in a protective case, together with extra mantles. The better of these provide excellent camp illumination. You can also procure one of the small electric lights which, draining little power, plugs into the lighter socket on the dashboard. At least one small flashlight is also advisable.

PERSONAL EFFECTS

Each camper should have preferably a waterproof duffle bag, opening along its entire length, in which to pack personal effects. A small suitcase will do, of course. You will probably want to include clothing for stormy or dusty going.

At a few public campgrounds you may wish to mingle socially with other parties, and some fairly presentable sports clothes may then be desirable. This will remain less wrinkled if carried folded in a regular wardrobe case or in one of the fabric containers that may be hung up at full length wherever you have the space. If a woman is along, she may particularly appreciate one of the Coleman gasoline irons.

While many campgrounds have bathhouses and showers, there may be other stopovers where you cannot get down to a stream or lake shore to wash up but may have to dress and perform your toilet in the privacy of your tent. You should be prepared for this. If you are accustomed to an electric razor, incidently, a small converter may be secured at small cost. Plugged into the lighter receptacle of your car, this will enable the use of your regular implement.

Then there is the sporting equipment; guns, rods, cameras, and other such choice companions of the outdoor hours which only the consideration of space, weight, and of our dwindling means ever give us the fortitude to resist.

SELECTING THE BEST ROUTE

Travel services are maintained by many of the principal oil companies. Among those concerns employing tourist representatives who—at no cost to you except a two-cent postcard—will map out special routes, suggest stopovers, list attractions and accommodations, and even furnish detailed information on hunting and fishing are: Amoco, Atlantic, Cities Service, Esso, Gulf, Humble, Shell, Sinclair, Socony-Vacuum, Sunoco, Texaco, Union, and a number of the Standard Oil Company corporations.

All these we have personally tried. Some, as a matter of fact, even furnish through their retailers stamped inquiry cards. Because the addresses of these free tourist bureaus occasionally change, the best sources for them are the various filling stations. There is no charge nor obligation, and usually a pertinent and comprehensive package of maps and literature is soon forthcoming by mail.

We have always found it profitable to present the same problems to several such agencies at once, because one often has information about detours and other conditions about which the others are not yet aware.

MAKING EXTRA SPACE

It seems all along that you are going to have plenty of room. Then all of a sudden, when you start to stow the outfit in your car, space becomes a problem. One answer may be a car-top rack, obtainable from most outdoor outfitters, on which anything from a boat to a hodgepodge of luggage can be carried without damaging the vehicle.

A simpler solution, that perhaps will afford just enough extra room, may be the removal of the back seat. Even if someone is going to ride there, filling in the gap with such essentials as tentage and sleeping equipment will provide, with a little arranging, a sufficiently comfortable vantage spot for not too long a journey.

TENT TRAILER

Two small and light trailer arrangements are also available to the camper who prefers mobility to even limited luxury. The first of these is the tent trailer. This is little more than a simple two-wheel box, covered by a tent that can be raised and lowered by a frame that folds flat across two permanent bunks when you are ready to roll. Storage space is provided beneath and between these beds.

TEARDROP TRAILER

Next along the path to sumptuousness is the small tear-drop trailer. With its permanent double bed, accessible through small doors at either side, this resembles nothing quite so much as a portable upper berth.

There is less living area. With the tent trailer, you can at least sit on the edge of your bunk with you feet on the floor. The two-wheel teardrop is all bed except for a rear compartment covered by a hinged panel which lifts into position as a sort of roof. Here some sort of cooking, refrigeration, and food-and-water-storing arrangements can be assembled to provide an always ready kitchen.

Prices for both of these highly mobile two-wheel camps range upward to about five hundred dollars, which does not include such considerations as hitch, insurance, and extra wiring.

FOR BENEDICTS

Before you set forth, go over all the preceding items. Unless you are a bachelor, make out a check list with three columns; one for the essentials, a second for things you will need only for special trips in certain localities, and the third for grub.

Paste this list, if that is what you have to settle for, on a durable card or board. Have it at hand when you pack for the start. At that time, check off items one by one as a safeguard against going off and forgetting something indispensable.

Such an oversight may mean back-tracking and even the endurance of a certain amount of ironic comment, particularly from the distaff side of the expedition. Once, after getting two hundred miles on our way and pulling over at an ideally sequestered spot for lunch, we found that because of someone's oversight the grub box had been left in the cellar. That was a calamity indeed!

FOR BACHELORS

Bachelors can take advantage of the visual and highly functional practice of building little piles at one end of the most convenient room—cooking equipment in one, clothes in another, flies and other fishing necessities in a third, and so on. When you find you are lacking a certain item, a note to that effect placed in the proper group will serve as a reminder.

BEING READY

Before you start on your trip, do you know how to use every piece of equipment? Even if you've been heading into the tall timber by yourself for years, you may be a little perplexed by the intricacies of a tent procured for family use. When you are accustomed to lonely campfires, even one of the simpler gasoline stoves may be puzzling at first.

A sound procedure is to do any necessary experimenting beforehand in the back yard. Let the entire group pitch in, each handling the particular assignments that will be his duty on the journey. Try a sample meal of the more difficult foods. Include washing all the utensils and repacking them when you finish. Time-check all chores so that you will know how early in the afternoon you will need to stop to make a pleasant camp. With such an outfit, there is no reason why everyone from eight to eighty can not be as agreeably comfortable as at home.

CHAPTER 20

PADDLE, POLE, and PORTAGE

THERE'S AN EXHILARATION, a rhythm, and a fierce clean freeness to canoeing in the wild places that takes it out of the realm of other sports.

Nothing brings you more alert. Every muscle responds immediately, with both power and delicacy, to the swiftly shifting demands of balance and steerage. You poise almost quivering with restrained energy, studying which racing bulge of water to ride around an onrushing boulder. Then you're driving your blade with fast, hefty jabs. You're fighting to swing the stern free of a suddenly chortling current that hungers to heave the craft broadside up against the froth-dampened projection and there snap it in two.

With a sudden lift and plunge, you're past. Instantly you're fairly met with another challenge to every last iota of your strength, judgment, and skill—and another, and still another. You eye ahead, brace yourself, and turn your instantaneous decisions into exultant action amid the rush and hiss of wind and contesting water.

Then you're through the last of this intoxicating craziness. The stream widens into a deep gentleness. It is so abruptly quiet that when your paddle scrapes a gunwale the brief clatter seems a desecration, although you know the current is merely bunching behind another rock-pierced narrowness somewhere ahead. You see the perfect birch under which to spread your eiderdown. Your legs quiver a little when you step ashore. You draw in a deep breath. You're ten feet tall.

We've only experienced one other sensation remotely comparable to the species of excitement and gratifying satisfaction you win by shooting the white race of a primitive river under your own steam. That's feeling the smooth, muscular speed of your own favorite saddle horse rippling beneath you along an open ridge trail as, in sheer exhuberance after a successful day's hunt, you're racing camp-ward in the first cool dampness of a wilderness evening.

I've been canoeing all my life, and so has my writing sidekick most of his. Back while I was a boy in the Adirondacks was when I had my first canoe. I built it myself, using flat barrel hoops for the ribs and covering the ten-foot frame with unbleached muslin, which was the only material I could get. With many coats of paint it sufficed, and the craft did two of us kids all one summer. We used it mostly on the Rock River which was a fine wild stream in those days, with deer along it, and trout in its waters, and lots of swamps productive of bullfrogs and ducks. Now I see they have dammed it up and have made what they call Lake Durant out of it, with a large public camping ground nearby and a paved auto road along one shore.

CANOE COUNTRY

Northeastern America embraces the finest canoe country in the world. Maine and adjoining portions of Canada, the Adirondacks in New York, and Wisconsin afford opportunities for long and short cruises through interesting silences. There are many small eastern rivers that tinkle and gurgle across lowlands into the Atlantic or the Mississippi, traversing regions where one can usually camp freely, all providing good fishing and sometimes good enough hunting as well.

The most superb canoe stronghold of all lies in northern Minnesota and in northern and western Ontario and Quebec. In these latter regions you find a practically unspoiled wilderness with almost as much water as land, and such myriads of small lakes and connecting rivers that it is literally possible on nearly any given day to paddle your little craft toward any point of the compass.

All this land has been Indian canoe country for hundreds of generations. Wherever there is an obstacle to water travel, you will usually find a trail or easy way through or around. Portages they are called, and in the North we have seen where they are worn a foot deep in the soil and where the very rocks have been polished by thousands of moccasins.

The only real practical craft for the sportsman who travels such waters is the canoe. This can be easily portaged around rapids, past thunderous falls, and between lakes; on one man's shoulders if need be. In it game can be noiselessly approached. Because the canoe is made to be handled with its occupants facing forward, it is the only satisfactory craft for running the usual rapids and for ascending swift streams. It can be paddled. It can be poled. It can be lined. You can wade it, too, handling it where waters momentarily deepen by swimming with one hand on the stern.

CONTINENTAL NORTHWEST

Throughout the great continental northwest, large rivers slant hundreds and sometimes thousands of miles through splendid and almost virgin country. Most of these rivers can be ascended a long way, almost to their sources, in canoes.

Because of the tremendous distances to be covered, long narrow wooden boats capable of carrying barrels of gas in addition to heavy outfits are more commonly used in many regions. Some of these are powered by inboard motors, often salvaged from some truck or automobile that has been finally neutralized by the primitive roads of the area. Others are kicked along by big outboard motors, sometimes operated from an elevated seat in back.

Along these streams by fall there is little game except for occasional moose, bear, and a few deer. Prospectors licensed to keep themselves in meat do all right in spring and summer, however. In the mountains, they sometimes even catch up to a swimming goat.

Trophy hunters travel these rivers until they are as near as they can get to good hunting range. They then back-pack into the mountain habitats of sheep, goat, caribou, moose, and grizzly. Such a trip is really an expedition, to be planned months in advance and to be undertaken only by experienced and strong outdoorsmen.

THE CANOE

The longest canoe journey I have made was for seventy-five days, about half of which were travel days, through the wilderness of northern Ontario. Our seventeen-foot canvas canoe weighed eighty pounds and our outfit, at the start, just about four hundred pounds more. Of course, the weight of the latter diminished daily as grub was consumed.

A fifteen-footer weighing just short of sixty pounds dry, and with its sleek cedar interior and canvas covering kept freshly varnished and painted to reduce the absorption of heft-increasing moisture, has taken the other of us and everything he wanted on a number of wilderness trips about half that long.

Today the new Grumman aluminum alloy canoes have it over other types in almost every way, although you'll probably want to subdue the glare with a dead-grass shade of paint, and to include

The Grumman aluminum canoe has fine, practical lines. The bow and stern are low so as not to catch the wind, and the seats are lower, making the center of gravity low.

the available rubber gunwale guards for both stern and bow paddlers in the interest of silence.

The size of the canoe to be chosen depends largely on the bulk and weight to be carried, on the skill and huskiness of the occupants, and on whether many large lakes must be negotiated. The particular craft must not be loaded so heavily that it will be sluggish, hard to turn, or slow to respond to paddle. It should lift with characteristic leaflike buoyancy over large swells rather than plough through with a resultant shipping of water. There must be sufficient freeboard so that the waves encountered on fairly windy days will not swamp it.

No canoe can be expected to weather a serious storm on a large body of water. You simply go ashore and wait for a calmer spell. But the craft should not be ladened so heavily that it will be unsafe in the chop and waves of an ordinary blow.

With an aluminum craft, you'll want to include one of the special kits containing patches, sealing compound, and rivets. Minor punctures can usually be temporarily repaired with cold solder, or with marine glue, or even with a strip of ordinary waterproof adhesive tape from your medicine kit. With a canvas canoe, pack along one of the waterproof glues, some heavy canvas, a can of copper tacks, some white lead, and maybe an old spoon and brush. We've also done pretty well in a pinch by using spruce pitch, melted along with a candle stub, in which to soak and cement on a strip of fabric requisitioned from the flap of a duffle bag.

TUMP LINE

The almost universal method of portaging grub and equipment across a carry is with a tump line, packsack, or combination of the two. The tump line consists of a broad band of thick, soft leather about three inches wide and fifteen inches long. Canvas is sometimes used instead. To each end of this headpiece is attached something such as a rope or a rawhide thong perhaps ten feet long. Tapering straps are so employed, too, their length being adjustable by buckles.

These two extremities are secured to the bundle to be packed, in such a way that at the proper height above the bundle the headband forms a loop. This usually goes over the forehead at about the natural hairline, while the bundle rests against the middle of the back just over the hips. The weight is thus supported by the head, the neck muscles, and the spinal column. It is steadied by pressure on the shoulders, back, and hips.

The sportsman will find the tump line a vexing way of packing until he develops strength and endurance in his neck muscles. He should never attempt it, except experimentally, on his first wilderness journey. But if he is to continue taking canoe vacations year after year he should learn to use this flexible accessory, for with it a greater weight can be packed than in any other manner.

The base to which the tump line is attached often consists of a roll of bedding or a sack of flour. This rests low down, almost on the top of the hips. When it is in place, other bundles such as flour sacks, duffle bags, and loose articles of most any kind are piled on

Portaging with tump line.

top. Reaching in some instances almost to the top of the packer's head, these go more or less between the two lines stretching up from the base bundle to the headpiece. The packer keeps everything in place by bending slightly forward. It's not as difficult to balance the load as one might expect.

In this manner, professional Indian and half-breed packers regularly take freight weighing up to 200 pounds over portages up in the Hudson Bay country. The weight record, so far as I know, is held by a big Cree Indian named Joe Morin who, in a contest between some Chippewayan and Cree packers at Pelican Narrows in Manitoba, packed for a hundred yards the incredible weight of 620 pounds of flour.

The tump line is at its best for short distances on plainly marked portages. Its advantages are too often offset when you have to pick your way over rough ground, for your head is bent downward in such a way that you can not turn it without swinging your whole body. You can not easily see what lies ahead, nor are you apt to spot game. Even if you do glimpse a retreating bruin, you can not get off a well aimed shot while movement and vision are so restricted.

The tump line's chief value lies in the fact that with it more can be taken over the portage in one trip. Only one tump line per man is needed. It is simply untied from one load and hitched to the next.

PACKSACK FOR PORTAGING

The other form of pack in most common use among experienced voyageurs is the packsack variously known by such names as the Woods, Poirier, Maine, Duluth, and Northwestern. Basically, it is simply a canvas bag or sack, approximately fifteen to twenty inches wide and twenty-five to thirty inches long, opening at the top. Shoulder straps extend from a central point at the top to the two bottom corners.

Many outfitters make it up in a reinforced boxlike bag of waterproofed duck, about eighteen by twenty-six by eight inches. Extra pockets are sometimes sewed on the outside and in the flap that covers the square top opening. In addition, provision is often made for attaching a tump line to buckles or D rings on the outer edges of the sack near the top. Use of the tump line is optional.

Camp duffle and grub are stowed inside the sack up to its capacity in weight or bulk, soft materials nearest the back and lighter goods at the bottom. One packsack commonly carries all cooking and eating utensils, as well as victuals to be used at the next meal. On arrival at the new camp, this is deposited near the site for the fire so the cook can get busy pronto.

Blankets can be folded and packed inside a sack, and so can the tent or shelter cloth. But, commonly, these are rolled and the bundle balanced on top of a fully loaded packsack where it is easily carried. Rations and other essentials are frequently packed in waterproof duffle bags, about nine by twenty-four inches, which are supplied by most camp outfitters. These bags can also be conveniently balanced atop the pack.

As the shoulder straps may at times have to bear a considerable weight, they should be broad where they go over the shoulders. It is also a good thing to pad them there with sheepskin to which the fleece is still attached. The tump line may be used to take some of

Portaging with packsack.

the heft off the shoulder straps. In fact, employing the support in this manner is the easiest way to get the hang of using it alone.

A mighty good pack for those kitchen goods is the old-fashioned pack basket, once so popular in northern New York and Maine. Strong and resilient, it protects breakable and crushable objects from being jammed together, at the same time riding easily on the back. In camp, you can hang it in a shady place along with perishables that need coolness and ventilation. I have frequently used these inexpensive, hand-woven baskets myself. The bedroll perches so easily on top of one that the two combined make a load that's light enough for almost anyone.

OTHER PACKS

Many other types of packs can be used for carrying fairly heavy loads short distances. Steer clear of those which have the shoulder straps attached far apart to the top of the sack. These will be continually slipping down on your arms. Shoulder straps should start very close together from the top of the pack; even from a single large D ring. Those of thick, oil-tanned leather are far superior to webbing.

The previously discussed Bergans type of frame rucksack and Alaskan pack board are excellent. Even though the former can not very well have bags piled atop it, one is convenient for packing valuables like camera and binoculars that have been safely tied within partially inflated plastic bags, and indispensables such as fishline, hooks, and a small supply of ammunition. You can stow this under your seat, buckling or snapping one strap fast if you want. If it'll float, and a sealer cloth at the open end may be enough to assure this, the better procedure may be to leave it free. Either way, you can get at it in a hurry if need be.

Probably the only reason why the especially adaptable pack board has not become widely popular among canoeists is because it has not yet reached the northeastern canoe country. It certainly is the best way to pack hard and unwieldy objects, particularly outboard motors. Instead, these last are often wrapped in some impervious cover and then in a tent, and packed with the tump line. I have seen several ingenious packs designed to carry a particular kicker, however.

Cans of gas and oil are often tied one to each end of an eight foot pole, and the pole then balanced over one shoulder in the Chinese coolie fashion. Loose articles such as guns, rods, and axes are carried by hand. It is not uncommon to note a bucket, filled with most anything, also so borne.

You see some odd sights on portages. One day on a carry just south of James Bay I met an Indian packing an old-fashioned trunk, about two-and-a-half feet square by four feet long, using a tump line. Seems he had just been married, and the trunk contained all his bride's trousseau.

PORTAGING THE CANOE

The average canvas canoe suitable for wilderness travel will weigh about eighty pounds and the modern light aluminum craft somewhat less. It is not nearly as difficult to take one of these crafts over a portage as anyone who has not tried it might expect, particularly as the load balances itself on your shoulders and presses straight down.

Almost invariably the experienced canoeist uses his two paddles to form the carrying yoke. These are lashed with something such as cod line or babiche between the center thwart and front seat,

Canoes up to 18 feet long are easily carried by one man.

blades to the former and handles to the latter. Where the upper portion of the blade is about three inches wide should come just in front of the thwart. The distance between two blades should be such that they will lay comfortably on the shoulders when the back of the neck is resting slightly against the thwart.

A well made canoe should nearly balance on the center thwart, being just a trifle heavier towards the stern. Then when your head and shoulders are in place and, reaching a little ahead, you grasp each gunwale and pull down slightly to balance the boat, its bow will ride about six feet above the ground. This clearance will enable you to choose your footing and to steer the craft past trees and other obstacles.

In the Adirondacks where I learned as a boy to handle a canoe, a wooden yoke, similar to that which encumbers milkmaids in some countries, is used to portage the local guide boats which have no center thwart. Similar yokes have been made for canoes, but we have yet to see one to which an experienced canoeman would give cussing room.

There are several ways to get a canoe up on your shoulders. Until you get the knack, any of these can strain you, especially when you're still soft from city living. Better get an experienced canoeman to coach you, and don't attempt anything beyond your strength. The easiest and safest method is to turn the canoe over. While your companion raises the bow at arms height above his head, step under, place your head between the paddles and the back of your neck against the thwart, and lift. For a carry of more than fifty yards or so, some padding for the shoulders will be desirable. I simply put on my mackinaw.

LOADING THE CANOE

A canoe should be loaded only when it is afloat or nearly so. The weight, preferably centered as low as possible, should be so distributed that when both men step in, the canoe will ride just noticeably deeper at stern than bow. It should always be so trimmed, of course, that the side balance is absolutely central.

If you figure to run rapids during the day, crowd the weight as close to the center as possible. Loaded thus, the craft will turn much more quickly.

Then, elbows ever straight and arms swinging naturally from the shoulders, you can control it with a stroke so basic that—in its customary unhurried rhythm—the first descending arc of each full-armed sweep can be largely maintained by gravity. The resulting intervals of relaxation before each final forward lurch of the shoulders keep you from seriously tiring although, toughening as you go, you continue along day after day.

FOR WET GOING

If you expect rain or rough going, place four light poles or a few spruce boughs in the bottom before loading so as to keep articles slightly above any water that may come aboard. This will then run harmlessly back to where the stern paddler can bail it out from time to time. It's also sometimes a good idea in such exigencies to make sure that what's at the base of the load is either something that will not be damaged by soaking or that it is in waterproof containers.

Another good angle in some water is to lay a light tarp amidships and to stow all but the heaviest articles in this. Finish by drawing the canvas up around the thus enclosed outfit and lashing it as securely closed as possible. The ax can be shoved within easy reach under these lashings and the strap of its sheath buckled over one or more as an extra safety measure.

Do not tie or otherwise attach this bundle to the canoe. Anything particularly cumbersome and heavy, like bags of canned goods (their contents identified by scratches in case the labels are soaked off), should be laid by itself directly on the bottom of the craft and the tarp-wrapped essentials packed atop them. Then if you happen to have a wreck, the latter will float and you'll have an excellent chance of recovering it with contents intact and dry.

This is particularly true if the highly buoyant sleeping bags are included within the tarp. The canoe can be loaded much more compactly, in any event, if these are so folded before being rolled that they can be wedged from side to side instead of being stowed lengthwise.

There is another angle to sleeping robes that it may be well to keep in mind. Those with down, fresh kapok, and similar fillers make good life preservers to grab in an emergency, especially if you have a stout strap or thong on them where you can grasp it in a hurry. A lot of bushmen keep their sleeping bags handy for this reason, often using them for a seat or for a pad on which to kneel while paddling. In a small canoe, however, an inexpensive life preserver cushion filled with kapok will serve the same purpose a lot more conveniently.

RIFLE PROTECTION

All our wilderness rifles have slings attached with quickly detachable swivels. In rough water it is easy to unsnap one swivel, pass the sling under a thwart of the canoe, and snap it on again. Then if we have an upset, and we've both experienced them, we do not lose a rifle.

Because of the dampness encountered during a canoe trip, it's a good idea to bring along a waterproof gun case. A plain plastic cover, that weighs scarcely anything and which folds as small as a handkerchief, will protect the rifle from rain. Used in camp, it will keep off the night dew which often wets weapons as badly as if they had been out in a storm. A wet or warped stock, as you know, can entirely change the zero setting of your rifle.

In camp, cut two short forked stakes, drive them in the ground alongside your bed, and lay the encased rifle across them. If you happen to be out without a case in misty or frosty weather, a dry place to cache it is between a full-length air mattress and a ninety-by-ninety sleeping robe. If you place it near the edge away from the side you get in, it will remain well protected all night, and won't be in the way.

HAVE A SYSTEM

Anything you want to get during the day, such as lunch or a boiling kettle, tuck conveniently into a side space. Cameras and fishing tackle should also be accessible. Tents and waterproofs should be on the outside of rolls and packs in case you have to make camp in a downpour. If you figure you are going to need your down jacket, wedge it up under the bow or stern deck where you can get at it easily.

The first individual across a portage should bring an ax in case any cutting has to be done. The fellow whose job it is to tote the canoe should go over a strange carry first with a pack to become familiar with it. When he takes the canoe over, another packer should go along with him if possible.

If two campers can reduce their duffle to just three packs, each of which they can carry without undue effort, the work of portaging will be greatly simplified. They'll then have to make but two trips. Each will take a pack load on the first. On the second, one will bring a pack and help the other where he can with the canoe.

Whether you adopt these methods of packing and handling your outfit, or have the fun of devising a routine of your own, adhere to a system. Have a place for everything and everything in its place. It means less labor, delay, and confusion in traveling and in camp, and you have more time to devote to your chosen sport.

Such a system also eases most of the drudgery out of portaging. It can even make a carry something to look forward to as a break in

The end of the portage. Ready to load up again.

the monotony of paddling, an opportunity to stretch the legs, and in chilly weather a chance to get some welcome exercise; all provided there are no confounded bugs. Skeeters and black flies can turn a portage into something else again. But you'll soon forget any discomforts at the next glittering challenge of open water.

I recall one occasion in that wonderful canoe country west of James Bay when we came on a very long, narrow lake down which a bitterly cold wind was whipping. We rigged up a blanket for a sail and ripped down the dozen miles in a jiffy, while I sat in comfort in my mackinaw. I even had some fusees in my pocket so I could have a smoke. Boy, was that ever travel de luxe after a day of bucking a swift river with many portages!

CHAPTER 21

SADDLE and PICKET ROPE

THROUGHOUT THE MOUNTAIN and foothills of western North America, from the dusty mesquite of Mexico to the Arctic Circle, almost all the good big-game country is at least two or three days travel from the railroad or the nearest auto or wagon road. Outdoorsmen have to pack their outfit and supplies into these regions, and the most common method of transport is with pack animals.

A large pack mule will freight considerably more than a horse unless it happens not to be in the mood. Pound for pound, so will a burro. But among the disadvantages to be encountered with both mules and burros is that it is almost impossible to make most of them ford rivers and even fair-sized creeks, or to transverse really boggy country, with the result that their use is confined almost exclusively to desert and high dry regions.

For general carrying on hunting trips the more amenable pack horse is commonly used. How much one can pack day after day depends on a combination of facts and imponderables having to do with terrain, weather, feed, equipment, type of load, skill of the human packers, and the temperament and aptitude of the individual animal. An average horse, to generalize, will pack about 120 pounds for weeks at a time along the steep trails to be expected in high country. This minimum can, many times, be increased. To load a horse beyond its limit for very long, however, makes for all kinds of trouble including sore backs. This limiting figure, whatever it may be where you are going, will indicate the number of pack animals needed to handle a particular outfit.

Pack horses and mules can be expected to travel from five to twenty-five miles a day in western mountains, again depending on such factors as country, trails, and weather. Along fairly decent going, the usual pack train we've ridden with can average about fifteen miles a day, starting about ten a.m. and stopping about four p.m. Burros are much slower. However, the location of good grazing is what generally dictates the selection of the camping sites and, thereby, the duration of each day's travel.

Most of the really fine mountain hunting country in the United States lies within the Forest Reserves, where luring horse trails wind along nearly every valley and across the passes. Throughout much of these western spaces, plenty of grazing exists. It is necessary that camps be chosen where there is good horse feed. Otherwise the animals, even though hobbled when turned loose at night, will stray for miles in search of fodder.

When there is ample grass, it is possible even in wilder regions to take a pack train through almost any country where steep cliffs, peaks, very heavy timber, and down stuff do not bar the way. Almost all the forests except on the thick southern slopes of mountains are open enough to ride through anywhere. Even where you do not see a good trail, your horse will often recognize one, especially if it is in familiar terrain.

THE MEMORY OF A GOOD HORSE

Some years ago I was hunting on the eastern slope of the Coast Range Mountains in British Columbia, and one afternoon I camped by a fine spring. I had with me a good pinto saddle mount named Chilly and a wise old pack horse called Loco. As was my custom, I chopped a saucer out of a fallen log and placed some salt and sugar in it for the horses. It both kept them around camp and made it easy to catch them.

Next morning I broke camp and went north for three miles through a flat covered thickly with jackpines. Mule deer had worn a game trail among the greenness of the conifers, and this dim path was the only easy way across the bench.

Neither I nor the horses had ever been in this country before. But two months later I came back from the opposite direction, wishing to camp at the same spring. There was now a foot of snow on the ground. The game trail was absolutely indistinguishable, and the jackpines looked unfamiliar in the heaviness of snow. I got off Chilly, put him in the lead, and drove the two horses ahead of me. Without hesitation, Chilly took that return trail for the three miles straight to the campsite, went up to the fallen log, nosed the snow off it, and started to lick.

Another time I was in the Rockies of northwestern Alberta with Stan Clark, who's now down by Jasper Park but who formerly had a spread up the Halfway River a few miles across country from Hudson Hope. We had a saddle mount apiece and four pack animals. We were driving the horses in front of us along a fairly reasonable route, when we came to a deep mud hole with a large stump just above it on the left. The leading horse left the trail and detoured the mud hole up above the stump.

Two weeks later we were following the same way back. During the fortnight, the mud hole had dried out. Across where it had been was a plainly marked way, tracked down hard by the feet of much game. Yet each horse, as it came to it, turned off to the right and took the same detour around the stump.

None of this is meant to imply that you can rely on a horse to keep you from getting lost, any more than you can on a dog, except in both's own neighborhoods. Even there, the abilities of various horses in this respect differ markedly. Chinook, a sorrel mare one of us rides, all the time waits for an opportunity to circle very, very gradually. If you're just daydreaming along through the bush in cloudy weather, you're apt to glance around and find yourself heading back to camp. Chinook, with the almost undetectable aid of her nose, follows a back trail almost hoofprint for hoofprint when given her head.

On the other hand, the wife of one of us has a saddle mare at the present time that gets turned around as quickly as the greenest tenderfoot. In a way, this is a redeeming characteristic. The reluctance with which a lot of cayuses leave their home grounds becomes an exasperation at times. Copper, once you've trotted her into the bush and circled her around a few times, travels with equal enthusiasm in any direction. She's as anxious as the next mare to get back to the bundle of oats which she knows will be waiting. But even when night is nearing, if you just sit motionless in the saddle when approaching a reasonably familiar trail, about half the time Copper will quicken her pace along the wrong turning.

PACK TRAIN

The prospective sheep and goat shooter who has not previously hunted with a pack train should understand certain details about the horse and his load, and some of the procedures of traveling, camping and hunting. These differ somewhat in various localities and among different outfits. Basically, though, they're much the same in that they are hitched to the proposition that keeping the horses in good condition is the primary essential.

You're already under canvas, let us assume. The party is going to break camp and travel on this day. At the first quickening of dawn, the wrangler starts out to find and drive in the animals which were turned loose the afternoon before to feed. Most of them, probably, have hobbles strapping their front legs together. The bells buckled around their necks have been unstoppered so that they will clang, bong, and peal the melody of their whereabouts.

The horses may be feeding anywhere from a few yards to five miles from camp, nevertheless, although the experiencd wrangler usually keeps an ear open. If before dark they start to drift too far, he'll often edge around and whoop them back. His own horse, if he can manage it, is staked out nearby in a lush patch of grass at the end of a picket rope.

Trouble comes when the animals are not all out of the same bunch. Then, in particular, they may be scattered in several groups. It can take a good half of the morning before the wrangler has located them all. Every once in a while delays of this kind must be expected. If a particular knothead becomes too much of a nuisance though, it may be tied short to a tree all one night so that it'll keep so busy eating the next it won't have time to wander.

When the wrangler drives the horses into camp, everyone on hand except the cook turns out to catch them, tie them to trees, and saddle them.

THE COOK

The cook, in the meantime, has piled out at dawn, although not with any bright song of joy. Because of various air currents put into motion by the blending of night with day, it's colder now than it was during total blackness. He maybe deposits a dead old pine stump, saved for the purpose, in the center of the last fading embers of the campfire.

This gives him a blaze like the light of a pressure lantern, and it also helps him to get some warmth into his extended fingers. Pretty soon he's thawed out enough to shove the coffee pot grumpily into the heat. He then begins banging pans around, a little more expressively than necessary.

One specially gregarious trail cook we know has a habit of carrying on a one-sided conversation, so provocative that anyone snoozing nearby is apt to hear himself joining in. Whereupon a grin

Only with pack horse can you take an outfit adequate for extensive roaming into such superb, unspoiled country as this.

spreads over this cook's face, for all he really wanted was company, and now he keeps exchanging remarks with such robust good humor that further sleep is impossible. The coffee smells too good, anyway, particularly when joined by the aromas of flippers and "tiger."

Sometimes none of these devices work. Then the cook, with a certain grim righteousness, sets about personally arousing one and all in time for hot porridge, bacon, eggs, flapjacks, fruit, and your choice between steaming pots of coffee and tea. A feminine member of the party he may call the "just once" that most trail cooks insist upon by the simple device of opening the valve of her air mattress.

The cook then sees to it that everyone gets his lunch, in many cases put up the night before. He washes and dries the dishes. He packs the kitchen and the food panniers, making sure that what he needs for the next meal is where he can get at it first. He may then turn to with the others to roll up the tents, so that when the wrangler gets back with the horses everything will be ready to be packed on them.

PANNIERS

There is no standard size for panniers. Most of them, the best ones, measure on the outside about twenty-two inches long, fifteen inches high, and nine inches deep from front to back. Packers prefer the bottom angled back so the pannier will not stick out so much on the animal and bump into trees. One six inches wide is functional.

The top, bottom, and sides can be made of three-eighths- or half-inch waterproof plywood, and the ends of seven-eighths-inch pine or spruce. To prevent mice or chipmunks from getting at the contents, the pannier can be lined with tin or with copper screening. Notches on the front edges are made for the lash ropes, that secure the pannier on the sawbuck saddle, to ride in. Hinges and fasteners can be either metal or leather.

I have two of these panniers. One is for kitchen and eating utensils. It will hold my nest of three aluminum kettles, frypans, plates, cups, bowls, and cans of salt, sugar, pepper, butter and lard. The other takes my personal and photographic equipment. Tent, sleeping bag, air mattress, and a big wash and mixing pan go on top.

Various camp outfitters sell panniers, or kyacks as they're also called, made of fiberboard and plywood. You can also build them yourself, as most bushmen do. Some are made of the heaviest canvas. Especially picturesque, although not as practical as wooden varieties, are those made of tough untanned cowhide laced together with the hair outside.

THE SPORTSMAN

An outfitter will usually assign one pack horse to each sportsman for carrying his personal outfit. Your rifle should go in a heavy leather scabbard slung the way you find handiest on your saddle horse. Camera equipment is also usually stowed on the riding horse. So are your binoculars.

Saddlebags are handy for this purpose in open country. If you're sidling around through trees, anything breakable is better wrapped in your extra shirt or other such clothing and tied securely behind the pommel. Watch it, too, when you stop, for a lot of cayuses

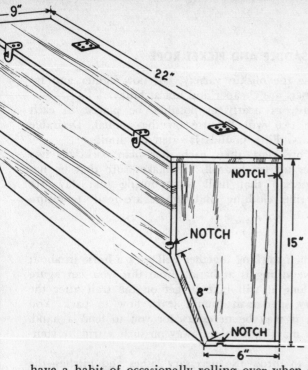

9"

22"

NOTCH

NOTCH

15"

8"

NOTCH

6"

Construction of wood or plyboard pannier for horse or mule (burro slightly smaller) The angle back at bottom is so it will not be continually bumping into trees on narrow trails.

have a habit of occasionally rolling over when saddled.

Fishing rods can be a problem. Often the best idea is to have a stout aluminum or fiber case for them and to trust their packing to the outfitter.

Sleeping bag and air mattress may be rolled in a tarpaulin about eight feet square, or in a small tent or shelter fabric, and tied with a rope. Such a bundle will measure about three feet by a foot and a half. Flat rather than round, it will be some seven or eight inches thick. It can thus be conveniently laid atop the saddle and panniers as a top pack. The pack cover of heavy waterproofed canvas, spread over the load before the diamond or other hitch is thrown, will protect the equipment from rain and from snagging in the brush.

If you're on your own, the ax in its sheath will want to go where it will be both safe and readily accessible. On a pack horse, it can generally be shoved under the lashings with the handle facing backwards and with the sheath strapped over a rope as an additional precaution against loss.

Most outfitters you'll travel with will furnish you with two panniers in which to carry extra clothing and other items for your individual use. Generally speaking, you place the most often wanted articles at the top. Shirts and such you use to wrap breakables. Possessions such as binoculars and telescopes, with which dampness can raise hob, you tie securely within slightly inflated waterproof bags. We used to use the oilskin variety, but now lighter and far tighter plastic containers are cheaper and not as bulky.

Equal weights must, as nearly as possible, be placed in each pannier so that the two will balance on the animal. Desirable maximum weights vary. Fifty pounds is often the limit.

Immediately after breakfast, then, each sportsman packs his two panniers and bundles up his bedroll. He makes sure that he has everything on his person that he'll want during that day. He checks to see if his rifle, clothing, and camera are ready to secure on his riding saddle.

PACKING

Two experienced men working together will pack a horse in about ten minutes when everything is at hand. From this, you can figure approximately how long it will take to get on the trail after the animals arrive. Every sportsman should learn how to pack. You can never tell when it may be necessary for you to lend a hand. Besides, one day you may want to get away on such a trip by yourself.

Anyone can learn to throw the necessary lashes and hitches—the diamond and one or two of the often ample simpler knots such as the half-diamond and the squaw—in two or three lessons if he'll do a little practicing with a piece of string during spare moments.

A good woolen blanket or an adequate pad goes on first. This must be smooth and soft. Next comes a saddle that fits the individual animal. It should have breast and breech straps and double cinches. Before you tighten these last, put a finger under the front center of the blanket and lift it slightly along the spine. Sling on the panniers, secure them, lay what you're going to across or between them, and spread your pack cover in place. Then with a strong half-inch rope braided to the ring of a canvas pack cinch, which at its other extremity has something such as a large wooden hook, bind down the entire load.

When the outfit is ready to hit the trail, the lead rope of all but the front horse is tied to the pack of the one ahead with a knot that can instantly be jerked free if something goes wrong. The wrangler holds the lead of the foremost animal and rides off.

Or the horses are turned loose, the wrangler starts ahead, and the cook closes up behind. Occasionally a horse bolts out of line, and the rear man urges him back. This he does slowly and quietly, so as not to excite the string. Some days may be full of all kinds of trouble; spooked horses, turning packs, and snagged or bogged down animals. Little distance will then be covered. On other days we've traversed as much as a rousing thirty miles.

The wrangler is the man to say where the next camp shall be made. He is responsible for the horses, and he must stop where feed is good, where there's water, and where he can hold the animals reasonably close.

SADDLE HORSE

Usually the sportsman and his guide will start off right after breakfast on their own horses, either to hunt or just to ride through the most interesting country. Often they'll arrive at the next camp after the train has pulled in, to find the shelters already pitched and

Throwing the diamond hitch.

the cook maybe sour-faced again because someone has had some jocose remark to make about the mulligan that is simmering. On some occasions, too, the sportsman will travel with the pack train, out front where he can spot game and keep out of the dust. In either event, he should see to the saddling of his own horse.

The natural tendency when saddling, especially with the heavier of the western jobs, is to heave the girth rings and stirrups too high. This causes them to bang noisily against such tender spots as leg joints and ribs. A lot of resultant shying and side stepping can be avoided by swinging these just high enough to land easily on your mount's back where they'll slide down smoothly. You can then reach underneath and finish cinching without going around to the off side to straighten things up.

A lot of outdoorsmen planning trophy hunts in the west don't have much opportunity to familiarize themselves beforehand with horses or with the design and function of the riding gear characteristic to that part of the continent. Maybe the following few hints which we have picked up from time to time, usually the hard way, will give those individuals a little better idea of what lies ahead of them.

When you're ready to get on, particularly if you and the horse are strangers, the main thing is to be in control. Horses differ. With a very few, you'll have to rein the head either in or around. Others begin to fret and sometimes to pitch if you're that heavy on bit. Mostly, a firm but light hold on the lines will be sufficient.

Unless you want to be bequeathed the deadest old plug in the remuda the next day out, don't like a lot of dudes, clamber up into the saddle and then yell for someone to hand you the ding-blasted reins.

A smooth and sure way of getting into the western saddle you'll probably be using is to take the lines in the left hand, stand by the head of the cayuse facing the tail, grasp the mane or saddle horn with the left hand, put the left foot lightly in the stirrup, grab the horn securely with the right hand, and then swing aboard in one fluid motion while using the horn as a pivot. This natural arc is spoiled, as you can readily understand, by the awkward if common mistake of grasping the back of the saddle with the right hand.

The knees are not used in western riding as they are meant to be in the East. With the western saddle therefore, you'll want the stirrups long enough so that you'll barely clear the seat when standing in them. You'll then be able to rely on balance and on the grip of your thighs, employing your partly tensed knees and maybe ankles as springs to absorb any roughness that would be otherwise jarring or jolting. Here, again, there is a tremendous difference in horses. Without exaggeration, some actually trot more smoothly than others walk.

Keep the lines low ordinarily, although if a knothead is inclined to pitch, you may want to curb that impulse holding its head high. Don't fall into the practice very common among dudes of knotting the ends of the reins together as soon as you climb on a strange horse. Then if anything goes wrong, or even if you hustle off to take a shot at game, you're apt to find yourself plumb afoot.

The times when you want to ride reinless, twist them a couple of times around the horn and maybe top off with a single half hitch. Then if anything goes amuck, the lines will soon be dangling; to halt the horse if it's been broken to ground-rein, or to impede it long enough for you to have a chance of easing around and catching it.

CLOTHING

When you're traveling with horses you hit a lot of extremes; hours of hard climbing often immediately followed by other hours of just sitting in the leather. Having the right sort of clothing, therefore, is at least as important as it is in other forms of wilderness living.

A man doing the relatively hard work of hunting perspires freely, and his clothing becomes more or less wet. Cotton garments are best for all hot and warm climates in that they are coolest. The perspiration which they absorb, however, makes them so cold that they chill one as soon as this function slows down. When cotton is worn, the outdoorsman should have a rub down and change of dry clothing as soon as he gets back to camp.

This is not difficult in a warm climate. In excessively hot weather, furthermore, the exudation of perspiration does not slow too perceptibly, and such a change is not so necessary. But if during the rigors of strenuous hunting or traveling you have occasion to stop for long in a wind, sitting on a lookout perhaps or riding atop an extended ridge, then cotton garments are not too good.

For a cold or even a chilly climate, the clothing should be wool throughout. Wool also gets wet from perspiration, but much of the water passes through it to be evaporated on the outside. Wet wool, moreover, does not feel particularly cold. It does not chill like wet cotton except when the wind is blowing very strongly. Under these circumstances a closely woven but still porous outside jacket of thin cotton may be needed to slip on as a windbreak.

Wool is warm chiefly because of the insulating effect of the dead air held in the numerous tiny spaces among its fibers. A pair of light wool garments are warmer than a heavy one of the same total weight because of the additional air contained between the two of them.

In extremely frigid weather one can freeze quickly in wet clothing. It is very necessary under such circumstances to keep from perspiring excessively. This you can easily accomplish by shedding layers of clothing as you warm up, thereby always remaining moderately cool.

The horseman or other outdoorsman in warm or tropical countries may well wear cotton underwear and khaki trousers. Roomy breeches made for walking and for outdoor living still have their advantages under certain conditions. The day of the knee-constricting riding

The horse wrangler.

breeches, however, is far past if you figure on doing any amount of traveling afoot.

For convenient and for safe wilderness wear, bush trousers should be stagged three inches shorter than city trousers, should have no cuffs to collect debris, and should not be baggy. In lieu of khaki, many individuals find blue denim work pants are very good once they've softened up. In a country with many thorns and prickles, canvas leggings and even briarproof pants may be desirable. While on a horse, you may want leather chaps.

Either a khaki or a light flannel shirt may be worn, as desired. The bird shooter usually wears a hunting coat of khaki or light canvas, with many pockets including a large game compartment in the rear. In very hot weather, this coat may be worn immediately over an undershirt. On cooler days a khaki shirt, or in frostier climes one or more woolen shirts, may be worn under it. For the bird hunter, the hunting coat takes the place of the rucksack, and in its large pockets he carries such necessities as his supply of shells.

The desert and plains hunter of big game will dispense with a coat and will wear either a khaki or a wool flannel shirt. He should also have a rucksack in which, among other daily necessities, he can carry a canteen of water if he leaves his horse for a stalk. If he wears a khaki shirt, he should carry a flannel shirt in his rucksack. Most desert country gets surprisingly cold as soon as the sun goes down and the heat, with little moisture in the atmosphere to beat it back, radiates out of the rocks and sand.

The hunter of big game in colder regions often makes the mistake of wearing extremely heavy clothing. Except for the canoe hunter whose guide does all the paddling, the late-fall duck hunter who does not stir around much, and the horseman who sits still in the saddle for long periods, this can be an extremely serious error. Very heavy garments induce perspiration, waste energy, and result in unnecessary and even dangerous coldness when one halts. Very heavy trousers will gall between the legs on a long hike.

Sensible clothing under these conditions often consists of light or medium-weight wool underwear, wool trousers of about the same weight you would wear in a city such as New York in winter, and a medium-weight wool shirt. This is enough for any man actively hunting on foot in temperatures above zero. Leave that heavy mackinaw with your horse, canoe, or other conveyance. In the rucksack should be carried another wool shirt, and perhaps a light, waterproofed, cotton, windbreaking jacket. This last should allow enough air to circulate through it to keep body moisture from collecting. The shirt can be donned when you stop or when the single shirt is not warm enough. The jacket will be appreciated in rain, snow, or blustery wind.

Some covering for the hands may be a necessity. Light leather gloves make horse handling more of a pleasure on frosty mornings when buckled leather is stiff and tightened knots are sometimes encased in frustrating blobs of muddy ice. Heavy, lined ones are usually enough for medium cold. Woolen gloves covered with roomy leather mittens are better for extreme cold.

A more practical scheme than wearing one-finger mitts, which in congealing going leave your trigger finger stiff, is to tie your regular mitts together by a long thong that loops over the shoulders behind the neck. In case a sudden shot at game presents itself, jerk the mitt off the master hand with the teeth. The thong keeps it from becoming lost, and you have a limber and unencumbered hand for operating the rifle.

ON YOUR OWN

The first thing that horses set about teaching you when you begin to handle them is that they're all individuals—some intelligent, a few knotheaded, most friendly, a handful downright cantankerous, others aloof, nearly all quicker on the home trail but a scattering equally ambitious in any direction, the majority placid, and too many just plain skittish. Certain others, intrinsically often the most gentle of all, are just downright dramatic.

The competent saddle horse is, in particular, a wonderful companion and an excellent sentinel as well. We've both shot considerable game whose presence was first sensed by our mounts. Once you become accustomed to hunting with a good horse, there's nothing else quite like it.

There is no reason why two men reasonably accustomed to handling horses, to camping, and to traveling with a map, should not take an extended pack-horse trip by themselves. It means a lot of work, for if you hunt persistently during the day, you will have cooking, tackle repairs, and odd jobs to take care of sometimes late into the night. Horse wrangling, too, will frequently interfere with a planned stalk.

Two men can rent, or often more cheaply buy, four horses and live the life for months at a time. One pack horse will be able to carry all the outfit needed. The other, if you plan carefully, will have no trouble in handling enough food for a couple of men for a month. As for taking care of your horses, lone trappers and prospectors often travel with six or seven.

In many states and in some of the provinces of Canada, however, the law requires a non-resident sportsman to be accompanied by a registered or licensed guide. Too, before outdoorsmen attempt such trips on their own, they should make sure by experiments in country safely close to civilization that they are competent. Generally speaking, furthermore, they must be of such a temperament that they will find as much satisfaction and delight in riding, packing, doing camp work, and attending to cooking, as in hunting and fishing.

CHAPTER 22

WOMEN
in
the
WOODS

By Vena Angier

THE WILDERNESS LIFE IS something that most women, particularly those of us from the cities, have to work up to gradually. Even the staunchest of our covered-wagon ancestresses faltered while still within sight of the old homes they maybe loathed but to which they clung instinctively. Most of us have what is probably the same feeling today, possibly because the accustomed if often tiresome bounds we are leaving are what we have come to associate with security. Isolation seems to lie ahead, somewhere beyond the edge of our small private worlds.

Yet wilderness living is as much woman's heritage as man's. The only difference lies in the approach. Not all of us have the male's instinctive urge for hunting and fishing. Most of us, however, can sincerely interest ourselves in some of the innumerable other outdoor diversions.

Then there is almost always the home-making urge. This takes on a deeper significance in the farther places. Here a woman who'll make the effort soon becomes really needed. A lot of husbands and wives don't need each other in the city. Don't we see it all around us? There are always restaurants, hotels, and a maid who'll come in to clean. If life gets too lonesome, there's always someone else in a city. But in the woods, after a day or two at the most, you can soon belong.

All this is when you fully participate in real, independent outdoor living. It does not apply to vacations in commercial hunting lodges. It has little relationship to trips when the outfitter takes care of even the smallest detail. It does not even include automobile and similar tenting excursions so much in civilization that you have little responsibility except to be present and pleasant.

When there is nothing much to do but sit around, boredom with even the sweeter tempered of us becomes deadly. What we may have dreamed of as a free life becomes one of unnecessary, then of disagreeable, and finally of fiercely resented inconveniences. Under such circumstances, women have disrupted more hunting and fishing trips than bad weather, contrariness of desired trophies, malfunctioning equipment, lumpy beds, wretched food, fatigue, and all combinations thereof—while, let it be added, being thoroughly and miserably unhappy ourselves.

This need not be. Woman is as truly made for the green woods, the fragrant hillsides, the shimmering mountains, the cool swamps, and a flickering warm fire at eventide as are her men folk. But she has got to be permitted, and she must permit herself, to be a full participant in the adventure.

If we like hunting and fishing of one kind or another, as many of us honestly do, fine. Otherwise, there is no particular reason, in the long run, to pretend such an interest. We can still be full partners by reliving the moments of decision with our sportsmen. By learning to appreciate fully the fruits of his pursuits. By cooking the prizes as they should be cooked—and because we want to! And, finally, by happily and wholeheartedly making the tent or cabin where we happen to be at the moment truly home.

WHAT ABOUT CLOTHES?

Women today are unsuited, both in nature and experience, for the task of outfitting for the wilderness. Before I went north for the first time, to live 150 miles from where the nearest railway ends and three miles from the closest neighbor on the bank of the Peace River in northern British Columbia, Brad had enthused to me across a heap of magazines and catalogs that every trip back of beyond is divided into three delightful segments; the joy of getting ready, the adventure itself, and finally the pleasure of reminiscing.

At that time, I'd never experienced the latter two phases. I couldn't form any logical opinion about them. But the first, I soon became aware, can be a nightmare, especially for someone who'd spent most of her years in big city hotels.

It had been bad enough during the first few indecisive shopping trips to paw through scratchy woolen breeches, heavy itchy socks, and rough shirts when I'd much rather have been choosing gay sheer frivolities. Even without any more outdoor experience than the usual musical show dancer and producer accumulates, I finally put my foot down as far as clothing was concerned.

"Granted," I said, as I recall in *Home In The Woods*, "that woolens are practical during cold weather and warm, wet days and dry. But I'm not in training to become a female Paul Bunyan. Granted, too, that riding gear if chic is too tight for walking. There's my morale to think of. Woolens can still be pretty, soft, and feminine. We'll just go around to that ski shop."

The selection of feminine clothing for the wilderness should in general take into consideration the same salient features advisable in outdoor masculine garb. Style assumes a somewhat greater importance, of course, if only for the sake of our men. Too, most of us make our selections with a view to staying around camp more than our male counterparts.

I always include some light, bright dresses that can be easily washed and ironed. The better of the numerous denims now available are very practical, I find, and they afford color and modishness as well as practicability. Don't make the mistake of buying clothing that is too heavy. Wearing several loose, comfortable attractive shirts and sweaters, for example, will afford you a lot more scope than can one bulky mackinaw.

A long warm robe is always appreciated in dry cool weather wherever one has the room for it. In wet or snowy weather a short robe is more practical. Nylon underwear washes and dries quickly. Seersucker pajamas look well without ironing. I find, too, that I like high fleecy slippers that can be worn indoors and out even in wetness and snow.

Loafers, with soft fresh wool socks for walking and variously hued cotton socks for lounging, are practical, too. So is a durable little plastic raincoat with hood. You'll probably prefer one that will fold up into almost nothing.

Extra buttons for the clothing I'm carrying go into my small sewing kit which also includes needles, thread, darning wool, thimble, hooks and eyes, snaps, a spare zipper, a lump of wax, and tiny excellent scissors. At our log cabin, I especially prize my gasoline-fueled Coleman Iron.

COSMETICS AND TOILET PREPARATIONS

Relaxing is one thing, letting yourself go another. Hands, for instance, need particular care in the bush. Trimming the nails shorter than may be desirable in the city will help to reduce the frequency of breaking and chipping. I find it reasonable to put on cotton or woolen gloves for rough work and occasionally to don rubber

gloves for the harsher indoor jobs such as cleaning our cabin stove. .
Hand lotions, particularly those abundant in lanolin, combat chapping and keep the skin softer than it would be otherwise. A white
nail pencil is a help in keeping clean nails clean looking in the bush.

Lipstick helps the morale as well as protects against chapping.
If you are accustomed to using perfume, it will not be out of
place in the wilderness, either. A light cologne is refreshing, too,
for all concerned. You'll want some good facial cream, as outdoor
living is drying for the skin. Unbreakable plastic jars and bottles
are fine for carrying these.

Provision should be made, too, for care of the hair. Bring an
effective, compact shampoo, particularly one that while traveling you
may have already found satisfactory under varying conditions. If the
water where you are is hard, you'll find rain soft enough for any
use. Incidently, the fact that it may be stained from flowing off a
well seasoned roof harms it not at all.

Your toilet articles will probably also include a mirror that can
be hung on a twig or leaned against a convenient log, toothbrush,
tooth paste, combs, hairbrush, nail file, tweezers, tissues, soap, and
whatever other small items you may personally require. Take a
reasonable supply of aspirin, small adhesive bandages, and any other
medicinals you ordinarily need. Towel and face cloth, you'll probably come to agree, should preferably be some dark shade or brown,
green, or red.

Snow is in the air. Vena Angier gets out her webs.

I like to hang a substantial little leather pocketbook, one of the small and often hand-tooled models with a zipper top, to my belt by its loop for carrying mirror, comb, lipstick, and other incidentals in the bush. Sunglasses stored here are well protected, as are any necessary prescription lenses. If you need to wear glasses, by all means bring along at least one and preferably two extra pair whenever you go into the wilderness.

If you'd like to include some provision for bathing, especially if where you're going the climate may be too cold for the enjoyment of some secluded stream, canvas tubs are available at sporting-goods stores which weigh very little and which fold into easily carried bundles. One I have is two feet in diameter and sixteen inches high. Made of strong waterproof canvas, it weighs only one pound and a half.

On the roughest trips, a small canvas wash basin weighing only a few ounces can be carried. I've even provided a washing receptacle by pressing a small square of canvas into a depression in the ground and filling that with water which I've occasionally heated, too, with hot stones from the fire.

Yet cleanliness in the wilderness is, when compared to that enigma in city life, a contrastingly simple problem. What dirt there is, such as carbon from the fire, is good honest grime. Everything in the deep woods, so far from human contamination, seems undefiled and even antiseptic.

SLEEPING

After a full day in the woods there is seldom any trouble in sleeping. I'll have to admit, though, that I did not look forward to my first night in sheer wilderness. Like many other women with whom I've later exchanged experiences, I found myself trying to maintain a wall of conversation against the shadowy forest that seemed to press in from every side.

I hadn't admitted even to myself how much I'd been dreading this initial night deep in the untenanted emptiness of what I had so often heard called the Silent North. The very name suggested a frightening void. Its implication was especially disturbing to someone who had always gone to bed in the reassuring, if annoying, company of a city's million nocturnal sounds.

Yet I found the sub-zero wind that engulfed our Peace River cabin almost comforting in its intensity. Puzzled, I decided the reaction must result from a sharpened appreciation of being so warm and sheltered in the midst of such savage grandeur. The soft and beckoning eiderdown robe, instead of being merely something to be

Vena and Bradford Angier "bile the kittle" on the bank of Peace River.

tolerated, proved to be the must luxurious bed I'd ever experienced. I have never changed this opinion, incidentally. With a softly in-flated air mattress easing every changing tangent of my body, the sensation was literally one of reclining on air. Almost the next thing I knew, it was morning.

The only concession to feminity that I've ever made as far as sleeping arrangements are concerned is to add a sheet to my down robe. It is, admittedly, a nuisance. It shifts position during the night. It has to be washed. It's unduly cold when I first get in on a frosty evening. But although men seem actually to prefer the soft fleeciness of many sleeping bag linings, I find the contact of wool, although not really annoying, not as pleasant as smooth fresh cotton. I have discovered that many other women in the woods feel the same way I do.

BUT AREN'T YOU AFRAID?

What is there is to be afraid of? Wild beasts? The truth is that the most dangerous animals in North America are the plain barn-yard varieties of bulls. No one in that part of the Far North where we have our home in the woods has ever been hurt by a wolf, grizzly, black bear, moose, mountain lion, or any other wild animal. One man has been killed in his own yard by his bull, however.

Others have been threatened and forced to climb to safety by domestic bulls.

An acquaintance back in Boston once asked me, in all seriousness, what I would do if an Indian chanced to pass while I was swimming alone, and presumedly ungarbed, in some wilderness water? Well, he'd either retire from that vicinity so quickly and softly that I'd never sense his presence, or he'd continue along without delay in the pretense that he was totally unaware of me.

The implications of the thus posed problem went deeper, of course. The whole answer is that a woman is historically a great deal safer from either minor annoyance or major violence in the wilderness than when strolling, alone or escorted, along the lovely Esplanade in Boston, or through New York's enjoyable Central Park, or in any other heavily frequented and accordingly well patrolled city rusticity. No woman we or any of our friends have ever known about has ever been molested in any way whatsoever in or around Hudson Hope, and that is that.

What else is there to fear? Sickness? That is a possibility anywhere, and the unfrequented farther places are far more healthy than civilized areas. Accidents? They are, of course, a constant threat in the wilderness as well as elsewhere. The main danger is that if you get hurt while back of beyond, you may really be in a predicament.

The fact that everyone realizes subconsciously that what may be only a minor mischance in the city can turn out to be fatal when there's no one nearby to help is, I now realize, the major reason why there aren't more mishaps in the woods. Anyone who lives for very many days in the farther places gets the habit of being careful.

AREN'T YOU LONELY?

The lonesomest I've ever felt was when walking up New York's crowded Fifth Avenue, alone and a stranger, one spring afternoon. I'm never lonely in the woods. I never have the time.

So many interesting things are always happening all around that it is difficult, for me at least, to find enough leisure. Like most wives married to men who'd willingly hunt and fish twelve months a year, I like a certain amount of shooting and fly casting. It's fun for me, too, to follow my husband and try to see how quietly I can walk in the woods.

Photography makes an engrossing hobby. Then there is reading. I like, too, to sit on the river bank and knit. When the men folk are out hunting is a good time to do your washing, so that you'll be free to listen to their adventures when they return.

There is always something to do: looking for minerals, hunting out various wild foods, seeing how many different flowers we can find, learning to identify trees, cleaning camp, carrying in wood, exploring, just plain ordinary strolling, distinguishing various birds, and riding if you happen to have a horse. I do, and this spring Copper had a long-legged, little colt.

"While I enjoy the friendship of the seasons, nothing can make life a burden to me," Henry Thoreau found, and so do we. "My days were not days of the weeks, nor were they minced into hours and fretted by the ticking of a clock. My life itself has become my amusement and never ceased to be novel, a drama of many scenes and without an end."

COOKING AND EATING

The biggest item of women's work anywhere, of course, revolves about cooking. There is no escape from this in the wilderness. Appetites, as a matter of fact, generally prove to be a whole lot healthier and more robust in the woods.

That means you have to cook more. It does not necessarily result in additional work, as I am the first to admit. You can just cook more of each dish. It's as easy to grill three pounds of steak as one third that amount. Potatoes can, as well as not, be roasting at the same time. Water for tea can be bubbling. These, plus some greens and some fruit, make a pretty good noonday meal.

If you can't clean up all the steak, any remaining tidbits will be especially tasty in mulligans. When we have plenty of meat, I try to cook too much rather than too little for this reason.

The bush cook, meager though her choice of materials may be, has one tremendous advantage over the most lavishly equipped city chef. The autocrat of the metropolitan kitchen too often has to stimulate the small appetites of dyspeptics. A pot and pan wielder in the wilderness has hearty appetites for an ally.

A big advantage I had in my first wilderness efforts was that I wasn't already a skilled city cook. There is a tremendous gap between the sort of culinary artistry that embraces electrical gadgets and delicately contrived automatic ovens on one hand and, on the other, a wood fire. I can understand why some really marvelous cooks, despairing early, never do span it. I had no such conditioned reflexes to unblock.

Water boiled over crackling sweet-scented poplar, too, except that it took longer. Cheese sandwiches also melted and bubbled deliciously in a reflector oven. Except for being able to draw a few such parallels, I started in practically from scratch.

As I later realized, I was lucky. Anyone informing an experienced cook, as an old trapper did me, that two tablespoons of fresh light snow will take the place of each egg in a batter would have been put in his place in no uncertain fashion. But I didn't know enough not to try it. It worked.

What culinary artist wouldn't have turned up a disbelieving nose when advised by a Hudson's Bay Company manager and his wife that the white of wood ashes, used part for part, is a satisfactory kitchen substitute for baking soda? I just took it as a matter of course when everything came out all right.

The best way to learn to get along with cooking in the bush is to follow directions. This I did automatically, in plain, common, ordinary, self-defense. I didn't know anything else to do. I've been fortunate enough, too, to be able to benefit from the on-the-spot advice of old-time prospectors and trappers. The kind of recipes to go by in the wilderness, of course, are the outdoor varieties such as those included in this book.

The main essentials in outdoor cooking are: to be fast when appetites and conditions call for speed, to make plenty for seconds and thirds and, most of all, to do a good job on the fish and game that is brought into camp. The results with these don't have to be fancy. In fact, most outdoorsmen prefer wild meat cooked so as to enhance its natural character and flavor. Nothing is as disappointing and eventually more infuriating to a hunter or fisherman than to have that sleek flashing trout or fast bounding deer ruined by thoughtlessness, carelessness, disinterest, or continued inefficiency.

CHAPTER 23

POTHUNTING and HUNTING METHODS

FOR THE PROCUREMENT of such meat as your country affords you need suitable tools—for big game, an adequate rifle; for lesser prey a shotgun, a small game rifle, or a handgun. The more efficient these weapons are and the more skilled in their use you have made yourself, the better will be your chance of obtaining pot meat. You should also know where to look for your meat, and the best ways of bringing it to bag. So let us get together and discuss these matters in this chapter. First, let us consider your weapons.

THE BIG-GAME RIFLE

On no piece of equipment I know of has more been written than on the big-game rifle. The discussion has been endless, much of it among authors who have never shot anything larger than a small deer in a forest close to civilization. There are just two phases of the subject about which I would like to talk to you. The first is the killing power of the cartridge. The second is the refinements of the weapon that will help you to make sure and humane kills, preferably with one shot.

No bullet—no matter how large in diameter, how heavy, or how high a velocity it is fired at—can be depended on to kill big game reliably and swiftly unless it strikes in a vital part of the anatomy. This means the brain, the spinal column, or the center of the animal's blood supply; the heart, the large arteries around the heart, and the lungs.

The brain and the spinal column present too small targets for anyone to be sure of hitting except under unusual circumstances.

The chest, containing the heart and lungs, presents the largest mark. A modern bullet at modern velocity penetrating into this boiler room disrupts so much tissue, and so fills the cavity with blood, that the animal either succumbs on the spot or drops after a wild race of perhaps twenty-five to a hundred yards, as soon as the supply of blood to the brain ceases.

This critical area is not a difficult target. Any hunter who can not be fairly sure of striking it with the majority of his shots has no moral right to hunt with the rifle, for he will cause too much suffering.

For such sure killing all that is then necessary is a cartridge having a bullet of such weight and construction that, at the velocity at which it is made to fire, it will smash through the heaviest shoulder blades and ribs surrounding the chest cavity and penetrate within. The minimum bullet that will do this on all species of American big game up to about two hundred yards is a soft point, jacketed bullet of .25 caliber, weighing at least 117 grains, and fired at a muzzle velocity of at least 2700 feet per second.

As the weight of the bullet goes up, a proportionately lower velocity will still assure the same smash and energy. The minimum is therefore, roughly speaking, the .257 Roberts, the .300 Savage, and the .35 Remington cartridges. With heavier cartridges, be sure that the recoil of the weapon does not preclude nail-driving marksmanship on your part. A properly constructed .30-caliber bullet of 180 grains at M.V. 2,700 f.s. (.30-06 U.S. cartridge) is adequate for any American big game if properly directed at the chest cavity. But not even it, nor anything larger, is sure unless accurately aimed.

American standard big-game rifles are almost invariably equipped with an open rear sight and a bead front sight, both of the vintage of about 1730. Such sights are totally inadequate for the kind of shooting, I trust, the wilderness-loving sportsmen will care to settle for. I have been coaching thousands of men in rifle marksmanship all my life, but I confess I can not teach anyone to shoot well with a rifle fitted with such obsolete sights.

Of course, you can knock down a deer at fifty yards or a woodchuck at fifty feet, if that is all you require. But in the open and in the woods the alignment of such sights is so affected by light and shadow as to cause prohibitive errors at longer distances. Moreover, in the hurry and the more or less excitement of shooting at game, scarcely anyone can depend on himself to make the careful alignment necessary with such sights. The common result is overshooting.

Such open sights should always be removed from any rifle you purchase. The rear one should be replaced with a Lyman-type (large peep in a small disc) adjustable receiver sight. We think the best hunting front sight is the Redfield flat-top Sourdough. For the way to aim with these sights, see any of the better manuals on rifle marksmanship.

Such sights can be seen more·clearly in poor light than can any other metallic sights. A few days of their use, aimed correctly, will result in much more accurate hitting ability. In the hands of a fair marksman, a lever- or pump-action rifle is capable of sure shots on big game up to some 150 yards, and the better bolt-action rifles on out to about 250 yards. So sighted, the old .30-30 Winchester and .250-3000 Savage rifles make fine weapons for deer in wooded country.

The experienced hunter-rifleman of today demands a more specialized rifle that will respond to his skill in marksmanship. At the same time, it must be simple and rugged enough for wilderness use. The past fifteen years have seen big strides in the development of such rifles. A bolt-action rifle of better grade is the Winchester Model 70, weighing about 8½ pounds, and chambered for the .270 Winchester or .30-06 U. S. cartridge.

Such a firearm should have a well-fitting and properly bedded stock, a shooting gun sling, and a single-stage trigger pulling off at between three and four pounds pressure without creep or backlash. It is best sighted with a four-power modern hunting telescope sight with a field of view at least 30 feet at 100 yards. By taking full advantage of its latent capabilities, an efficient hunter can make sure hits in the boiler room on big game out to about 350 yards. This is the artist's weapon.

No rifle can be properly sighted at the factory or by a gunsmith except by sheer luck. You must sight it in yourself, both for your way of holding and aiming, and for the ammunition you will use in the woods. Until this has been done, you can place no reliance whatever on your weapon. The task should be taken care of before your trip, and it should be verified several times. Rifles shooting cartridges having a muzzle velocity of 2500 to 3000 feet per second should have their sights adjusted to strike the point of aim at 200 yards. They will then not overshoot more than three inches at 100 yards. By accurately aiming just a trifle high at 300, or at the top edge of a large animal at 350 yards, you can be sure of a good hit.

POTHUNTING

The full-charged factory cartridge will blow small edible game and fur bearers all to smithereens if the bullet strikes in the body. Throughout the wilder parts of the United States and Canada, grouse are not particularly alarmed by human beings. It is common to come on them strutting or dusting on the ground, or to have them fly up onto a lower branch of a tree and offer a standing shot at ten to fifteen yards. You can then decapitate them with your rifle if you know exactly where the bullet will travel with relation to the point of aim at these short distances. Usually it strikes an inch to half an inch low.

But the full charged cartridge releases a lot of noise to echo around a game country, and it is rather like using a sledge hammer to drive a carpet tack. Such cartridges are not particularly good getters of such pot meats.

THE ALL-AROUND RIFLE

Most of you, I imagine, would not care to be burdened with more than one rifle or gun in the woods. In many localities it is preferable to have a weapon well suited to both large and small game. Such an all-around rifle is the king of weapons for the chronic wilderness lover and loafer. It is based on a .25- to .30-caliber rifle, adapted to use both a light load for small game as well as the standard big-game factory load. This adaptation does not detract in one iota from its effectiveness on large animals.

The small load should be adequate for all game from quail and squirrels to turkey and beaver, killing neatly but having no more destructive effect than the .22 Long Rifle cartridge. The best light loads are based on the use of the lighter jacketed bullets with sharp points. Muzzle velocity should not be greater than about 1600 feet per second. Such a bullet will not expand at this low velocity. Passing through the body of a grouse or weasel, it will neither destroy too much edible meat nor ruin a trophy skin.

For forty years I have used such a load in my .30-06 rifle with the greatest satisfaction. It consists of the 150-grain, full-jacketed, pointed (M11) service bullet with a powder charge of 18 grains of Du Pont No. 4759 powder. Even better loads are the .25-caliber 87-grain, and the .270-caliber 110-grain, bullets with slightly lighter charges of the same powder.

These loads have slight disadvantages. They give a little louder report than it is desirable to let loose in a terrain where your anticipated and wished-for trophy is a big-game animal. They require a different adjustment of the sights from that needed for the big-game load, so that you have to shift both cartridge and sights. Finally, these reduced loads can not be bought on the market.

You must handload them yourself or have a custom handloader make them up for you. Handloading ammunition, however, is a most interesting hobby.

For some years now, my favorite all-around rifle and my constant afield has been a bolt-action rifle of 9 pounds weight, chambered for the .270 W.C.F. cartridge, and sighted with a four-power Bear Cub scope. For big game, either the 150-grain Sierra boat-tail bullet, or the 150-grain Speer sharp-point bullet loaded to M.V. 3,000 f.s., is used.

With the elevation dial of the scope set at two minutes, this load shoots to the point of aim at 200 yards. At 100 yards it strikes two inches above aim. At 300 yards it drops about six sinches, and it is about a foot low at 350 yards.

The small game load is the 110-grain Sierra pointed, soft-point bullet with a charge of 16 grains of 4759 powder. With the reticule dial of the Bear Cub scope set at seven minutes, the bullet strikes three-tenths of an inch below aim at 25 yards, one inch above aim at 50 yards, and three-fourths of an inch above at 100 yards. At this latter distance a five-shot group will be in about 1½ to 1¾ inches. The report is quite light and the recoil nil.

THE SHOTGUN

If you care nothing for big game or are in a country it does not frequent, then the shotgun should be considered for the procurement of small pot meat. It is the most effective on all birds and on most small animals, when a size of shot suitable for the particular game is used, up to its sure killing range of about 40 yards for 20-, 16-, and 12-gauge guns. The .410 bore has a maximum killing range of about 30 yards.

With a rifled slug, a single-barrel gun of 12 gauge is also quite effective on deer up to about 50 yards. You must equip it with adjustable rifle sights, however, to make sure hits.

The drawbacks of the shotgun are only its loud report and the rather heavy weight and large bulk of its shells. An expensive shotgun is not at all necessary for pothunting. Way back in 1930 the sales manager of the Stevens Arms Company sent me a common single-barrel gun.

He wrote me: "Don't think I am giving you a valuable present and thus putting you under any obligation. This gun retails at $15.00, and it cost us less than half that amount to make it. But I would like you to try it in comparison with the finest British shotguns costing around a thousand dollars. I think you will find that

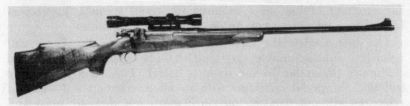

Col. Whelen's wilderness rifle. .270 caliber, for big and small game.

it will pattern just as well, and we think here it will prove just as durable and stay tight just as long."

After having used this little, light, cheap, single-barrel piece for twenty-five years on countless trips afield as a pot gun, I will be darned if he was not right.

THE SMALL-GAME RIFLE

From many viewpoints the little, light, and inexpensive lever-, pump-, or bolt-action rifle using the .22 Long Rifle high-velocity cartridge is the most convenient gatherer of small pot meat. The ammunition is light and inexpensive. The report is not apt to disturb big game 300 or more yards away.

It kills neatly. Even on the larger small game, such as turkey, the high-velocity cartridge with hollow-point bullet performs quite well. It is the logical weapon for eastern Canada where about the only pot meat is grouse and muskrat, the latter being most decidedly edible, and where handguns are in general prohibited.

This should have the same metallic sights as those suggested for the big-game rifle. Using the .22 Long Rifle high-velocity cartridge with sights adjusted to strike point of aim at 75 yards, either a solid or hollow-point bullet hits one inch high at 40 yards, one inch low at 85 yards, and 3½ inches low at 100 yards.

With such a rifle you can also have a lot of fun safely plinking around camp. Practice with it is the least expensive way of arriving at a high degree of skill in marksmanship. Everyone should own a .22.

THE HANDGUN

The most practical answer for a multitude of outdoorsmen is the light, high-grade .22-caliber pistol or revolver. It is conveniently and easily carried at all times, even while hunting with the big-game rifle. Besides furnishing you with pot meat, it will account for varmints including poisonous snakes. It can be used for securing large fish not protected by law. It is also ideal for the casual plinker.

The .22 Long Rifle cartridge, particularly the highspeed type, has excellent killing effect on birds and small animals. The report is not too loud. The ammunition expense is insignificant.

The best models for such use are the lightweight pistols and revolvers with adjustable target sights. The short 4½-inch barrel is slightly preferable to the six-inch barrel. The .32 S & W Long and the .38 Special cartridges with round-nose bullets and standard velocities will not damage too much meat, but they are noisy and rather expensive.

Before 1910 there were no full-sized .22 revolvers made. Phil B. Bekeart, a San Francisco dealer, had confidence in the future of such a handgun. He gave Smith & Wesson an order for a thousand of them, and in 1910 they produced what has since been known as their .22-32 Target Revolver. That year Hartley & Graham in New York got hold of one of these, and I immediately bought it.

Several years later this handgun won for me the aggregate of all the pistol matches at the annual outing of the Camp Fire Club. In 1912 I took it along on a two months hunting trip in the primitive area at the head of the South Fork of the Flathead River in Montana. I carried it all the time while hunting, fishing, and even when I went to a stream for water. On that trip I shot exactly forty grouse with it, and we ate them all.

I have this little revolver still. It has gone on almost every trip I have made in the United States since those early days, has brought a large amount of small game to our table, and has given me a world of pleasure.

If I were selecting a new handgun for pothunting today, however, I believe I would choose one of the lighter autoloading pistols with a 4½-inch barrel, target sights, and grip with thumb-rest. This I would do mainly because it would be lighter, smaller, easier to care for. Such weapons, too, have much better hand-fitting grips than any standard revolver.

I regard adjustable target sights as being absolutely necessary on such a weapon and, indeed, for any handgun that is to be interesting and satisfying to shoot. To kill small game neatly and surely, you must hit it in a vital spot, just as in target shooting you must hit close to the 10-ring—a nine at least.

Each make of ammunition will shoot to a slightly different spot. Likewise, any difference in the manner and tension with which the handgun is held will cause it to center its bullets differently. If the pistol is to hit close to where it is aimed, it must be possible to adjust the sights according to the ammunition and the manner of grasping the gun.

CARRYING THE PISTOL

Look up the laws regarding the carrying of a pistol before you take one anywhere. Throughout most of the United States it is perfectly legal to carry one provided it is not concealed. In New York State, however, even the owning of a pistol is practically prohibited, and a license to possess one is extremely difficult to obtain. In Canada, too, the possession and use of handguns is to a large extent restricted.

The best way to carry a pistol is in a stout leather holster. This should have a flap. At first I had an open Mexican holster for my .22, but one day I almost lost it when I tripped and the pistol fell out. My collaborator actually did lose a prized one of his in the East when inching along at full length across some frozen beaver ponds at twilight. A flap also does a lot to protect the gun from dirt and rain. Carry the holster on a rather wide belt worn low down on the hips, not tight around the waist. You can also stick it in your rucksack or packsack.

Take plenty of ammunition, at least a thousand rounds for a two-week trip. You won't need anything like that much for pot shooting, but you are sure to do a lot of plinking which is lots of fun, particularly on rainy days, and good for your marksmanship.

LEARNING TO HIT

You should not kid yourself about pistol shooting. Until you have made yourself into a fair pistol shot, it will be an absolutely useless weapon to you. Almost all American males think that they inherit an ability to shoot well with a pistol or a revolver, due probably to their romantic reading when kids. Nothing could be further from the truth.

If you have never before shot a handgun, all you have to do to cure yourself of this notion is to go out, put up any kind of a target, and start to shoot at it. You will find that literally you can not hit the barn. Moreover, the more undirected practicing you do, the worse you will shoot. Good pistol shots are made, not born. You can make yourself into a good shot, but you have to start the right way, and it is going to take a little time.

You don't necessarily need a coach to teach you. If you can understand and apply what you read, then a good manual will do to guide your practice. One of the best is *Pistol Marksmanship,* available for seventy-five cents from the NRA Book Service, 1600 Rhode Island Ave., N.W., Washington 6, D. C. But for a starter, let me give you a hint here.

You can not hold a pistol steady at first. No one can. If you attempt to aim at a target, you will find your sights trembling all over a three-foot circle at fifty feet. If during this wobbling you attempt to pull the trigger when for a fleeting instant the sights seem to be directed towards the mark, there will be no use in going up to the target to see where the bullet hole is. That would be like going in swimming after a hearty meal—you won't find it there.

When you first get your pistol, there is no use in hustling out to a range to "see how it shoots." That would be a sure waste of time and ammunition, and besides it has ruined a lot of morales. Instead, practice in your home holding your empty pistol in the right position at arms length and aiming at some small mark. You will find that you quiver all over the landscape.

But keep it up. Practice for five or ten minutes three or four times a day, attempting merely to hold the pistol steady. In just three or four days, a tremor which at first covered a three-foot circle at fifty feet will have been reduced to something like an eight- or ten-inch variation.

Then it is time to think about that trigger. While you are trembling over this reduced area, without letting up a bit in your effort to hold still, start placing pressure on the trigger. Continue with a very slow and gradually increasing pressure, until the hammer falls quite unexpectedly. Now you are going to find your hypothetical bullet somewhere within the radius of your tremor fairly close to the bullseye, which is considerably better than not hitting the whole barn.

With continued practice of this sort day after day in your home, dry shooting without ammunition, you will get better and better. But your squeeze on the trigger must be so gradual, building ounce by ounce while you endeavor to hold still, that you never know when the hammer will fall. Every time you try to pull the trigger when the sights appear to be aimed right, you are probably going to miss the whole darned target.

At the start it will likely take you at least ten seconds of this gradually growing compression. That's all right. The finest revolver shots in the world average about three seconds to squeeze the trigger in slow fire. *The hammer must fall unexpectedly.* Before very long it will do that while your sights are trembling over a mark the size of a grouse. Then it's time to step outdoors with ammunition.

There is one more lesson to be learned from this master pistol shooter. He does ten times as much dry shooting at home as he does firing on the range with ammunition, and he continues it all the time. It is the most necessary and valuable practice always, and it costs you nothing but a few minutes daily. But get that manual, study it, and apply it.

WHERE AND HOW TO HUNT

In a country that is known to contain a certain species of game, you won't locate it everywhere. There will be large sections, in fact, where you'll never see it at all. Wild game is just like the human species. It is concerned mainly with food, shelter and sleep, and at appropriate times it will be found where these can be obtained.

Birds take to roost at night, but during the day they do not hesitate to go where their food is, for their flight enables them to escape their enemies. Mammals, except in rare areas, where they are undisturbed and where there are no predators, tend to feed at night when they can escape observation and during the day to lie hidden in some safe retreat.

It is entirely unproductive to hunt in places where no self-respecting wild game ever ventures. One way to find out where to go is to ask local residents where they see game and to concentrate thereabouts. Lacking that information you must study the habits of game, one way or another, to determine the sorts of habitat in which each is likely to be.

Beaver and muskrats will be found only where there are ponds and streams. Woodchucks are not travelers or roamers, and will be seen only where there is succulent grass. Their burrows will be close at hand. Squirrels live only where there are nuts and masts; rabbits only where green vegetation abounds.

Sheep, goats, and to a large extent caribou are animals of the high open places. They prefer high meadows where their wonderful eyesight will warn them of any nearing danger. Moose are very partial to certain foods, mainly willows, and will be found mostly in low and wet places where such succulencies occur. When not feeding, they bed down in thickets adjacent to such areas, a favorite resting place being near the top of a largely open slope where they can not be approached unawares and where they can trot away in either direction. Deer are browsers, not grazers, and their food is small bushes, leaves, plants, and shrubs. They feed where these are and in the middle of the day bed down also in nearby thickets.

TRACKS AND TRACKING

Besides looking in the right kind of country for the game you want, search for any signs indicating its presence. If you come upon reasonably fresh tracks in fair numbers, there is a locality that can be profitably hunted. Each species of animal leaves its distinctive mark on ground that is favorable for an impression, and it is generally easy to distinguish the track of one species from another.

Unless you are a woodsman of long experience, you probably will not notice tracks unless they are made on a more or less bare and fairly soft piece of ground, rather free of leaves, grass, and moss. Of course, you are interested only in fairly recent tracks; those made within a couple of weeks. A track newly made on soft and more or less moist loam usually appears clear and distinct, with sharp outlines and edges.

As soon as the imprint has been made, it begins to get dull and to be more or less obliterated from the effect of sun, wind, and insects crawling over it. Its precise edges become blunt, perhaps, and crumble. It dries. Dew or raindrops mark it. Dust may blow into it. Before many days, it disappears.

Sometimes, however, a very old track may look perfectly fresh and fool you momentarily. I remember several acres of ground on the edge of a park in the Montana Rockies so tracked up by elk that it looked like a barnyard. Each impression was distinct, with sharply defined edges. But those tracks were made in a gumbo soil that had been wet at the time, and the impressions were preserved as though they had been pressed in wax. I examined them in September. The elk that had left these tracks had done so in the early spring, and now they were high up in the moutains near timberline.

Tracks made in snow, particularly fresh snow, will be perfectly apparent to anyone. Some of them, however, may appear only like holes made by snow spilled from branches. You have to go along them a little way sometimes to find a clear cut impression at the bottom which will show what animal passed that way. If it is storming at the time, the amount of loose, fresh snowflakes in such tracks can inform you approximately how old they are. The snow in a perfectly fresh track may also be soft. If the thermometer is below freezing, however, it will be glazed over with a crust.

It is comparatively easy to follow a fresh trail in the snow for a long distance. If you are tracking the animal with a view of getting a shot at it, you must be particularly alert and noiseless. You must keep watching ahead and not have your eyes continually on the track.

Take heed of the wind, too. If it is at your back, instead of following the trail directly, proceed parallel to it but a hundred yards or so to one side, checking back once in a while to make sure that you are continuing in the correct general direction, and looking where the animal will probably be. Animals watch their back trail. Moose, for one, zigzag a bit and then circle back into the wind before lying down. Of course with the wind blowing directly from you to them, any will get out far in advance of your arrival.

Tracking an animal on ground free of snow is almost always un-profitable, not because it is impossible, but because it usually takes too much time. The tracks may be perfectly distinct for a short or long distance on bare earth. Then the animal comes to terrain covered with leaves, grass, or moss where you have to search minutely and slowly for each telltale indication of his passage. Nevertheless there are times when this must be done, as when you are following a wounded animal.

If you get a shot, say at a deer, and feel quite confident you hit it in the boiler room even though it ran off out of sight, be sure to note the direction in which it disappeared. Then go to where the animal was when you shot at it, and look for hair and blood. All of our hoofed animals have very brittle hair. If your bullet has con-nected, some of this hair will have been cut off and you will dis-cover it in the ground, grass, or bushes if you look closely enough. You may also find blood, although bullet wounds do not always bleed externally.

If you are sure that the animal has been hit, the thing to do, unless you are in a forest jammed full of other hunters, is to relax right there for half an hour before you start to follow the spoor. This is to allow the animal time to get over the worst of its scare, to bed down, and to stiffen up. Otherwise, you may drive it right out of the area and lose it to predators.

In country where there are many other hunters, on the other hand, to delay following the wounded animal means running the risk of having another licensed individual come on it and tag it as his own. It may be, too, that approaching darkness makes it desirable to fol-low the tracks at once.

In any case, you have a most interesting little piece of tracking on your hands. The tracks as the animal ran off may be clearly ap-parent on favorable ground, or they may be just mere impressions, not more than what would be caused by pressing down with a stick. You can find those dim marks if you look closely. A leaf may be pressed down or, disturbed, its damp edge turned up. Grass may be bent or bruised. Dirt or sand may be thrown up a little. Even a single particle adhering to a blade of grass may identify a trail.

When you get two or more tracks in succession, measure the dis-tance between them. This distance, marked by a broken switch if you find that device handy, will tell you where to look ahead for an indi-cation of the next impression. Tracking in moss is particularly diffi-cult. There may be hundreds of holes. Look with suspicion on any that is not the correct distance ahead of the last sure print.

In the early morning a fresh trail through grass that is covered with dew or frost will show a very distinct white trace that can be seen from a distance, but this will all disappear as the vegetation dries. Conversely, when temperatures are far below zero, the frost brushed from trees and bush by a passing animal will leave a bare dark indication of his passage.

To develop skill in identifying fresh spoor, make sample tracks in all kinds of country at all times of day and weather. The end of your ax handle will suffice to make sure imprints. Examine them hourly to see how wind, time, sun, heat, and frost alter them. Animals, too, will often scrape or bruise twigs, buds, bushes, and branches as they pass. Reproduce such abrasions and fractures and watch how they discolor and disintegrate with time. One old hunter who was the most skilled tracker we have ever known told us that he had been making these test marks for twenty years and was still learning from them.

You can not learn tracking merely from such suggestions as these, but they may be of some help if only by showing you where to start. Tracking is an art learned only by long experience aided by unusual powers of observation. Game tracks will be of the most assistance to you in the meantime by indicating a particular little locality where it will be most profitable to hunt.

CHAPTER 24

FUR, TROPHIES, and RAWHIDE

EACH FALL THE RETURNING venison hunters among our friends like to tell about their success. They bring back a lot of fine meat and occasionally a nice rack of antlers. But ninety per cent of them throw away the skin. From the viewpoint of old woodsmen, this is a sinful waste.

It is true that the skins of the deer tribe, which in addition to the great humped moose includes elk and caribou, do not make very satisfactory rugs or robes when tanned with the hair on. They are attractive to look at for awhile, but the hair is very brittle. Some breaks off. More falls out. For years you have it all over everything.

Did you ever hunt in the cold North where caribou hides are often used for bedding and for insulation under sleeping bags? Hair is constantly in everything, including your tea and mulligan. On the other hand, the skin of the Rocky Mountain goat when tanned intact makes a most attractive cover so long as you keep it clean. Bears, too, make notable rugs. So do coyotes and the great wolves of the frozen stretches.

But for the bare hide of any animal there are many uses. A number of firms will convert deerskin, for example, into buckskin for you and cut it into most attractive and functional hunting shirts and gloves. One of us is still wearing such articles made from deer he killed in New Brunswick a decade and a half ago.

Or you can take the skin yourself and turn it into rawhide, a material for which any outdoorsman will find a dozen useful applications. Rawhide is simply the skin of any animal, with the hair removed, that has been naturally dried without any preservatives.

243

You can use rawhide for soling moccasins and, in an emergency, any footwear. You can utilize it in making strong containers and boxes such as panniers, saddle holsters for rifles, belt holsters for pistols, knife sheaths, and so on. Rawhide is also most useful for strongly and swiftly repairing broken articles such as a split gunstock.

SKINNING

How do you make rawhide? It's really quite simple. You start by carefully skinning the animal. To skin a deer, first remove the lower legs or shanks. The novice is likely to begin too high at what most of us think of as the knees. Cut deeply through skin, flesh, and muscle about an inch below the joints. Then brace your knee against what are actually the ankles. Pull forward briskly in the case of a front leg, backward with the hind leg, and the shank will snap off.

Your taxidermist can make very attractive gun and clothes racks, lamps, and other nostalgic items from the shanks with attached hoofs. Skin these all the way down. Cut all meat off the bones but leave the latter attached. Then salt thoroughly and send to the taxidermist, either with instructions or with a request for his suggestions.

Now we come to the actual skinning. Slit the hide along the inside of each leg to meet the belly cut. Extend this latter incision on up to the neck just short of the jaw. Then cut completely around the neck close behind the jaws, ears, and antlers. If you may want to have the head mounted, however, you proceed a bit differently at this stage, as we will presently consider.

Slit the underside of the tail, also. Then start at each of these cuts in turn to peel the skin from the flesh. If you are working on the ground, use the hide throughout as a clean rug on which to keep the meat unsullied. Generally, the skin will come away neatly, particularly if the animal has just been shot. In places where it adheres rather firmly, such as along the neck, use your knife carefully to cut it loose.

Avoid as much as possible making any nicks in the hide. You will notice between skin and flesh a thin, white film resembling parchment which, as a matter of fact, it is in a sense. Touch this film with a sharp blade, and the skin will continue to peel off. If anyone is helping you, have that individual keep the hide pulled taut while you free it with the long easy sweeps of a keen knife.

FLESHING

Despite all your care, there will be a few places where thin layers of meat and fat will adhere to the skin. When you have the latter off and can find some time to work on it, perhaps leisurely beside the campfire at night, neatly flesh it. One way to make this task easier is to stretch the section on which you are working tightly and comfortably across a knee.

Fleshing consists of cutting, scraping, or peeling off all pieces of meat, fat, and muscle that adhere to the hide. You can do this with your knife if you are careful not to cut the skin. Or you can use any tool with a scraping rather than a cutting edge. Indians made scrapers out of bones and stones. We even came upon an ancient one last year along British Columbia's Fraser River that, now one of our choicest possessions, had been laboriously ground with sandstone from green nephrite jade.

IF YOU WANT A RUG

If a rug is what you want, lace the skin to a frame. Or stretch it, with the hair against a building or big tree, with nails around the edge. Or, leaving the fleshed side up, stake it out on clean and dry ground by pegs driven around the perimeter through little slits made six inches apart. Let it dry away from moisture and sunshine. If there are blowflies and bugs around, rub the inside with salt to discourage them. A day or so later, wipe the wet salt off and let the skin dry as before.

You may be on the go, however, and unable to stretch the skin. It can still be kept in fine shape for a rug by salting it thoroughly all over the fleshed side, turning the ends and edges in, and rolling the whole thing into a limp bundle that may be stowed in a loose burlap bag if one is handy and hung in a cool dry place. The hide does not have to be fleshed too closely when handled this way.

HEADS FOR MOUNTING

In case your game has excellent antlers and you want to have the head mounted as a trophy, instead of skinning as previously indicated proceed in this manner. Starting at a point atop the shoulders, slit the hide down over each shoulder until the two incisions meet at the point of the chest between the forelegs. Commencing again at the top of the shoulders, cut forward along the top of the neck to a point just between the two antlers.

From these cuts, peel the skin off the shoulders and neck right up to the skull. Run the point of your knife deeply into the cartilages between the skull and the first vertebra, cutting this junction as free as you can. Then push the head hard one way and then the other, and the skull will break free of the backbone. Now you have the head with the cape attached.

Proceed to turn the skin inside out over the head, first cutting very closely around each antler. Then slice away down in the orifice of each ear, leaving these members on the skin, of course. Skin around the eyes, placing a finger in each to make sure you do not cut the lashes. Then cut to the junction of the upper gums close to the teeth, and in front of the front teeth or gums, leaving the nose on the skin.

Salt the ears, eyeholes, nose, and gums very thoroughly. Roll up the scalp, flesh side to flesh side, and leave it for two days while the salt works in. Then wipe as much wet salt off as possible. Hang up the scalp by the nose to dry in the shade, using a bent stick like an extemporized coat hanger. Do not stretch the scalp.

In the meantime, remove all flesh from the skull and the lower jaw. Incidently, this meat is adjudged by many to be the tastiest on the animal. Using a small stick shaped like a small spoon, remove the brains through the hole where the skull was separated from the backbone. Brains, too, are a fine delicacy, scrambled for instance with eggs. Send the dry or nearly dry scalp, the skull with antlers attached, and the lower jaw to your taxidermist.

IF YOU WANT RAWHIDE

Let the skin remain stretched in the shade until it is dry. Use no salt or other preservatives for skins to be made into rawhides or into garments without hair, although you may find it necessary in warm weather to use salt and occasionally alum or arsenic soap for skins to be tanned with the hair or fur on to keep them from spoiling. For rawhide, as a matter of fact, the stretching and drying are not absolutely necessary. The fleshing is. The skin must also be dehaired.

DEHAIRING

To remove the hair, immerse the skin in a container of preferably warm but not hot water into which you have thrown and stirred a couple of shovels of wood ashes. Let the skin remain in this water, swirling it about with a wooden paddle every now and then, until the hair starts to loosen. This will ordinarily take from one to three days.

As soon as the hair has slipped sufficiently so that you can pull out tufts with your fingers, remove the now slipping skin from the water and put it on a dehairing or fleshing log. This is simply a convenient log some eight or nine feet long and at least six inches in diameter, with one end stuck in the ground and the other leaned against a tree about four feet above the roots. Lifting the top of this smooth log slightly, place the edge of the neck of the skin between it and the tree. The hide is thus clamped handily for dehairing.

The skin now drapes soggily down over the log with the hairy side up. For removing this hair, use any object which has a dull scraping rather than a cutting edge. An old flat file, with one edge ground like a skate blade and with a wooden handle shoved onto each end, will do nicely. So will a drawknife with a scraping edge formed on it. Some bushmen drive a smooth piece of wood onto the point of a long sheath knife for a second handle and use the back of that blade. Aborigines often still find shells, stones, and bones satisfactory.

Straddle and sit on the log below the sodden skin. Using the tool of your choice, scrape off both the hair and the epidermis or grain under the hair, taking care not to cut the skin proper. You will be working *with* the hair, not against it. Loosen and move the skin where it is pinched at the top of the log so as to be always working and scraping down along the slanting log. If the hair is very difficult to remove, the soaking process probably hasn't been continued long enough. In this case, merely return the hide to the water for a few more hours.

STRETCHING

When the hair has all been eradicated, wash the skin again to clean it. Then stretch it on a very strong frame, punching little holes about every three inches along the hide's edge and lacing it to the frame with stout cord such as cod line or with leather thongs. A satisfactory small frame can be made by bending some limber wood such as a husky green willow in a hoop; a larger one by lashing four poles into a rectangle of the desired size.

Pull up on the various strings until the skin is drum tight on the frame. Then let it dry in the open air, preferably in sunlight this time, until all moisture is gone from it. It will then be as stiff and hard as a somewhat battered sheet of thin rusty metal.

You now possess rawhide. This will keep indefinitely so long as you keep it dry and safe from insects and animals. Northern sled and pack dogs, incidentally, can make it disappear in a very few minutes, and if you have been using a bone scraper, they are apt to top off the feast with that—which, in a wink, is what happened a dozen years ago to one of us.

MAKING RAWHIDE ARTICLES

You must make a form or pattern of the articles you wish to make of rawhide. Over this you will stretch, lace, shrink, and dry the hide. In this case, you do not have to dry the hide first but can stretch it wet over the form and let it dry and shrink there. Or if your hide is dry, soak it in water beforehand to make it pliable and soft. For a pannier, this form may be a wooden crate with dimensions similar to the inside of the pannier desired. For a scabbard or holster, it may be a wooden replica of a gun, a trifle larger than the actual weapon so that this may be easily inserted and withdrawn from the resulting holder.

As the rawhide dries, it is going to shrink very tightly on the form. The latter, therefore, must be so constructed that it can be taken apart inside the dry rawhide. The crate for the pannier for example, can be built with its components fastened together with screws accessible from the top. The model for the holster can be made of three pieces of wood, the middle one being in the form of a wedge that can be pulled out when the hide is dry so as to collapse the entire form and permit it to be withdrawn.

When the particular form you desire is ready, cut out a piece of the dry rawhide large enough to cover it amply. If you are a new hand at this, a sensible way to get started is by practicing with a piece of wrapping paper.

Soak this piece of rawhide in water, and then pull and stretch it, working until it is soft and pliable. While it is still wet, stretch it very tightly over the form. Pull it tense and so shape it so as to eliminate any wrinkles, much as you would do when wrapping a

Revolver holster and knife sheath of rawhide.

parcel very neatly in paper to go by mail. Then through holes punched along its edges, lace the hide on the form as tautly as possible with leather thongs.

Let the skin dry thoroughly, in the sun if you like, and the article is finished. The thong lacing that binds the rawhide will remain a part of the job. Inasmuch as it will probably be conspicuous, it should be neatly done.

For lacing scabbards and holsters, it's a good idea to assure equal spacing of the holes by measuring the positions of these accurately. A pair of dividers can be easily improvised, for example, and a barely discernible prick made where the lacing hole is to be placed. You can then form these holes with a one-eighth-inch leather punch available at most hardware stores.

To make sure that the holes line up through the two edges of the hide, I hold several inches of these together with a hand vise while punching through the two thicknesses at once. Such a vise can also be used to pull the hide up very tightly on the form.

HOW TO MAKE BABICHE

For the thong lacing, you may use leather shoelaces. These may be secured in lengths of six feet and more from dealers in high topped boots. You can also employ the rawhide belt lacing obtainable from some hardware stores and from the big mail-order houses. Better still, and at no expense to yourself, you can make your own thongs from your rawhide. The Indians call this rawhide lacing *babiche*.

Take a piece of rawhide roughly circular in shape and of preferably uniform thickness. A convenient size to work with is one about eight inches in diameter. With a sharp knife, cut along the periphery of this to start a thong about one-eighth of an inch wide.

Now drive a spike into a board. Stick a very sharp knife beside the spike so that there is a space, say one-eighth of an inch wide, between the spike and the knife edge. The width of this gap will be, of course, whatever you wish the resulting thong to measure. If you do not have a board and nail, a smooth log with a projecting stub can be as easily utilized. Although improvisations will be limited only by ingenuity and by the materials at hand, this is the simplest principle for the setting up of a die for cutting thongs.

Start the thong attached to the large piece of rawhide through the slit between the guard and the knife edge. Keep pulling on this string, and your die will continue to cut lacing neatly off the edge of the section of rawhide. If you started with a rough circle some eight inches across, you will end up with a strip about seven or eight yards long.

Place this string in a can, cover it with neat's-foot oil, and allow it to soak overnight. Then remove the thong and work it with your hands until it is soft. The result will be babiche, an exceedingly strong form of leather string.

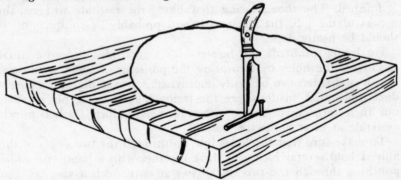

Method of cutting babiche or rawhide thongs and laces.

RAWHIDE IN GENERAL

If you ever have the bad luck to fall and break the stock of your gun at the grip, wrap some wet rawhide around it. Pull this up tight with thongs, and allow it to dry. The mend will be nearly as strong as iron.

In fact, all these rawhide articles completed as described will be extremely rugged and almost as hard as metal. Items like panniers are in the main all the better for being left firm and rigid, for they will then better protect their contents.

But if you want to make rawhide scabbards and holsters a little more flexible and attractive, this can be accomplished by painting them once daily for several days with neat's-foot oil to which just enough animal lard is added to make it a bit creamy. The scabbard in particular, though, should be left rather stiff. The holster can then be rubbed with an oily cloth, however, to smooth and soften it a little and to render it more water resistant.

In the case of some holsters and nearly all saddle scabbards, the ordinary deerskin does not make rawhide that is quite thick enough. For the rawhide in the revolver holster shown here, I used a heavy bull hide. This was almost an eighth of an inch thick.

On the other hand, you can easily thin down rawhide with sandpaper while the material is stretched flat on a small piece of board. Extremely heavy rawhide can also be planed thinner with a regular capenter's plane.

SKINNING FUR ANIMALS

Fur bearers, some of which make particularly fine eating, are skinned either open or cased, according to the species. Among this continent's animals which are usually handled open are beaver, badger, and moles. The others are generally cased, although a few such as the raccoon and wolverine may be either open or cased depending on the quality of the fur and to a large extent on the section where they are taken.

If the animal is to be skinned open, the skin should be slit from the point of the lower lip along the center of the chest and belly to the vent. From this cut, run the knife down the insides of the four legs. The skin can then be pulled off with very little difficulty.

The beaver, however, is skinned by making the cut from the point of the chin down the middle of the chest and belly to the vent. The pelt is then worked off the legs. These are pulled through after they have been lopped off at the first joint. It is then quite easy to finish removing the pelt.

CASE-HANDLING FURS

If the skin is to be cased, slit the insides of the hind legs from the paws to the vent. Skin out these legs, the rump, and the tail. Hang up the animal by tying the hind feet together over some projection such as a ridgepole or the limb of a tree. It will then be found easy to work the skin off, inside out, with very little use of the knife—pulling it over the head much as one shucks off a sweater.

When the forelegs are reached, push them back and work them out of the skin until the paws are completely skinned out. Clean the gristle out of the ears after the pelt is off. Particular pains should be taken when cutting the skin around the eyes and the lips to guard against their being mutilated or stretched too far.

The tails of most animals should be split and thoroughly cleaned out. Never leave the bone in a tail and the gristle in the ears or, rotting, they may damage the pelt. The tails of the beaver and muskrat are of no value and should be cut off unless the animal is to be mounted. Commercially speaking, the same thing applies to their paws as well.

CLEANING

It is always better to skin an animal as soon as possible after it is killed. The pelt will then have a better appearance. If a fur bearer freezes before it can be skinned, it should be thawed out very slowly and never brought into too warm a place.

Remove every shred of fat and flesh with the dull edge of a knife or a similar tool. Some trappers use a piece of hardwood, shaped as a knife. A few others still rely on bone scrapers. Opinions vary on the preferable direction in which to scrape.

It is usual, however, to start with the top of the pelt, and to work toward the tail, being careful neither to nick or multilate the pelt nor to allow grease to get on the fur. Where fat and dirt do get on the fur, they can be removed while fresh by the use of ordinary soap and lukewarm water. Never use hot water.

If all the fatty tissues are not entirely scraped off and the skin thoroughly dried, damaging grease burn may result from these fatty areas being in contact with one another without any redeeming circulation of air, as when furs are stored.

STRETCHING

No matter how prime and full furred a peltry may be, it will

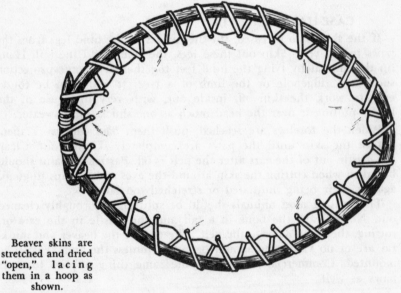

Beaver skins are stretched and dried "open," lacing them in a hoop as shown.

shrink in value if it is not properly stretched. There are many good stretchers on the market. Homemade stretchers, however, will answer the purpose equally well.

All open skins should either be tacked to a flat surface with the flesh side up, or laced in a frame such as one that can be made by bending a supple green willow about two inches through into the shape of an oval hoop. For cased peltries, use a wedge-shaped stretcher made of stout wire or soft wood. Two examples of these latter are illustrated.

All pelts should be stretched as nearly as possible to their natural size and shape. If the stretcher is made too large, it will over-expand the skin and make the fur look thin. There is only a certain amount of give in a skin. No matter which way a pelt is pulled, it will only give this certain amount. Seeking to stretch it too far will only defeat its own purpose by diminishing the quality.

If on the other hand the stretcher is made too small, the pelt will wrinkle and not dry properly. This will not only detract from its appearance but may also cause the fur to slip in places. Wooden stretching boards should be made of a soft wood from three-eights to three-quarters of an inch thick. The edges and the nose should be rounded off and the board made perfectly smooth.

Place the skin on the board so that the back will lie flat on one side and the belly on the other. Pull the peltry to its full length and tack down the edge of the butt. If you have difficulty in putting the skin on the stretcher, the latter is too wide and should be narrowed so the fur will go on without much resistance. Insert pieces of wood in the forelegs to stretch them. Tack out the edges of the hind legs and tail, if any, so they will dry properly.

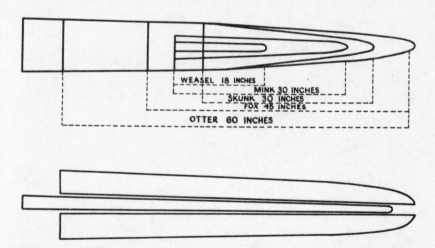

Stretchers for cased skins. The lower one has a wedge in the center so it can be made wider to stretch skin to proper width. They are one-fourth to one-half inch thick, with rounded edges.

DRYING

Never expose drying skins to the direct rays of the sun nor to the heat of a stove or campfire. Allow them to dry slowly in a cool and shady place.

Cased skins are dried with the fur inside. If you want to turn them, they should be removed from the stretcher as soon as they have dried enough to hold their shape. Start by folding in the nose. Work the pelt over it bit by bit. Replace the peltry on the stretcher until it is thoroughly dry.

Incidently, with the finer furs the trader usually tends to grade down for safety's sake a peltry whose skin has been left out. His psychology is that if the fur was choice, the owner would be displaying it to its best advantage.

Skins should not be folded if it is reasonably possible to avoid this. Beaver skins should preferably be laid fur to fur and pelt to pelt, and packed flat or rolled. Fine peltries should be kept separate from greasy or dirty skins. Never place one pelt inside another. Finally, keep any raw furs you may be fortunate enough to secure in a cool, dark, airy place.

FOR THE GOOD OF THE VENISON

CHAPTER 25

A LOT OF PEOPLE, particularly women, sincerely believe that they don't care for wild meat. Many such individuals are convinced that they especially dislike the flesh of any of the deer tribe. They complain that what they describe as venison's gamy taste is too strong. Not a few try to make the meat more edible, to their way of thinking, by horribly overcooking it.

When people honestly and open-mindedly react this way to venison, you can bet the animal was not butchered properly at the right time or that the meat was not cared for as it should have been afterwards.

Sometimes a buck or bull secured at the height of the rutting season is not as good as it might be. A paunch-shot animal that has run a long distance before falling will not make the best venison. Otherwise, given proper and timely butchering and care, all venison should be tempting to even the most critical tastes when suitably cooked upon reaching the kitchen.

Venison, it is true, usually does not taste like our domestic meats. Young bear, when properly stewed or roasted, can not be distinguished by the average individual from choice beef. Mountain sheep always does have somewhat the savoriness of lamb, while mountain goat resembles mutton. But the aristocrats of the deer family have a quality of their own. They are always delicious and never tough if reasonably prepared. Particularly, there is no strong or gamy taint to them.

IS BLEEDING NECESSARY?

When you shoot a large animal, it is ordinarily useless to run in and cut its throat or stick it in the point of the chest with the

255

motive of bleeding it. A modern bullet so disrupts the chest or abdominal cavities that they fill with blood almost immediately. Little or none of this blood will come out if the throat is cut.

Besides, you are going to open the animal without delay, anyway. At the very least, if for instance you have to follow a second wounded quarry, you will slit open the abdomen and chest and leave the animal, preferably across branches or otherwise in some well ventilated position, so that it will both drain and cool as soon as possible. In an emergency, all this can be done within a couple of minutes. Under favorable conditions, in cool dry weather when there are no flies, the meat will still be good days later.

In any event, the blood should be drained out just as soon as possible. If you're going to use the skin, don't spill blood on it, as it is difficult to remove. When the animal has been cleaned out, take fistfuls of grass, moss, or leaves and wipe the chest and abdominal walls free of moisture. The blood itself acts as a good solvent in doing this. Get the inside walls as clean and dry as you can. Never, never use water.

BUTCHERING

When you come to your kill, don't try to hang the animal up unless this can be easily and quickly accomplished. Ordinarily, the job is apt to be difficult and unreasonably time consuming. If this is the case, it will be sufficient to have the carcass with the head uphill and the rest of the body slanting downwards. If that is not possible, get the animal's chest up on a rock or log.

Turn the animal belly up, securing it in that position with rocks, logs, stakes, or whatever else may be handy. Then make a three inch cut at the lower end of the breastbone just below the lowest ribs. As soon as the knife cuts through the skin, fat, and meat into the body cavity, insert the first two fingers of whichever is your master hand into the opening.

Hold the intestines down and away so that the knife will not penetrate them. Then extend the incision down to the rectum, circumventing the active external milk glands, if any, and then returning to lift and cut away these easily disengaged tissues. Cut around each side of the major sexual organ and around the rectum, taking care not to puncture either. The contents can quickly taint the best meat unless any areas of accidental contact are immediately trimmed away. Carefully free the ducts leading to each, and tie them off with a piece of string or lace so that nothing will escape from them.

Then with your sleeves rolled up and any wrist watch removed, reach up into the upper end of the abdominal cavity and cut the diaphram loose all around. This is the membrane that separates the organs of the chest from those in the abdomen. Now reach with your secondary hand into the top part of the chest. Find and pull down on the windpipe, gullet, and large arteries. Cut them off as close to the neck as you can. This is one operation where, because of the close and obscure quarters, you have to take particular care not to slash yourself.

Now the entire contents of the chest and abdomen are free except for occasional adhesions along the backbone. These can be quickly torn free by hand. You can now turn the animal on its side and dump out the viscera. As you work down towards the stern, take care to poke the two tied ends free so that they will fall out with the remainder. It is after this that you wipe the inside of the animal as dry as possible, once you have dragged it away from the discards.

DELICACIES

Save the heart, cutting it free of the little pouch of membrane in which it is lodged. Be sure to lay the liver carefully beside it on some clean area such as a piece of bark, a rock, or a patch of snow. Secure the two kidneys as well. All are delicious. You may also care to save the white sheets of abdominal fat which will render into excellent lard for cooking.

Unless you are going to have the head mounted, slit the underneath of the jaw deeply enough so that you can pull the tongue down through this opening and sever it near the base. When we are hunting, we both carry a bloodproof bag in which to stow the heart, liver, kidneys, tongue, and fat for carrying back to camp.

COOLING

Now turn back to your animal. What you do next will depend to a large extent on circumstances such as weather, weight, and terrain. You may be able to hang it up by the head. You will at least be able to turn it so that the body opening can be propped open with sticks in order that the meat will cool as soon as possible.

Covering the carcass with a mass of well leaved boughs will protect the flesh to a large extent from the shifting sun, as well as from birds, such as Canada Jays, which may be already waiting for a chance to peck away at the fat.

If blowflies are bad, you should either have enough cheesecloth to cover the cavity or one of those cheesecloth bags available from outfitters in which the entire animal can be placed. Bluebottles and other winged pests will still probably get at it to some extent. When these have been particularly thick, we've found it effective to douse the underneath few of a mass of evergreen boughs with one of the effective and unobjectionable personal fly dopes such as 6-12 or Pellent, taking care of course to keep this off the meat. You can examine all openings and exposed spots when you pack the animal out, in any event, and wipe away any eggs and young larvae.

If rain is threatening, a better procedure is to turn the animal so that it is draped back up over a rock or log. The body cavity must be freely ventilated in any exigency. Turning a freshly butchered deer on its belly in the snow, for example, will even over-night cause the meat to start to putrify noticeably despite temperatures well below zero.

DANGER FROM ANIMALS

At this point, you will probably leave and go back to camp to secure companions or a pack animal to help in getting your venison out of the woods. If you are in country where bear are thick, it may be a good idea to discourage their presence by leaving some article of clothing flapping nearby. One of us has had a big blacky and her two cubs clean up the hind quarters of two large bucks shot just before sunset and returned for the next forenoon.

Wolves are far more cautious. We've cleaned out a moose during an early northern night with a pack howling only yards away in the blackness. Sure they would not bother the meat before we returned, we just left it on the snow. Tracks, when we went after the animal with a horse the next morning, showed that the seven in the pack never did venture closer than fifty feet.

One other time, however, we had to leave a butchered moose out a week in the mountains because of the weather. When we got there that time, the snow for a hundred feet all around had been flattened down as slick as a skating rink. Only one shin bone remained within even that area. That was the only instance when timber wolves have ever troubled any of our meat.

PACKING

The easiest way to get the venison out of the woods is with a horse. This is a common practice in the West. In the East, some hunting camps keep a horse for this purpose. If the animal is spooky, stroke and pet him some and during the process rub a little of the blood on his nose.

Ordinarily, you can tie a deer across or in front of the riding saddle. With something such as a moose, you'll perhaps cut it up and divide the sections between two pack animals. If the snow is on the ground, you may drag the unskinned quarry by its head after cutting off the legs at what is usually thought of as the knees but which are actually the ankles. Dragging is most easily accomplished with a harness.

However, you can take a half hitch high around the tail, bend back the hair, and then take a second half hitch around the now doubled tail. The usual saddle horse will then skid even a good sized moose out without' any discomfort if conditions are halfway good. If the experience is a new one, the horse will probably settle down better if you remain in the saddle as much as possible. Snugging the rope around the saddle horn is not such a good idea if you're going more than a few feet.

MANPOWER

Deer can be dragged headfirst by a couple of husky hunters. They are often carried on a stout pole, back hanging down and feet tied up over the timber. The head should also be lashed up so that it won't dangle and continue to throw the load off balance. As a matter of fact, a deer lugged more than a short distance in this fashion will swing so much that you will very probably soon be weighing the advisability of cutting a second pole and using the two of them as a stretcher. This, once the animal has been tied on solidly, can be carried at any height.

One ordinarily rugged man can carry a deer by himself unless it dresses out a lot too far above one hundred pounds. There are two handy ways of accomplishing this. We prefer to drape the animal over our shoulders like a scarf and to hold on to the legs. This way if you start to slip or stumble, you can get rid of the load in a hurry.

If you've tied it into a pack by lashing the legs together, you may fall and find an uncomfortable amount of weight pressing you down. A common way of carrying deer, nevertheless, is by tying all four legs together and then running your head between body and legs, with the shank ends held down in front of your chest with one hand. The flats on the sides of one fore and hind leg then rest on your shoulders and do not cut in. It is almost impossible to carry a heavy deer any distance piggyback because of the way the sharp bones bite into the shoulders.

If under any circumstances whatsoever you carry a deer through a forest frequented by other hunters, tie a red bandana handkerchief or strips of bright red cloth conspicuously around it. It isn't a bad idea, either, to sing in a loud voice.

SKINNING

If your are an old-time hunter, you'll very possibly prefer to complete the skinning on the spot, as described in the chapter on Furs, Trophies, and Rawhide. You may pretty well have to do this if your trophy is big. There are exceptions, of course, depending generally on the available methods of transportation and to some degree on the weather.

In any event, you'll want to get the hide off as soon as reasonably practical. The meat should be allowed to cool thoroughly with the least possible delay. Unless the animal is a small one and is opened wide, it won't cool quickly in temperate weather with the skin on. And if you're in a cold climate, you'll want to complete the skinning before the hide freezes on, or what would have been an hour's work may very easily develop into a cold and disagreeable all-day chore.

For the good of the meat, don't toss a whole deer—skin and all— on the warm front of your car to motor it back that way. It's a very pleasant feeling all around to drive back to friends and family with the entire animal on display, and in some of the big old cars with high sweeping fenders you could get away with it. In far too many instances, however, the fine delicate flavor of the venison is tainted if not completely spoiled by this practice.

QUARTERING

Once the carcass is free of the skin, which you have been shifting about so as to keep the meat as clean as possible, quartering will be in order. Unless you intend to save the head, ease the point of your blade deeply into the cartilages between the skull and the first vertebra, severing them as well as you can. Then twist the head abruptly in one direction and then in the other, and it will snap free.

With an ax or ideally a meat saw, split the bone from the belly cut to the neck. Open the neck longitudinally on the same line and remove the windpipe and gullet. Then split the backbone from neck to tail. The animal will now be in two halves. Quarter it by cutting each of these halves along the line of the lowest ribs.

PROTECTION

You may now choose to rub flour on these quarters and to wrap them in cheesecloth to discourage pests. Sprinkling black pepper on the flesh will also help to keep bluebottles and such annoyers off. You will also probably want to examine the meat every day or so to make sure that it remains unbothered, giving particular atten- tion to bullet wounds and to folds and nicks in the flesh. Any eggs or larvae so detected can be quickly and harmlessly scraped, wiped, or if you wish cut away.

In any event, the quarters can now cool quickly, especially if you hang them high in a tree to hasten the chilling the first night. Some of the pack trains in the Canadian Rockies, hunting early so as to be back down in the lowlands before snow sets in too deeply, keep fresh game sweet by trimming the branches out of the tree and pulling the meat up into the clear twenty feet or more from the ground where blowflies do not operate.

A meat tent is a handy thing to pack along in hot weather if you have a large enough outfit to warrant its inclusion. A handy model, often seen in survey camps in the wilderness, consists of canopied netting with a zipper opening. This shelter is customarily tied in a dark, well ventilated spot by a single rope that runs from its top center.

REFRIGERATION

Keep these quarters as cool and as dry as possible. If you are heading outside, get them into refrigeration as soon as you can. If a long and warm auto trip lies ahead, try at the earliest opportunity both to pack each quarter in a carton of dry ice and to secure those containers in larger ones with crumbled newspapers between for insulation. Circumstances may be such, too, that you'll prefer to travel in the comparative coolness of the night.

If the weather is hot and the distance far, you will probably do well to lay over a day in some locality where you can have the meat frozen solid. This may be a desirable time to cut and wrap it in plainly labeled packages that can be retrieved from the freezer and used one by one. Odd portions can be ground into hamburger, along with a desirable proportion of beef fat if you want.

It should then be an easy job, with the help of dry ice which these days is obtainable along most routes, to bring these packages frozen to your cold storage cabinet, drawer, locker, or butcher's cold room. You'll have some really fine meat.

CHAPTER 26

MEAT FOR OUTDOORSMEN

THERE IS A SAYING that all meat is grass. This is literally true. The carnivora live on the herbivora. Man lives on both and on grass, in the form of vegetation, as well.

Since meat is grass, it is entirely possible for man to live on meat alone. This has been demonstrated in innumerable instances over the ages, the only requisites being that the meat is largely fresh, that it is not overcooked, and that it is sufficiently fat—the best guide for the latter requirement being the diner's own appetite. When in the normal unhurried course of a meal you have eaten enough fat, you will want no more.

No particular parts of the animal or fish need be eaten. Sizzling plump sirloins, if that is what you prefer, will supply you with all the food ingredients necessary for good health even if you eat nothing else whatsoever for a week, or a month, or a year.

Vilhjalmur Stefansson, the eminent arctic explorer, lived in the North, for an aggregate of more than five years on meat and water alone. In fact, skins also provided much of his parties' clothing. Under medical supervision centered in New York City, he later showed the complete sufficiency of such an all-meat diet by living for a minutely observed and painstakingly tested year exclusively on this food of our more or less remote ancestors and of certain primitive hunters who still so subsist today.

It is a fascinating thought that even in this age of the balanced diet a skilled woodsman and hunter could live completely off the wild meat of a good game country, provided of course that the laws of the region permitted it. Some, as in the North, in fact do. I say "fascinating," but I am not so sure it would be for long, for in many areas you would have to spend an important part of time hunting, with often no opportunity for anything else. Hunting for mere subsistence can become a pretty strenuous occupation.

You fellows, young and old, who go into the woods and mountains for your vacations, or on rivers and lakes, can get along very nicely for a week or two on imperishable meats such as bacon, ham, dried beef, and the endless canned varieties. But the day soon comes when you crave real, fresh meat to supplement your other foods.

Too, we've both left camp a lot of mornings with no provision for lunch but a blackened pail and a little bundle of tea, figuring to dine and almost never failing to do so on some prevalent small game such as ptarmigan or partridge—spitted on a stick, thrust briefly into flame both to seal in the juices and so set the flavor as to obviate any need for salt, and then roasted as slowly as our patiences would allow.

You will often find an opportunity to obtain fresh meat in your vacation land when the game laws permit. These are subject to annual changes, and at the end of this book you will find names and addresses of the offices where you can obtain information for everywhere on the continent north of Guatemala and British Honduras.

All is meat that comes to a hungry man's table, and all animals and birds in North America are edible. Some taste better to each of us than do others. Perhaps none surpass the ungulates or hoofed animals. Of these, mountain sheep meat is usually considered the most choice, and then in order caribou, deer, antelope, moose, and goat. Such large animals will provide a lot of nourishment for a long time for many people, and it would be nothing less than a crime to kill any for food unless all the meat is really needed and can be utilized.

Individual animals and birds of the same species are not equally fine eating in the sense of being tasty and tender. Male animals shot during the rutting season, as a rule, are not so good. The most magnificent trophy that adorns the walls of my hearth room is that of a mountain caribou that I shot one September during the height of the rut. Its meat was something else again. Paunch-shot animals that have run some distance before falling and animals that have been poorly butchered are not such pumpkins. The proper preparation and care of wild meat for food is discussed in another chapter.

Coons, possums, rabbits, and squirrels are all good. In the tropics there are many small exotic animals, among which I would give first place to the sloth despite its unattractive appearance. It is a pure vegetarian, and a far cleaner animal than any pig. Its meat is like delicious pork.

Then there is the whole feathered tribe, all good eating and most of them delicious, although I personally would draw the line at the turkey buzzard. I did try an Amazon parrot once, but I think it had been feeding on a rubber tree; at least, my teeth sort of bounced off. The wild turkey is the most preferred of all wild birds, but you must remove its craw as soon as you have shot it or you are in for a disappointment. As a matter of fact, all birds should be drawn as soon as they are bagged.

The one dish that has lingered longest in my memory was comprised of six-inch brook trout with many frog's legs which two of us twelve-year-old kids prepared alongside a brook in the North Woods. The iguana, that five-and-a-half-foot lizard that looks like the dragon of mythology and which is plentiful in our tropics, is almost the equal of the northern bullfrog. The meat of all the water turtles makes delicious stews.

Then of course there are fish, but I shall not touch on such obvious food here except to say that, even if you are not a confirmed angler, it will pay you to include some simple light tackle even in a back-packing outfit in case you pass promising waters in your wanderings.

Don't be squeamish in your eating or you will pass up a lot of really delicious pot meat. Most prejudices have their foundation in ignorance. Stefansson once said that he much preferred "well-brought-up young men" to more sturdy backwoodsmen on his expeditions, mainly because the latter looked on an expedition as a sporting venture and were willing to try anything, while the backwoodsman rebelled at anything that he had not been accustomed to all his life.

The fact is that every animal in the far and near places of this continent, all the fish that swim in our lakes and rivers and streams, and each bird that inhabits the air is good to eat. Nearly every part of North American animals is edible, furthermore, even to the somewhat bland antlers that are not half bad roasted when they are in velvet and to the bitterish gall that has an occasional use as seasoning. The only exception may be polar bear liver which becomes so excessively rich in Vitamin A that it is poisonous to some degree at certain times and is usually as well avoided.

BEAR

Our carnivora—the meat-eating bears, cats, and wolves, and such—are all edible, some individuals more so than others. Summer-killed grizzlies that have been subsisting along the salmon streams would not appeal to many, but a young grizzly I shot at timber line one fall was consumed in its entirety by my companion and myself with great gusto.

As for black bear, those of us who dine on it regularly, whenever we can, are just about unanimous in the opinion that the mountains and woods afford no more palatable and delicious game meat with the single exception of mountain sheep. Not even cubs and yearlings furnish really good steaks, it is true. But even an oldster cooks up into moist and savory roasts and stews. The meat then so resembles prime beef that you can serve it as such to individuals who are rabidly if unreasonably prejudiced against bear, and actually have them coming back for third and fourth helpings.

SUPERIOR SHORTENING

Any excess fat, and there will ordinarily be considerable except during the latter stage of hibernation and within the first few lean weeks following, should be trimmed off before the bear meat is cooked. This fat should then be heated in open pans to extract the grease. Strained into tins, this hardens into a clear white solid that is the best shortening we or any other user we have ever talked with has ever found.

It is not unusual to get some forty pounds of such lard from a large black bear downed just before the long winter sleep. The shortening procured from a grizzly is also excellent but, when similarly rendered, remains an oil which is not so easily carried. Some backwoodsmen still make spreads for their bannock and flapjacks by mixing some sweet such as honey or molasses with bear grease.

KIDNEYS

Bear kidneys, when the fine membrane about them has been removed, come apart in small individual segments. Stewing these with butter, salt, pepper, celery, dried parsley, chopped onions, a dash of cloves if you happen to have any, and a bit of flour for thickening makes one of the choicest wilderness delicacies available.

Some recipes recommend soaking kidneys, liver, heart, tongue, and other such tidbits in cold and sometimes salted water for an hour or so before cooking. Actually, although you can suit yourself, there is no good reason for this, and it takes away a certain amount of flavor and nutriment.

THE MAIN COOKING SECRET

Most wild meat, unlike bear, is apt to be rather dry. For venison as venison *should* be, therefore, make sure that the steaks, chops, and roasts are not overcooked. A good general rule is to time deer, moose, caribou, elk, and similar meat one-fourth less than you would lamb.

The tougher portions such as the neck and the lower hams can be reserved for stews. The neck, incidentally, also makes the most praiseworthy mincemeat. The ribs are best broiled very quickly over a charcoal or wood fire, so you almost burn the exterior but leave the inside almost raw.

To keep your meat juicy and appetizing, always try, except in the case of soups, to sear the outside quickly in flame, extreme dry heat, very hot fat, or in furiously boiling water. Then only minimum amounts of the juices will escape. For the same reason, do not ordinarily use salt until the very end.

COOKING ON A STICK

This is the easiest, quickest, and often the handiest way to cook tender meat, and there are no dishes to wash afterward. Take a peeled stick, perhaps a half-inch through and some three feet long, and sharpen both ends. Impale on it chunks of succulent meat about the size of baseballs. Best for this purpose are the long outside strips cut from either side of the backbone; next best, the pair of tenderer but less flavorful tenderloins that lie along the inside of the spine. Between each such segment, stick a thick piece of fat or bacon to baste the lean meat.

You can have your fire burning up with a high blaze if you want. Plant the stick upright, close enough to the flames so that the outside of the meat will be quickly seared. Rotate the holder frequently, leaning it at different angles so that the tidbits will cook evenly and rapidly until they are a little bit charred on the outside but still rare and juicy in the middle. Eat from the stick, salting to taste.

STEAKS

Steaks may also be cooked without utensils by extending the meat over glowing embers on forked green sticks. One of the campfire grates available from most outfitters is handy for such broiling, too, although those which have folding wire legs that can be shoved into the ground may as well be divested of these if weight is any problem. It is a simple and often safer matter to lay such a grid between logs and rocks.

Cut the steaks an inch and a half thick if that's the way you like them, sear them first in flame, and then allow them to broil three or four minutes to a side some three inches above live coals of preferably some hardwood such as oak, birch, or maple. The softwoods make poor coals, so it is just as well not to try to broil with them if some better fuel is available. Steaks can also be well broiled atop a dry metal sheet or in a dry frypan.

A lot of campers like to fill a frypan with plenty of sizzling hot lard or bacon grease. Steaks about half an inch thick are then dropped into the pan one at a time, gradually so that the fat will not stop sputtering. Then remove to a hot dish, season, and serve.

BOILED MEAT

Cut meat for boiling into about two-inch cubes. Drop these one by one into rapidly bubbling water. Don't salt until almost ready to serve. Meat can be relished after it has been boiling only five minutes, but many get the habit of letting it simmer for an hour or more.

Often rice and other vegetables are cooked along with it, and these dictate to some extent the amount of cooking. In any event, the addition of any such components should be so staggered that everything will be done at the same time. Any additional fluid that needs to be put in should be boiling, not cold. You will, no doubt, prefer to keep the pot well covered.

STEWING

Stew meat, which can be the toughest in the critter, is best browned at the onset with grease, chopped onion, and any desired spices in the bottom of the kettle. You can then, if you want, stir in enough flour to make a thick smooth gravy.

The liquid comes next. You can use at various times any fluid in which vegetables have been cooked or canned, broth from boiled meat, or just plain aqua pura. Season, bring to a boil, and then place tightly covered where it will simmer all morning or all afternoon.

A Dutch oven is a handy receptacle for stew inasmuch as you can dig a hole, always in a safe place where fire can not spread, and leave it buried there among hot coals while you spend the day hunting. But don't ever take any chances when doing this.

MULLIGAN

The preceding is the basis of a stew, and from that point forward you're on your own. What the end result will be depends more or less on ingenuity, imagination, and the materials at hand. Available vegetables go well in such a stew. So do odds and ends of steaks and roasts.

When a lot of us are off by ourselves, the tendency is to go in for one-dish meals. This we can easily accomplish with numerous such

mulligans, even to the extent of making bread unnecessary by adding a starch such as rice, potatoes, noodles, macaroni, one of the
cooked cereals, or perhaps a steaming soft dome of dumplings.

SOUP

If you are making soup with a meat base, put the meat in cold
salted water. Include any bones you may have, opening the larger
of these to get to the marrow which in terms of energy is the most
nutritious part of any animal. Using a saw will do away with sharp
splinters. Bring to a boil and let simmer, the longer the better.

"TIGER"

"Bacon," a sourdough friend of ours translated when asked what
he meant by saying he'd gouged himself with vast quantities of
tiger. "That's because it's striped. Sounds nobler when called tiger."

The main troubles that camp cooks experience with bacon arise
from their submitting it to a lot too much heat. Not only is the bacon
thus burned and toughened, but very often the frypan becomes a
mass of leaping flames. Aside from resulting offenses to taste and
digestion, this is wasteful if nothing worse. The nearly three thousand calories per pound that fat side bacon contains lie largely in its
grease, any excess of which should be saved, particularly in the bush.

We'll do better to fry the bacon slowly over a few coals drawn to
one side of the blaze. More satisfactory still is the practice of laying
the strips well apart in a pan and baking these evenly to a golden
brown in a moderately warm reflector baker.

Slabs of bacon have a tendency to mold. This can be harmlessly
wiped off with a clean cloth moistened either in vinegar or in a
solution of baking soda and water.

LARD

The lard pail can be replenished by pouring in your surplus
bacon grease. Excellent lard can also be secured from game fat not
eaten along with the lean. Cut this into small cubes and, if only
in sparse amounts, melt these down in the frypan over a very slow
fire.

Pour the liquid grease into some handy container where ordinarily
it will harden and become easy to pack anywhere. Half-pound pipe
tobacco cans with pressed top lids are fine for this and other food-
packing purposes. Save the cracklings to eat with lean meat or to
munch for lunch some cold noon.

LYNX

Lynx meat, served up to hearty appetites alongside a campfire, is except for fiber almost indistinguishable from the white meat of chicken. Because the larger lynx in particular are apt to be somewhat stringy, we like to cut the meat into very small pieces and to fricassee these.

This you can do in a Dutch oven if you want, preparing the meal before you leave camp in the morning and leaving it to reach a state of perfection by the time you return ravenous at night. Or if someone is going to be in camp during the morning or afternoon, the meat can be trusted to cook slowly in a big kettle suspended over the fringes of the fire.

Start the meat as you would a stew in the bottom of a large receptacle. Allow to simmer gently until tender. Such vegetables as onions, carrots, chopped celery, and in fact any you'd include with chicken go equally well with this dish.

You can make gravy on the side if you want by blending six tablespoons of flour with a small amount of cold water, then adding three cups of the liquor from the pot and stirring until a thick sauce is the result. This may be poured over the lynx and vegetables. The fricassee goes well atop mashed potatoes, hot steaming bannock, or fresh fluffy rice. A little paprika will give it character. The flavor is surprisingly delicate.

BEAVER

Among the small animals the cream must be handed to our beaver, from the tip of its nose to the end of its tail, although few of us today will have an opportunity to indulge in this delicacy. I still lick my chops thinking of the meals I made from amisk on three separate occasions.

One way to collect a luxuriant grizzly robe in the continental northwest is to accompany a trapper when he goes out in the spring for beaver. The great bears are so fond of fresh beaver meat that it is not unusual for them to raid a camp while the trapper is elsewhere on his line. Once you've sat down to a feed of amisk after a day of making your way past steaming snowdrifts and flooded streams, you'll better appreciate why.

Beaver meat is particularly rich. It's best when possible to stick to the tender youngsters. If you ever do cook up one of the big fellows weighing forty or fifty pounds, a good thing to remember is that the meat will become more and more fibrous and stringy the longer it is cooked.

The ordinarily moist dark flesh is reminiscent of plump turkey.

It is particularly excellent roasted, and when so cooked it has the advantage of not requiring any basting. Cold, it is still moist and tasty in sandwiches.

Beaver tails are the piece de resistance that impelled Horace Kephart to note regretfully when the Twentieth Century was newer, "This tidbit of old-time trappers will be tasted by few of our generation, more's the pity!"

The first such tails that my collaborator ever saw in a detached state were presented to him by a northern trapper who'd strung a dozen on a cord. In this form, they look like nothing quite so much as scaly black fish whose heads have been removed. Heat causes the rough dark skin to puff and lift away, exposing a white and gelatinous meat. Somewhat resembling pork when boiled, this goes particularly well with such dishes as baked beans and thick pea soup.

"Noble creatures," Dudley Shaw, still this particular outdoorsman's nearest neighbor on the Peace River, decreed once at lunch, anchoring a slab of roast beaver between two slices of bread. "Glutted himself joyously with poplar."

"How can you tell?"

"Amisks who bog themselves down on willow," the seventy-year-old trapper and former Hudson's Bay Company man explained, "are permeated with a bitterish flavor. And if they're crowded back into spruce, as happens on some congested ponds, the result is notoriously ghastly. Then the only thing you can do is parboil it copiously. Indians still scrape fat for a quick snack from even those hides, though. They roast the blinking stuff on green sticks propped by a fire while finishing skinning out the plunder. Cheers them up nobly."

PRESERVING MEAT

If you're camping in one place and have a quantity of fresh meat you'd like to preserve with a minimum of trouble, cut it into strips about the size of the average forearm, following the membranous divisions among the muscles as much as possible. Pull off as much of this parchment as you can.

Roll the pieces in a mixture made in the proportions of: three pounds of table salt, five tablespoons of black pepper, and four tablespoons of allspice. You can then either drape the strips over a wire or similar support where they'll be safe from animals small and large, or you can pierce one end and hang each with a piece of string.

The meat must be kept dry. About a month is needed for it to shrink and season properly. After that, it will keep indefinitely. Moose we've preserved in this way has lasted several years, by which time the last chunk has been eaten. This tastes good when thinly sliced and chewed on the trail. Scraped and trimmed some, it goes well in mulligans.

JERKY

Jerky is very concentrated and nourishing. A little goes a long way in rations light in weight and high in nourishment. This pioneer standby is not by itself a good food for long continued consumption, however, as it lacks the necessary fat.

The fat, which would turn rancid, should be trimmed away from the meat before the drying operation necessary for jerky is commenced. A conservative procedure is to render it, either for later use as a food supplement or for more immediate employment in the making of pemmican.

Jerky is lean meat that has been divided into strips and dried over a fire or in the sun. Its manufacture is commenced by cutting lean beef, venison, or other fresh red meat into long and wide strips about half an inch thick. Hang these on a wooden framework about four to six feet off the ground.

Under this rack, build a small, slow, and smoky fire of any nonresinous wood. This fire should not be hot enough to cook the meat at all, its chief use being to keep flies away. Let the meat dry in the sun and wind. Cover it at night and if rain falls. It should dry in several days.

When jerked, the meat will be hard, and it will be more or less black outside. Protected from dampness and from insects, it will keep almost indefinitely. It is best eaten just as it is. Bite off a chunk and chew. Devoured thus, it is quite tasty, especially when ambling along a wilderness trail gives you the time and the relaxed perspective necessary for fully savoring it. Jerky may also be cooked in stews and soups.

PEMMICAN

Pemmican is little known and eaten these days. Any manufactured products labeled "pemmican" that we have sampled have been a long cry from real pemmican. Without doubt, however, this is one of the most perfect foods there is, especially for use during long journeys in the remote regions.

To make pemmican you start with jerky. Pound this into small shreds, perhaps with the back of your ax. Then take a lot of raw animal fat. Good beef fat, for example, can be purchased from your butcher at very slight cost. Cut the fat into small pieces about the size of walnuts. Fry these out in the frypan over moderate heat, never letting the grease boil up.

When the grease is all out of the lumps, discard these. Pour the hot grease over the shredded jerky, mixing the two together until you have about the consistency of ordinary sausage. Then pack the pemmican in waterproof bags. The Indians used skin bags. No salt at all should be added.

Ideal pemmican is, by weight, approximately one-half rendered fat and one-half well dried lean meat. Approximately five pounds of fresh lean meat is required to make one pound of jerky suitable for pemmican.

True pemmican of this sort comes close to being the one perfect food for any length of time, as it contains all the elements for perfect nourishment with the single exception of Vitamin C. This antiscorbutic ingredient you can do without for close to two months at least if you are already in good health. However, supplementing the pemmican with fresh fish, fresh rare meat, or any other fresh and not overcooked food such as the rose hips you can often pick while walking along, will supply the Vitamin C needed to prevent scurvy.

PORCUPINE

Many campers would pass up a porcupine, and yet he is one of the purest of all vegetarians. Again my memory goes back, to when Bones Andrews and I were compelled to spend several weeks in a region where there was no game. At the end of that time we had about the worst case of meat fever you can imagine. So we saddled up our little pack train and made tracks for higher altitudes and game country. On the way up, I shot a porcupine. I skinned it, starting at the smooth underneath, and tied it to the back of my saddle.

That night we made it into a stew. First, we cut it into small pieces and boiled these an hour. Then we added a handful of rice and salt, a dozen small dumplings of biscuit dough, and covered all that to boil twenty minutes longer. This was tall country. With air pressures lessening with the altitude, the higher you climb, the longer you have to boil. We finally finished by adding a little flour to thicken the gravy and by stirring in a teaspoon of curry powder.

Then the two of us sat down and finished the whole pot in one sitting. That pot held nine quarts and was full. The quill pig, incidentally, should be a young one.

CHAPTER 27

PROVISIONING FOR CAMPING

WITH APPETITES SHARPENED by the sort of robust outdoor living for which man was bred, meals afield can be just as nourishing and tasty as those in the city, and maybe more so—when you take foods that keep well, cook quickly, and are easy to carry.

If you have automobile or powerboat transportation and your camp is not more than a convenient fifty miles or so from provisioners, what to eat will be no particular enigma. You can have all the variety and luxury that you would expect in the big town—fresh meat, vegetables, fruits, and pastries, some of the quickly frozen products, and all the canned goods you want. Your menus will be limited only by the ability to cook, probably on a gasoline stove.

But under the more primitive conditions of which we write, your problem in selecting food will more than likely be complicated by meager transportation, lack of refrigeration, troublesome combinations of hot days and cool if not freezing nights, and by having to cook over a wood fire. Under these circumstances, much of your grubstake may well be largely dry. There is no sense in packing a lot of water along in your food. Besides, with dehydrated rations the weather poses no serious difficulties.

We do not suggest any particular grub lists or daily menus, for what suits one will not always satisfy another. You'll do best to take what you personally like and what you know how to prepare. Experimentation is the best way to find out how much you need of each item to round out a satisfactory meal.

THE STAPLE FOODS

The standard foods carried by most experienced campers on extended trips into the wilder portions of North America, and which in general should form the bases of most grubstakes, include flour, baking powder, compact cereals such as oatmeal and rice, dry beans and peas, powdered milk, powdered eggs, sweet chocolate, side bacon, salt pork, lard, oleomargarine or canned butter, dried soup powders, sugar, and dehydrated vegetables and fruits. All these are practically water free.

Some of the more nourishing spreads such as peanut butter, jam, and honey work in well. Practical beverages are concentrated tea powder or tea itself, one of the instant coffees, cocoa, and bouillon powders and cubes. Seasonings such as celery salt, onion salt, ordinary salt, perhaps iodized if you live in one of the goiter belts, pepper, a favorite spice or two, as well as a shaker of an unseasoned vegetable enzyme meat tenderizer may be desirable.

SCURVY

Many oldtimers have camped for years in the wilderness with no store grub other than a few of these staples. But over periods of more than two months or so, unless these are supplemented with some fresh food, living on them alone can cause scurvy.

If you go into the wilderness in good health, it will take usually from two to three months for even a bad diet to cause, through its shortcomings, recognizable scurvy. This, it is now realized, is a deficiency disease. If you have it, taking some Vitamin C into your body will cure you. Eating a small amount of Vitamin C regularly will ward off scurvy in the first place.

You won't find any appreciable amount of this antiscorbutic vitamin in long-bottled lime or lemon juices, in other words, nor in salt pork, nor in fresh meat that is fried to a crisp. In all these, the Vitamin C content will have deteriorated to the point of uselessness. None of these foods, consequently, will either prevent scurvy or cure scurvy.

This vitamin is found in all fresh food, be it venison, trout, wild onions, blueberries, or newly squeezed orange juice. Eating a small amount of fresh rare meat daily will, for example, prevent scurvy and every other food-deficiency disease. The vitamin C present in all such foods, however, is lessened and eventually destroyed by age, by heat, and by salt.

CANNED GOODS

Canned goods are usually ruled out except on trips when transportation is of little worry. Otherwise, their weight and bulk quickly adds up to prohibitive proportions. If you can not expect to procure fresh game or fish, however, you may care to pack along a few of the canned meats.

Canned butter remains sweet and fresh, but now there is nutritious oleomargarine whose taste soon becomes practically indistinguishable from butter and which stays good for months at ordinary temperatures.

The most economical way to heat canned vegetables is to puncture the top of the can slightly, as with a small nail, and then to place the container in a deep pan of water. This should not cover the tin, which should be left in the hot water only the brief time necessary to heat the contents thoroughly. It will then give no trouble in opening.

Nutriment that you may as well capitalize on to' the fullest, especially after packing it for miles, is wasted by emptying commercially canned vegetables into a pan for heating. But if you do this, simply warm them before using. Boiling destroys much of their food value.

Don't throw away any of the juice in the can. Containing both vitamins and minerals, it can be profitably used in sauces, gravies, and soups if you don't care to eat it all along with the vegetables. Seasoned if you want, it also makes a tasty beverage, especially in the bush.

HOW MUCH OF EACH

No one can give you much more than an idea of the quantities to take of various items. The tables near the end of the book will provide you with specific and definite information, however, by which you personally can arrive at a reasonable and practical estimate. Detailed grub lists as such are ordinarily of little value, for they seldom suit anyone but the compiler. It all depends on the number of meals you expect to make of each food, how many are to be in the party, and how much of each particular nutriment it. will take to make a satisfying portion for each individual concerned.

To determine quantities, you can experiment at home. If you want oatmeal porridge every morning, for example, find out just how much rolled oats are needed to make the breakfast you will likely eat in the woods. Just as a suggestion, take at least double the amount of sugar and sweets you would use at home, for your desire for them in camp will be out of all proportion to that in the city.

Here's a. yardstick that you may find valuable. Generally speaking, the total weight of reasonably water-free foods you will want to eat should not be less than two and one-quarter pounds per man per day. This does not include fresh vegetables and fruits. For purposes of figuring, consult the previously mentioned tables to ascertain the weight relationship of these to their dehydrated equivalents.

THE MOST WITH THE LEAST

Fat is, in calories, the most concentrated food. It is also the hardest to come by when living off the wilderness. Butter, oleomargarine, lard, and bacon drippings have more than double the amount of calories than does such a quick energy food as honey. If you plan to supplement what you carry with wild fish, meat, fruits, and vegetables, the foods to take should include a large proportion of edible fats.

Other concentrated foods that have figured conspicuously in rations where space and weight have been at extreme premium are peanut butter, chocolate, dried whole eggs, dried whole milk, and malted milk tablets. If you want a bulky starch, rice is one that cooks up appetizingly with nearly everything.

CALORIES

You can, if space and weight are at extreme premium, consider the provisioning chart near the end of this book in the light of the several fundamental dietary facts already considered and figure out how to go about packing the most nourishment with the least trouble.

Briefly, you're burning up a certain amount of energy every second. Any not supplied directly by a sufficiency of food is taken from the body's carbohydrates, fats, and proteins.

Even when you're sleeping relaxed in an agreeably warm sleeping bag, your system is consuming heat units (or calories) at the proportionate rate of about ten calories a day per pound of body weight. With a 150-pound individual, in other words, the least number of calories he'll use up each day is roundly 1500. These basal requirements diminish but little, as a matter of fact, even when a man is starving.

The more you move around and the more energy you use up in keeping warm, the more calories you consume. Even invalids increase their basic caloric needs by some twenty-five per cent. The city man who gets very little exercise uses on the average fifty per cent above his minimum requirements. To maintain his weight, therefore, such a 150-pound individual needs about 2250 calories daily.

It is reasonable, both from these facts and from experience, to generalize that a healthy and fit human being leading a robust outdoor life can require twenty calories of food a day per pound of body weight—and perhaps more, depending on his activity and on the climate. Cold weather, for instance, forces the body to put out more and more inner heat to keep itself warm. The same 150-pound city man, hunting in the north woods, can very easily use up 3000 or 4000 calories a day and trim down lean and hard on such rations.

THE LIMITING FACTOR

Available transportation will, of course, be the limiting factor in provisioning. A pack horse can balance 120 pounds or so for day after day over mountain trails, while a full-sized burro can double that. A canoe should not be loaded so deeply that it will have less than five inches of freeboard, depending on the water. This should be increased to at least six inches for windy lakes.

A husky man fresh out of the black-top jungles can without any particular difficulty shoulder about seventy-five pounds at a stretch over short portages, and he can take his time in making several such trips. He should not usually pack more than thirty-five pounds, of which twenty pounds may reasonably be food, when hiking all day for pleasure over high country.

HOW TO PACK

Dry foods such as flour, cereal, beans, salt, and sugar may be packed in small waterproof sacks which are available in a variety of sizes from most camp outfitters. You can make them, too. Each should be plainly labeled.

Dried meats may be wrapped in wax paper or aluminum foil. Lard, butter, and the like travel well in tightly closed tins such as half-pound and pound tobacco cans. Plastic jars and bottles made for carrying liquids are safer and lighter than glass for syrup, oil, and such. Powdered eggs and milk will keep indefinitely in snugly closed receptacles. Beverages in powder form should also be kept tightly covered.

VEGETABLES

Onions, potatoes, oranges, and apples, when you have the room for them, can be carried in gunny sacks. Size and color do not affect an onion's flavor or quality, but any with wet necks should be avoided. The Bermuda and Spanish types are milder than the very hard, long-keeping varieties. If you can, try a few potatoes first to make sure they're what you want. Pass up any with wastefully deep eyes. Choose oranges heavy for their size. Thinner, smoother skins usually indicate more juice. With apples, find out what variety you prefer for cooking or eating. Good color usually signifies full flavor.

Cabbage and head lettuce will keep fresh for several weeks if wrapped in wax paper and then in several layers of ordinary brown paper. Select heads that are heavy for their size. Avoid cabbage with worm holes, lettuce with discoloration or soft rot.

Eggs, cushioned with crumpled newspaper, can be packed in the more stable types of their own cartons. Fresh eggs keep several weeks. If you're camping in one spot, arranging them with the large end up will keep the yolks centered. Lettuce plus cold boiled potatoes, hard boiled eggs, onions, seasoning and mayonnaise or oil and vinegar spells potato salad.

FOOD IN CANS

If there are any cans without distinguishing markings except for paper labels and if there is a reasonable chance that your outfit may become wet, scratch the identity of the contents on an end of each tin. One of us neglected to take this precaution on a month-long river trip in eastern Canada. We had ample room, no portages, and plenty of hunting and fishing to do in preference to cooking. Therefore, we had an abundance of canned goods, packed loosely in burlap bags so we could trim the canoe more easily. After paddling mostly in rain the first day, and shipping some water in rapids besides, we had to try from then on to pick what we wanted from a perfectly blank array of tins.

The cleanest and safest place to keep the contents of an opened can, incidently, is in that can. Cover, perhaps with one of several elastic-rimmed little plastic fabrics brought for the purpose, and store away from squirrels and their like in as cool a place as possible. Unopened canned goods should preferably be kept at ordinary moderate temperatures.

KEEPING COOL

Foods can be kept cool by placing them in a bucket that is partly submerged in a shady portion of a brook, lake, or spring. Small amounts of fresh meat will keep for several days this way if air is allowed to reach it. Cooked meat, broth, mulligan, greens, etc. will stay better if covered individually. Include several yards of cheesecloth in your outfit to protect food when flies are troublesome.

You can also knock a couple of bottom strips out of a wooden box so that water will circulate through it. Weigh down the bottom of the box with large flat stones, and on these place a few perishables. If there is danger from slightly rising water, put these in containers that will safely float. It is usually a good idea to have a partially screened top for this box, which can be held in place by another stone.

ABOUT FREEZING

Some of these foods will spoil if allowed to freeze. Days these can be wrapped with bedding. Nights they can be stowed near enough to the reflected warmth of a fire. When traveling with a small outfit and sleeping out in temperatures sixty degrees and more below freezing, we have kept a few canned goods that otherwise would be burst by the cold stowed out of the way at the foot of the sleeping bag.

When food does become frozen, it preferably should not be thawed until it is to be used. The flavor and texture of fruits such as oranges are best preserved by letting them then thaw in cold water.

Frozen potatoes, which take on the look of marble, should be dipped in boiling water and their skins scraped off. Then drop them one by one in boiling water that is kept bubbling constantly. Cold weather, it happens, increases their sugar content, so you may find the resulting flavor especially appealing.

Fresh meat and fish keep well frozen. So do eggs and cheese, although their flavors are impaired.

DEHYDRATED VEGETABLES

Old-time outdoorsmen in years past did not have much use for most of the commercially dried and condensed vegetables. These were usually not appetizing, and, more important, they did not give enough energy and staying power.

But there has been a tremendous development and improvement in all dehydrated foods since the start of the second World War. Both of us have come to use them more and more since that time. Everyone who plans to camp in country where transportation is difficult, and where extreme temperatures are a problem, should certainly look into the subject of dry vegetables, for among these now are a large number of desirable additions to the staple foods.

Particularly, they afford a greater variety of tasty dishes than the average camp cook would otherwise be able to prepare, and this can mean a lot to outdoor appetites. Most of these dehydrated vegetables are extremely easy and quick to prepare, in most cases requiring only water and heat. Few now need presoaking. The majority take not more than ten to twenty minutes to get ready.

Above all, there's a tremendous saving in weight and bulk. Only the choicer portions are packaged by reputable concerns, eliminating entirely the need for any consumer waste. Zero temperatures are no longer hazards. And why stow twenty-five pounds of fresh pumpkins in your canoe when twenty-four pounds of water and one pound of yellow powder will give you the same results with a lot less bother.

Tastes vary. It is suggested that before you outfit with dehydrated products, you try out at home everything that you are considering using on your trip. Most taste very good, especially to outdoor appetites. A few, reasonably enough, you're probably not going to like. On the other hand, a dehydrated product will sometimes play a trick on you. One of us would rather have a second helping of something else than that first dish of fresh turnips. But when it comes to dehydrated turnips, these are not far from being our favorite vegetable.

Dehydrated foods may be obtained from many sporting-goods stores, from the larger outfitters which deal to a large extent via catalogues and the postal service, and from other sources often well advertised in the large outdoor magazines.

The prices, at first glance, may seem high. A better perspective is gained by figuring just how much of the edible parts of the raw material were needed to make that six ounces of powder which, in reverse, will regain its original weight and bulk once the water extracted from it has been replenished. Leon L. Bean of Freeport, Maine, sells postpaid for twenty-eight cents, to cite an example, a two-ounce jar of dehydrated onions that are the equivalent of a dozen fresh onions weighing three pounds. And all the eye-irritating and hand-scenting cleaning, peeling, and slicing are done.

VARIETIES OF DRIED FOODS

Such names as jerky, buccan, parched corn, pemmican, and pinole remind us that dehydrated foods were important on this continent back during pioneer days. The formula has not changed. It is to remove as much water from the edible part of the particular food as may be practicable. Drying by wind and sun often extracted no more than three-quarters of this moisture. Present processes sometimes leave less than a fraction of one per cent. Here are a few of the available items that you may want to consider for your next grub list.

POWDERED MILK

Whole dry milk is the camper's best substitute for fresh milk and cream. We always take it into the bush. It is especially handy in the north if only because the quality of evaporated milk, even when it does not burst the can, is injured by freezing. Besides, evaporated milk is still three-fourths water. Condensed milk is one-fourth water and nearly one-half sugar. One pound of milk powder makes one gallon of liquid milk.

Dried skim milk has all the nourishment of fresh skim milk. It has the calcium, phosphorous, iron, and other minerals, the B vitamins, natural sugar, and protein that makes liquid skim milk such an important food. Powdered whole milk has all these, plus the fat and Vitamin A found in the cream of whole milk. Adding two teaspoons of butter or margarine to a cup of reconstituted skim milk, however, will make it equal in food value to a cup of whole milk.

Containers should be kept tightly closed, as milk powder attracts moisture and becomes lumpy if long exposed to air. It also picks up odors unless care is taken, as some of our trapper friends using pack dogs here found out.

Milk powder is sometimes a little difficult to mix with water, but there are several ways to get around this. When you open the container, stir the powder and take up the amount you want lightly and without packing it down in any way. Even measures are best obtained by leveling off the top of the cup or spoon with the straight edge of a knife. Place the powder on top of the water with which it is to mix. Then stir with a spoon until smooth. The mixing can be speeded somewhat by having the water slightly warm. You can also shake the water and powder together in a tightly closed jar which will then serve as a pitcher. Dehydrated milk is now on the market that dissolves almost instantly.

Powdered milk, mixed dry with the flour, makes a valuable addition to biscuits and other breadstuffs. When you're in a hurry to get away hunting or fishing, milk powder can be mixed directly with cereals such as oatmeal and the breakfast food then cooked as indicated on the package.

POWDERED EGGS

An egg is eleven per cent waste unless you are going to bake the shells and then pulverize them as a lot of bushmen do for increasing the calcium content of their dogs' food. Seventy-four per cent of the remaining yolk and white is water. Yet a dried whole egg has practically the same food values, includes no waste whatsoever, and is only five per cent water.

Varying somewhat with different brands, one pound of dried eggs is the equivalent of three dozen or more fresh eggs. Two level tablespoons of the powder mixed with two and a half tablespoons of water usually equals one hen's egg. Used in such dishes as cakes and puddings, desiccated whole eggs can not be detected from eggs you have to crack open.

Cooked by itself, the flavor of egg powder is different from that of fresh eggs. Most of us on this continent are accustomed to the latter, so our natural reaction is that the former is inferior. But with a different premise it works around the other way, too. In any event, powdered eggs scrambled with chopped liver, kidneys, or dried meat make appetizing dishes.

Scrambled eggs made from the powder come to taste mighty good in the bush, too. Dissolve egg powder and dehydrated milk in luke-warm water to make the proportions of fresh eggs and milk you ordinarily use. Add salt, pepper, and a chunk of butter or oleo-margarine. A little flour may be used for thickening. Scrambling all this with bacon gives the dish added flavor.

POWDERED BEVERAGES

Powdered instant coffee is far preferable to the ground article for camp use. It is more economical in weight and bulk, cheaper, better lasting, and both quicker and easier to prepare. It can be made to individual order and without waste. Furthermore, there is no coffee pot with its darned spout to clean afterwards.

There is considerable difference in flavors, and you should ascertain your favorite before outfitting. Habit will do the rest. Powdered cream may be carried along, too, if you want.

If you'd like to provide for a quick pickup that you can take without the bother of stopping, as when you're hot on the trail of a moose, mix a teaspoon of your favorite powdered coffee with two teaspoons of sugar. Two or three of these combinations can each be wrapped in a bit of foil and stowed in a pocket. One, plopped dry into the mouth, will afford the same stimulation as would a cup of similarly based coffee.

Tea was something we long preferred to carry in the usual form, if only for the pleasant rite of tossing a handful of palm-measured leaves into the bubbling kettle. Besides, some of the early concentrates we tried were pretty sad. Now, however, Standard Brands, Inc., has a powdered tea on the market that mixes immediately with warm water and which tastes a lot closer to regular tea than any of the powdered coffees taste like regularly brewed coffee. This tea can't reasonably be spoiled by improper making, although I suppose some camp cook by trying to make enough for everyone at once can still somehow manage to boil it.

Fruit juices are particular treats in the bush. Lemon, for example, is also sometimes welcome with fresh rainbow trout. A number of consolidated fruit juices are now available, both dried and in concentrated liquid.

Boullion cubes and powders make hot drinks that taste good around a campfire. A lot of times you'll appreciate them a lot more than you would either tea or coffee. They are also useful for flavoring broths, soups, gravies, and stews. Other worthwhile beverage concentrates include cocoa, malted milk, and chocolate.

SWEETENING

You can buy a so-called sugar substitute, one tiny pellet of which will sweeten a cup of coffee to the same degree as would a teaspoon of sugar. Don't do it, however, unless for dietetic reasons. The little pills provide the taste, certainly, but they add no fuel to the body.

The various natural sweets, such as sugar, are one of our most quickly assimilated energy foods. Granulated white sugar provides 1,747 calories per pound. An equal weight of brown sugar contains 1,676 calories. The same amount of pure maple sugar has 1,580 calories. A pound of honey has 1,400 calories. Jams average about 1,262 calories per pound, jellies slightly less. For comparison, one pound of fresh lean venison runs about 633 calories.

THE BEAN FAMILY

The various dry beans and their cousins, the dry peas and lentils, are favorite old-time dehydrated foods. All provide hearty nourishment because of their carbohydrates which the human body transforms into energy. They contain some B vitamins. Besides such minerals as iron and calcium, they furnish protein which the body needs for building and repairing its organs and tissues. They are, furthermore, both inexpensive and fairly easy to prepare.

Although split peas and lentils may be cooked without soaking, beans and whole peas should be soaked preferably overnight. However, they can be started by first bringing the water to a boil for two minutes. After they have then been soaked for one hour, they will be ready to cook. The brief cooking, too, will guard against any souring if they are to be soaked overnight in warm weather. Cooking should be done in the same water, so as to preserve flavor and to conserve vitamins and minerals.

Canned baked beans leave me sort of cold for camp use. It is true they can be prepared "in just a minute or so," but look at the bulk and weight of the cans. I much prefer the old-fashioned dried variety with salt pork. Although it takes hours of preparation, I like to eat a big mess of genuine baked beans every three or four days in camp. They stick to the ribs. And the cooking is a good occupation for a rainy day when you have to keep the campfire going anyway.

COOKING DRY BEANS, PEAS, AND LENTILS

Start with 1 cup of	Soak in water	Add 1 teaspoon salt and boil gently	Will yield at least
Black beans	3 cups	About 2 hours	2 cups
Blackeye beans	2½ cups	½ hour	2½ cups
Cranberry beans	3 cups	About 2 hours	2 cups
Great Northern beans	2½ cups	1 to 1½ hours	2½ cups
Kidney beans	3 cups	About 2 hours	2¾ cups
Lentils	2½ cups (no soaking needed)	½ hour	2½ cups
Lima beans, large ...	2½ cups	1 hour	2½ cups
Lima beans, small ...	2½ cups	About 45 minutes	2 cups
Navy (pea) beans	3 cups	About 2½ hours	2½ cups
Peas, split	Best made into soup as they break up easily during cooking		
Peas, whole	2½ cups	1 hour	2½ cups
Pinto beans	3 cups	About 2 hours	2½ cups

PEA AND BEAN PREPARATION

But if you are bean hungry and don't want to waste that much time hanging around camp, you can heat up a meal of seasoned precooked beans now on the market in less than ten minutes.

Like the old German Erbswurst, pea and bean powders now available make excellent and filling soups in a few minutes. Stir these concentrates in hot water and bring everything to a boil, making the soup as thick as you like it.

DRIED FOODS UNLIMITED

Dried apples, pears, peaches, apricots, and prunes have long been camp favorites. So have raisins, currants, dates, and figs.

The numerous soup powders now on the market include onion, tomato, chicken, potato, vegetable, beef, and various combinations thereof. When it comes to dehydrated clam chowder, there are even the much debated Boston and the New York versions, the first rich and smooth with powdered milk and the second colorful with dehydrated tomato. There are also stews.

There are instantly mixed puddings from among which you may select chocolate, banana, lemon, butterscotch, orange, coconut, vanilla, pumpkin, maple, and even tangerine. A jelly is available that requires only water. So is a dehydrated applesauce.

A french-toast mix is for sale. So is a pizza mix. Other combinations place bran muffins, various regular breads, gingerbread, biscuits, flapjacks of one type and another, waffles and cakes at the camper's disposal. You do not even need a reflector oven for some of these latter, and there are packaged frostings that need only to be mixed and spread on.

Spaghetti, macaroni, noodles, and the like are already pretty well dehydrated, but now one can purchase different sauce mixes with which to season and flavor them. Hashes are available, of course. Both instant and quick-cooking rices will, if you want, save your time. There is a powder that, dissolved in hot water, makes maple syrup satisfying enough to even these couple of campers who've spent a good many months in northern New England.

PACKAGE THEM YOURSELF

Some items, such as bannock, you may care to package yourself at home in portions just large enough, for example, for a hot noonday lunch beside the trail. When you are ready to eat, all you need is water. Recipes suggested in the chapter on breadstuffs can be used.

A dry chocolate pudding mix can be blended at home by mixing and sifting three times: ¾ cup sifted flour, 4 cups skim or whole milk powder, 2 teaspoons salt, 2 cups of sugar, and 2 cups of cocoa. To use, add to each one cup of mix 1½ cups of water. Cook over boiling water fifteen minutes, stirring. Add a tablespoon of edible fat and a half teaspoon of vanilla flavoring, if you want, after the pudding is cooked.

Excellent for packaging all such home mixes are the small plastic bags, available very inexpensively from outfitters, which can be readily sealed by a hot iron. If you want to use them again, however, you can close them with Scotch Tape.

McNAY MARINATED STEAK

If one day on your hunting trip you'd like something a little different, especially with meat that hasn't enough age on it for your taste, you may care to try the following marinade used by Nettie and Orval McNay of Cambria, California, for steaks charred over open fires but still rare and juicy within.

Blend at home and pack, preferably in an unbreakable plastic bottle, 2 tablespoons of olive oil, ½ cup of wine vinegar, 1 rounded tablespoon of oregano, and dashes (less than ⅛ teaspoon apiece) of salt, Italian red pepper, black pepper, and cayenne pepper.

This marinade will flavor and tenderize seven or eight pounds of steak cut at least 1½ inches thick. Pour it into a flat dish in which it will lie about half an inch deep. Place the meat in this about suppertime, topping it with a thinly sliced, medium sized onion. Cover the dish. Just before you crawl into your sleeping bag, turn the meat over. The steaks will be ready the next day for searing in leaping flames and then broiling slowly over hot hardwood embers.

PINOLE

Pinole is a flour ground from parched corn. It was used by our primitive Indians and early frontiersmen as an emergency food. As such, it is still valuable. Back packers who have to strip down to minimum weight and bulk may find it useful to include some in their outfits.

Two tablespoons of pinole stirred into a cup of cold water make a rather insipid and tasteless gruel which, nevertheless, sticks to the ribs at times when you need energy. To make it more appetizing, you can add a spoonful of milk powder and another of powdered chocolate to the mixture, at the same time doubling the amount of water.

CHAPTER 28

ON A CAMPING TRIP loaves brought from some store near the fringe of the wilderness soon become stale and unappetizing. Campers enjoy hot and fresh bannocks, biscuits, sourdough bread, corn pone, muffins, buns, rolls, and other such toothsome breadstuffs more than almost any other class of foods.

These are all easily cooked over an ordinary wood fire under the open sky. You don't need a stove with a regulated oven. There's not even anything tedious or difficult about the preparations. Let's pitch in and see how these various basic staples are best prepared over a campfire.

BANNOCK AND MALE COOKS

Bakery bread is balky when it comes to molding. Its airfilled softness is unreasonably bulky when it comes to packing, especially when you consider that any of us can break himself off a chunk of warm, steaming bannock after a few minutes of practically foolproof effort.

The basic recipe for sufficient bannock for one hungry camper to use as a pusher for his mulligan follows. If you want more, just increase the ingredients proportionately.

> 1 cup white flour
> 1 teaspoon baking powder
> ¼ teaspoon salt

Mix these dry, taking all the time you need to do this thoroughly. Have everything ready to go before you add any liquid. If you are going to use a frypan, make sure it is warm and its interior greased. Why?

287

A lot of us grow up regarding cookery as some secret, scarcely to be mastered by mere man. This is often a conditioned reflex dating from hungry boyhood days when women, in usually well justified self-defense, have driven us from working kitchens. It stems in some part, our wives tell us, from girls' natural urge to impress us with their own importance in what, at that age, seems predominantly a boy's world.

There is actually no mystery about cooking. The way to attack it is like a problem in chemistry. You measure. You time. You follow other directions. Bannock furnishes a good example. Once you understand what happens with this, you'll have no further misgivings.

When you add liquid to the dry bannock mixture, it releases gas from the baking powder. This gas is the same harmless carbon dioxide that gives such beverages as ginger ale their bubbliness. Its function in breadstuffs is to raise the dough. Without some such effervescence, you'd end up with a flat, hard, dense chunk of hardtack.

It follows, of course, that you want to prevent as much of this gas as possible from escaping wastefully. You can go about this in several ways. Cold water, for example, releases the carbon dioxide much more slowly than hot, affording you more time to get the dough effectively over the fire. Some cooks go a step farther and use chilled mixing pans. It is better, too, to do the necessary stirring with a cold spoon or a clean pealed stick rather than with the warm hands. Why not just use more baking powder? The answer is that food both tastes better and is more digestible with a minimum of these acid-alkali ingredients.

Working quickly with the bannock from now on, therefore, stir in enough cold water to make a firm dough. Mold this rapidly, with as little handling as possible, into a cake about one-inch thick. If you like crust, leave a doughnutlike hole in the center. Dust the sticky loaf lightly with plain flour, so that it'll handle better, and lay it in the hot pan.

Hold it over the fire until a crust forms on the bottom, rotating the pan a little so that the loaf will shift of its own weight and not become stuck to the metal. Once the dough has hardened enough so that it will hold together, you can turn it over. This, if you've practiced a bit and have the confidence to flip high enough, you can do with a slight swing of the arm and snap of the wrist. You can also use a spatula, holding the loaf long enough to invert the frypan over its uncooked top and then neatly turning both together.

It is usually easier at this stage, however, to prop the pan at a steep angle in front of your fire so that the loaf will receive a lot of heat on top and bake some more. Once crust has been formed all around, you can, if you want, turn the bannock over a few times until it has baked evenly on both sides to a rich golden brown.

After you've been cooking bannock awhile, you can tap it with a finger and gauge by the sound if it is done. In the meantime, you may want to test by shoving in a toothpick or twig. If any dough adheres, the loaf needs more heat. Cooking can be done in about fifteen minutes. If you have other jobs to do around camp, twice that time a little farther from the heat will allow the bannock to crisp more evenly.

BAKING POWDER

Some outdoorsmen tend to use more than one teaspoon of baking powder for each cup of flour. Strengths of this manufactured leavening agent vary. Furthermore, baking powder tends to become weaker with age, particularly if the container is not kept tightly closed and in a dry place.

Directions on the particular can, if the contents are fresh, experimentation if they are not, will provide a reasonable yardstick. The ideal, so far as taste and digestion are concerned, is to use the smallest amount of baking powder that will raise the breadstuff enough for your liking.

OTHER COOKING METHODS

Instead of slanting the pan in front of the fire, you can use an existing boulder or build a wall of large rocks about a foot from the blaze. When the reflecting surface is piping hot, lean the pan with its back to this and its face to the conflagration.

You can dig a pit in front of the fire, rake some red coals into it, and place the frypan in this where it will be heated by the embers below and by the blazing forelog of the fire above.

When you have a lot of baking to do with a limited amount of utensils, as soon as a loaf gets a firm crust on each side, you can remove it from the pan and lean it vertically on the ground close to the fire. In all these instances, the forelog of your fire should be a well burning one several inches off the ground, so that it will blaze upwards with a fairly vertical flame.

REFLECTOR BAKER

Light and compact varieties of the reflector baker, which our ancestors used for baking in front of open fireplaces, are valuable outdoor equipment. The modern articles for campers are made of brightly reflecting metals such as aluminum, and they fold flat for easier carrying. Because these operate on the principle of reflecting heat to all parts of the food being cooked, their efficiency diminishes when they are allowed to rust or to become dull. Outfitters supply these in large sizes which will do for parties of four or five.* You can buy one-man models, too.

Such a portable oven presents the easiest and most convenient way of baking and roasting with a wood fire. Not only breads and biscuits, but fish and game as well, come out appetizing. You simply stand the reflector before a blazing fire. The heat you regulate merely by moving the contraption toward or away from the warmth. Food is placed in a usually greased pan on the shelf of the reflector oven and occasionally turned end for end so that the cooking will be more uniform.

Here is a fine way to cook bannock in loaf form. For instance, you want some handy slices between which to sandwich cold venision for the next day's hunt. Use the same basic recipe, but mold the :lough into an inch-and-a-half thick loaf about nine inches long and five inches wide. Dust this lightly with flour. Lay it in the warmed and greased bake pan, and shove this into the oven. Bake with frequent turnings until you get a good looking crust and the testing sliver comes out without any dough adhering.

HOT TRAIL BREAD

Fresh bannock is a simple thing to cook on the trail, even though the nearest pan may be a dozen miles away in camp. The handiest method is to mix the dry ingredients before leaving the base of supplies. The same basic recipe will do. The mixture may be carried in a small, tightly closed plastic bag.

After the fire is going and everything else is ready, mix in enough water quickly to make a firm dough. If the bag is waterproof and large enough, the simplest procedure is to roll down the sides and use it as a mixing bowl. A clean section of bark will do, however.

Wind this dough on a stick, so trimmed that several projecting stubs of branches will keep the ribbon in place. A particularly sweet wood for the job is birch. The evergreens may give the dough a predominant taste which, although entirely wholesome, you may not personally care for. The bitterish flavor sometimes imparted by poplar and willow is also harmless although to some unpleasant.

---

* Large size from D. T. Abercrombie Co. Large and small size from Smilie Outfits. See appendix.

Baking with folding aluminum reflector baker.

Particularly in cold weather you may want to preheat the stick before using it.

We like to start this trail bread by holding the ribboned bannock in ardent heat, occasionally turning it, for a couple of minutes Once a crust has been formed, it may be leaned between the fringes of the fire and some reflecting surface, such as a log or cliff, for the fifteen minutes or so required to form a tasty brown ribbon. Or you can just shove one end of the stick into the ground beside the heat and turn this holder now and then while readying the rest of the meal.

VARYING A RECIPE

Basic recipes may be varied in innumerable ways. Substituting milk for water, to give one example, will improve both the taste and the food value of bannock. So will the addition of powdered milk to the dry ingredients. For every cup of flour, stir in the amount of powdered milk that it would take to make a half cup of liquid milk. Bannock so prepared will turn a more golden brown.

A little whole egg powder, say the equivalent of one egg for every two cups of flour, will add richness. Some like to include a tablespoon of sugar with each cup of flour. Pressing and stirring a tablespoon of shortening per cup of flour among the dry ingredients helps any bannock. This is especially true in cold weather when an even greater proportion of fat will prevent the breadstuff from freezing hard on cold trails. The shortening may be butter, oleomargarine, commercial lard, any of the hydrogenated vegetable oils, bacon drippings, or grease rendered from animal fats.

Such fruits as raisins, currants, and blueberries make campfire bread tastier and more nutritious, although their inclusion requires a bit more baking powder to raise the loaf. Spices, especially cinnamon and nutmeg, are particularly zestful when their odors mingle with those of conifers and of wood smoke. A few of us occasionally look forward to the pumpernickel effect that can be imparted to camp breads by dusting them with the tiny black seeds of the pigweed, more formally known as lamb's quarter.

Bannock, in any event, never tastes better than it does when eaten fresh and hot after a hard day in the open. It should then be broken apart, not cut with a knife. A cold bannock sliced in half, however, buttered, and made into a man's size sandwich with plenty of wild meat in between is the best lunch ever.

BISCUITS

For biscuits, follow the basic bannock recipe. Into those dry ingredients, work two tablespoons of one of the edible shortenings among which we like none better than the pure white grease rendered from the fat of a black bear. Using a spoon or fork, rub the shortening in thoroughly. Then add enough water or milk to make quickly a thick dough just soft enough to be handled easily. If it becomes too sticky, add a little more flour.

Without wasting time, flatten the dough out about three-fourths of an inch thick. A cold bottle makes a good rolling pin if you want one. From this sheet of dough, stamp out the biscuits. The top of the baking powder tin will serve as a cutter, or with a knife you can make small squares. Dust each with flour. Place on a lightly greased pan or metal plate and bake until a rich brown, by which time they should have risen about two inches high. You may have to turn each biscuit carefully several times during the process to assure even cooking.

DUMPLINGS

If you are making a mulligan or other stew, wait until it is nearly done and then bring it to a bubbling boil. Take either the bannock or the biscuit recipe and quickly drop gobs of the resulting dough from tablespoon on top of the stew.

Cover the pot and allow the contents to continue boiling. The dumplings will be soft, puffy, and ready for eating in ten or twelve minutes. If you prefer, however, keep them on until they taste right to you, taking into account that those left in the hot liquor after the first servings have been ladled out will continue to cook. We only make enough of these at a time to eat at one sitting.

CORN BREAD

Steaming hot chunks of yellow corn bread, particularly when eaten in the flickering ingratiating glow of a campfire, helps one to appreciate more fully what a boon is this silk-eared vegetable which our pioneer ancestors discovered in use in this New World. Follow either the bannock or biscuit recipe, using corn meal and flour mixed in even amounts instead of straight flour. Add a fresh egg or its equivalent in powdered whole egg. However, naturally sweet corn meal needs no added sugar. Mold the dough into a sheet about three-fourths of an inch thick, and cook like biscuits in a reflector baker.

SNOW FOR EGGS

In the North when we have lacked eggs for this and other bread-stuffs, we have successfully used snow instead. Fresh dry snow is best for this purpose. It is rapidly stirred in just before the bread-stuff is put over the heat. It must not be allowed to melt until the cooking is underway, for its function is entirely mechanical.

The flakes of snow hold the ingredients apart, a physical effect that is heightened when warmth expands the minute blobs of moisture to steam. Cooked while these are so separated, such bread-stuffs come out airy and light. Egg is able to accomplish the same end result, as you can appreciate by watching the way an egg readily beats up into air-holding froth whose elasticity heightens its raising and spacing powers. Two heaping tablespoons of fresh dry snow will take the place of every one egg in a batter.

HOT CAKES

Use the preceding bannock, biscuit, or corn bread recipe. Add slightly more liquid, however, so as to make a dough that will pour lazily from a large spoon. Have your frypan hot. Grease it very lightly, just swiping it, for instance, with a piece of bacon rind. Incidentally, one of us has eaten these with a prospector who, having forgotten his skillet, used a long handled shovel instead, first scouring it in sand and then dousing it in the Peace River. The results were equally good.

Drop a spoonful on your pan or other receptacle to form each cake. Place or hold over hot coals until small bubbles form on the top of these. Then turn each over to brown on the other side. For dessert, try a stack of four or five of these, one atop of the other, each heavily buttered and sugared. Delicious!

SELF-RAISING FLOURS

Many of the prepared mixes are handy for camp use. A good plan is to try first, at home, any you figure you may care to pack into the bush, although after a little experience a reasonable idea of the finished product usually can be gleaned from the directions and suggestions on the packages.

Among the mixes available are those which will turn out hot rolls of many varieties including the Parker House favorites, cakes innumerable, pie crusts which can be filled either with dehydrated fruits or wild berries, numerous cookies, waffles, pancakes, muffins, cupcakes, pizza, and a gingerbread with which we both occasionally enjoy topping off an outdoor meal. Some companies even prepare special mixes for use in high altitudes.

HOMEMADE DRY MIXES

You can, of course, make and package your own dry mixes. Plastic bags, which can be sealed by a hot iron or Scotch Tape, may be secured from outfitters and used for this latter purpose. If space is no particular problem, it will be even better to store these mixes in jars or cans so as to avoid packing them down. In any event, they should be kept tightly covered. If the powder does become massed together, loosen it before use by lightly stirring, shaking, or sifting.

In these recipes, the nonfat dry milk keeps somewhat better than does the whole-milk powder, although we have used both under the most primitive conditions for years and have never had any difficulty with either.

For a dry biscuit mix, sift together several times eight cups of already sifted flour, one cup of whole or nonfat dry milk, one-quarter cup baking powder, and three teaspoons salt. A cup of one of the commercial shortenings that requires no refrigeration, sold under various brand names, may be cut or rubbed in at this time, or a cup of any edible fat may be so added later.

For biscuits, add to every one cup of this mix one-third cup of water, sufficient to make a soft dough. Knead this swiftly, patting or rolling it to the desired thickness. Cut with a handy can top. Bake in the reflector oven until done.

In berry season, some shortcake may be a pleasant change. You can make it from this same dry biscuit mix, augmented if you want by one tablespoon of sugar. Add the one-third of a cup of fluid necessary to make a soft dough. Flatten this to one-quarter inch thickness and either cut out squares with a knife or punch out ovals with something such as a can top.

Brush half of these with melted buter or oleomargarine. Cover each with one of the remaining pieces. Bake in the reflector oven. Then butter and add the berries or some other fruit. One cup of the dry mix makes six medium-sized shortcakes.

SPOON BREAD

This is the recipe that Colonel Whelen's daughter uses for spoon bread that is good eaten with butter along with the main meal instead of a vegetable. Or it can be served with syrup to provide a special treat for dessert.

½ cup corn meal
2 cups milk
3 eggs
½ teaspoon baking powder
1 tablespoon melted butter
1 teaspoon salt

Scald the milk by heating it nearly to the boiling point. Stir in the corn meal very gradually. Continue cooking in the kettle for several minutes, stirring so as to avoid scorching. Then add the baking powder, salt, melted butter, and the yolks of eggs beaten until light. Fold in the whites of eggs, beaten stiff.

Pour the now completed batter into a buttered baking dish, of such size that the mixture will lie about two inches deep. Bake for thirty minutes or more in the reflector oven, until the spoon bread is roofed with a nice thick brown crust.

If you do not have fresh milk, powdered whole milk will do. In the absence of fresh eggs, stir in an equivalent amount of powdered whole eggs.

HUSH PUPPIES

2 cups yellow corn meal
¾ cup flour
2½ teaspoons baking powder
1 teaspoon salt

Mix these ingredients and add one cup of water to form a medium thick dough. Drop big gobs of the dough into deep hot lard or, better still, into hot peanut oil. Cook until a rich brown. These are good to eat with fresh fish. In fact, some prefer to cook them in lard in which fish and perhaps onions have previously been fried.

BREAD IN THE NORTH

It is an old dodge in the whitened wildernesses at the top of the continent to keep bread fresh by freezing. A lot of trappers and prospectors set aside a baking day at the start of the winter. Perhaps a hundred loaves of bread may go through the oven at this time.

These are cooled to give the steam time to evaporate. Then each loaf is either individually wrapped in paper or lodged in a paper bag and put out in the cold to freeze. There they stay, protected from animals. If a chinook makes everything balmy, they may be buried temporarily in a snowbank.

The loaves are brought in one by one as needed. Each is then quickly thawed and at the same time lightly toasted in the oven, whereupon it recaptures the aroma and the taste of freshly baked bread.

SOURDOUGH BREAD

When a certain musical show participant and producer married one of these two writers and went to live in the wilderness of northern British Columbia, the most trouble she had with cooking was in learning how to make flour, salt, sugar, water, and leavening come out bread. But let Vena Angier tell it for herself:

"Sourdough bread was what I wanted, a seventy-year-old trapper, who is still our nearest neighbor, eventually told me. Oldtimers in the gold lands of the north are still called sourdoughs, the name borrowed directly from that mining-camp bread that early proved its ability to rise in any temperature short of freezing. On very cold nights, though, this particular sourdough admitted seriously, he still takes the batter to bed with him.

"During the gold-rush days at the turn of the century, when gravel punchers stampeded past our Peace River homesite toward where nuggets lay yellow and beckoning beneath the aurora polaris, prospectors used to bake sourdough bread in the shallow steel vessels they used for panning gold. Some of them still do, for that matter.

"A shallow hole was scooped in the ground, often in the heat-retaining sand of a stream bank. A fire was allowed to burn to coals in this cavity. Dough, in the meantime, was rising between two gold pans. Some of the glowing embers and hot sand were shoveled out of the hole. The pans were sunk in the depression and covered with the hot residue. One hour's cooking, in this makeshift Dutch oven, was generally the minimum. The bread wouldn't burn if allowed to remain longer. The crust would just thicken and become more golden.

"A simple bush method for starting the sourings which are necessary for this breadstuff. Dudley Shaw said, is to mix four cups of flour with enough warm water to make a thick creamy batter. Two tablespoons of sugar may be added. So may two teaspoons of salt.

The mixture should be placed in a warm spot for upwards of two days to sour. Yeast cake dissolved in warm water can be introduced to hasten the fermentation which will then usually take place overnight. Some find it handy to include, instead, a tablespoon of some cooking acid such as vinegar, also used to revive aged sourings.

" 'Cover the sourings loosely,' Dudley cautioned cheerily, 'or they'll explode frightfully all over the place. Makes a ghastly mess. Remember they bubble copiously to better than double size, so use a container that's vast enough. A lard pail's our favorite up in these jungles.'

"The initial loaves are made, Dudley went on, by mixing three-fourths of this sourdough with a tablespoon of melted fat and a cup of flour in which a teaspoon of baking soda has been well stirred. Then add whatever additional flour may be necessary to make a smoothly kneading dough.

" 'Keep attacking,' the trapper cautioned, eyes blinking amiably behind thick lensed spectacles. 'Don't gentle it. That is where most women make their mistake. Too much pushing and pressing lets the gas escape that's needed to raise the stuff. Just bang the dough together in a hurry, cut off loaves to fit your pans, and put them in a warm place to raise.'

"The batch, once it has plumped out to double size, should be baked from forty minutes to one hour in a warm oven of one sort or another that is, preferably, hottest the first fifteen minutes. Baking should redouble the size of the loaves. One tested 'in the usual way.' He elucidated that the usual way is to wait until the loaves seem crisply brown, then to jab in a straw. If the bread is done, the straw comes out dry and at least as clean as it was when inserted.

" 'How about the quarter of the sourdough I don't use?' I inquired, scribbling down the formula.

"That would be my start for further sourdough if it weren't for something else, the trapper told me. These sourings I could keep going by dropping in chunks or left over bread, flippers, and such, or just plain flour and water. About a cup should always be left out to keep going with.

"When the mixture got too rampageous, a touch of baking soda would gentle it. I should not use soda too copiously, though, or I'd bog down the noble sourdough for good. As a matter of fact, if too much soda is used, it makes the breadstuff yellowish. But if you don't get in enough, then the food tastes sour. A certain amount of experience is required, in other words.

" 'That would be your start for future sourdough," Dudley Shaw said friendly, 'if it weren't for the fact that I'm going to give you some sourings that are fourteen years old.'

" 'Fourteen years?' I gasped. 'Isn't that a lot?'

" 'They've just started nicely,' Dudley beamed proudly."

BASIC
OUTDOOR
COOKERY

CHAPTER 29

ALTHOUGH I SPENT all my boyhood summers camping, hunting, and fishing in the Adirondack and Allegheny Mountains, it was not until I went West at the turn of the century that I learned anything much about camp cooking.

Then I fell in with one of the very last of the old mountain men of the breed of Jim Bridger and Bill Williams. Bones Andrews, with whom I later hunted and prospected, was born in Pike County, Missouri, like so many of the early western pioneers. He learned to cook there in his mother's cabin, mostly with what the country provided in those early days. He picked up the rest of his culinary lore from his trapper associates in the Rockies all the way from old Mexico to Alaska.

It has been the personal experience of us both that the trappers, prospectors, and other outdoorsmen of this continent's western mountain country have it all over most easterners when it comes to cooking. For one thing, they are more accustomed to baching it and to doing all their own work all the time. The majority of the easterners, except for the short periods they may be in the bush each year, spend their time at home where they rely on their women folk to handle the kitchen chores.

THE OPEN FIRE

All but a very small proportion of our own outdoor cooking has been done over the campfire. Food tastes so much better when it is prepared over the red gleaming warmth of wild wood. It is so easy to regulate the open cooking fire so as to take advantage of quick roaring heat, or to provide a ruddy bed of coals that will break ardently apart for broiling, or to conjure up such fringe benefits that a dumpling-festooned mulligan will either simmer or just keep temptingly warm.

When you want to start those food smells tantalizing your sensibilities in a hurry, the various dry softwoods, especially when split, will chortle into a quickly flaring blaze. For steadier and more conservative ardor, the hardwoods are more satisfactory. For an enduring expanse of glowing coals, you will probably choose such fuels as oak, hickory, and ash. Or perhaps you'll split up one of the sweetly black-smoking birches with its inherently hot, fiery enthusiasm even when green.

SUBSTITUTION

Here are a few tried and proved recipes that will provide you with good basic meals, and with little effort or fuss. Using them as a foundation, you will be able to figure out numerous others so as to take advantage of the materials you may have at hand. Don't be afraid to substitute. And, by the way, the old idea that some combinations of food, such as lobsters and milk, may be injurious has long ago been debunked.

All kinds of combinations suggest themselves to the wilderness camper. For example, what housewife would think of serving her men a one-dish breakfast made by putting salt, sugar, butter, and either minced dates or apricots into hot water, bringing this to a boil, and then stirring in enough oatmeal to make a fairly thick mush. Yet outdoorsmen will gobble it with gusto.

SUBSTITUTE MAPLE SYRUP

You can even make a maple syrup substitute for your pancakes that's so much like the real article that no one ever credits this fact until he's made a portion himself. Start by boiling six or seven medium sized potatoes with two cups of water until but a single cup of liquid remains. Take out the potatoes for table use.

Stirring until the fluid commences once more to boil, pour in one cup of white sugar and another of brown. Place this on the fringes of the fire to cool. The first spoonful you taste will seem to justify your suspicions. The concoction has to be bottled and tucked away for a couple of days to age. Try it again at the end of that time and see if you, too, aren't amazed.

RICE

Rice, as you know, swells to beat the band. Wash a cup of this grain in cold water unless directions with the particular brand you are using instruct to the contrary. Then pour the seeds gradually

Brad Angier getting ready for chow

into a pot containing at least a quart and a half of boiling salted water. Let it boil hard for twenty minutes.

Watching out for steam, hold the cover on and pour off all the liquid. This contains nutritious starch and minerals and may well be used in broth or mulligan. Place the kettle to the side of the fire where the rice will steam without danger of scorching and where it will keep hot until ready.

Don't get started stirring rice, incidentally. We never cook this dish but what we are reminded of a recipe for rice pudding that we once read somewhere. Part of the instructions went: "Simmer on the back of the stove for six hours, stirring every few minutes from the bottom so the rice will not stick."

My own rice pudding recipe is based on: 2 cups cooked rice, 3 cups reconstituted whole milk, 1 tablespoon egg powder in a little water, 1/3 cup sugar, ½ teaspoon salt, ½ cup raisins, and your own idea of enough cinnamon or nutmeg. Grease a deep pan well with butter or lard, combine all the ingredients, and bake in an oven or reflector baker with moderate heat about half an hour until a light brown crust forms on top.

POTATOES

One good way to cook this native American vegetable is to bake the large ones in their skins in hot ashes, not glowing coals, until they have become pretty well blackened on the outside. Then break in half and eat with butter and salt.

The most tasty way I know of to fry potatoes is first to boil them peeled for twenty minutes, then to slice them into three-quarter-inch cubes. Have a quarter-inch of lard or other cooking fat sizzling in the frypan. Put in several onions that have been chopped up fine. Before these aromatic little bits have become much more than a light brown, add the cubed potatoes while the grease is still very hot.

Now remove the frypan to a part of the fire where the fat will just simmer. Cover with a lid or tin plate. Let the contents bubble and cook in their own steam, occasionally giving them a turn with a spoon. Add salt and plenty of black pepper. Serve just before the potatoes begin to get hard on the outside.

HASH

Chop up cooked meat with an equal quantity of boiled potatoes. Salt and pepper to taste, and add one or all of the following: chopped onion, celery or a little celery salt, and dry parsley flakes. Moisten the mixture with soup stock, bouillon, thin milk, or water. Spread thick on a greased pan. Set over slow heat for twenty minutes until the bottom of the hash is well browned, or bake in a reflector baker with moderate heat.

BAKED BEANS

Take three cups of dried navy beans. Pick out any small pebbles you may find. Soak the beans overnight in cold water, and the next morning put to boil in a large kettle with a tablespoon of salt. Boil for about two and one-half hours, adding boiling water as the fluid level goes down.

Then drop in about a dozen one-inch cubes of salt pork or bacon with the rind on it. Keep bubbling for about an hour and a half more or until the individual beans are soft but not mushy. You have been keeping about two inches of water on top of the beans in the kettle. This water is now the finest of bean soup. Pour most of it into another container and serve while hot, but leave enough so that the beans are still quite damp.

Then, usually the next day, place these beans about two inches deep in a pan, shift the cubes of pork or bacon to the top, sprinkle a little sugar over the entire surface, and bake in a reflector baker or oven for an hour or more, until they become a little brown on top.

SOUTHERN FRIED GROUSE

Either quarter the grouse, ptarmigan, or similar bird, or cut into small pieces. Roll in flour mixed with a little salt and pepper. Fry in sizzling hot deep fat, turning once during cooking, until well browned. Be sure to have fat hot and sputtering as you put each piece in.

EGGS, ONIONS, AND TOMATO

This nourishing and easily digestible dish with a mild and provocatively elusive flavor has always been a success whenever we've cooked it, partly because its preparation is both simple and swift. It's particularly good when someone hauls into camp late. Proportions, which in any event are not stringent, may be varied according to appetites.

For two campers, brown a couple of sliced or diced medium-sized onions with a little grease in a frypan. When these have been cooked to a dark blandness, add a small can of tomatoes. Let these become hot. Then break in six eggs. Season with salt and pepper. If you have some parsley flakes, add a sprinkle of these as well. Keep scrambling over a moderate fire until fairly dry.

BUSH ICE CREAM

Ice cream is one of the quickest and easiest of all foods to make in the bush, especially right after a fresh snow. Best for the purpose are fine dry flakes. Empty a can of evaporated milk into a large pot or bowl. A similar amount of reconstituted dry milk will do as well. Add two tablespoons of sugar and some flavoring. Lemon or one of the other extracts will serve. So will cocoa, powdered coffee, chocolate malted milk powder, and the like.

Then go outdoors and stir in clean snow to taste. More sugar and flavoring may be added at the end if you want. Three varieties that come out especialy well, if you happen to like them, are the universally favored vanilla, chocolate with overtones of peppermint extract, and banana made with that particular extract.

TROUT AND SIMILAR FISH

Open and clean as soon after catching as possible, saving the hearts, livers, and any roe. Unless you object to them too strenuously, leave on the head and certainly the tail where, in that order, lies by far the sweetest meat. Keep cool, dry, and well ventilated.

Cook over medium heat, preferably in butter, until the meat flakes away from the bone. The heart, liver, and any ova will then also be well done and tender. Transfer to a hot plate and, if you want, salt if the butter hasn't already taken care of that sufficiently.

FISH GENERALLY

The way you cook fish may be determined to some extent by how fat they are. The plumper ones such as salmon, lake trout, ling, and whitefish are best for baking in a reflector baker or Dutch oven and for broiling over the bright coals of a campfire.

Leaner fish such as pike, bass, perch and greyling, are preferable for chowders and for general boiling because they remain firmer. They may also be baked or grilled if they are basted with melted fat. Strips of salt pork or bacon will take care of this, too. All fish is suitable for frying. The main thing is not to overcook it. When the flesh is easily flaked, the fish is done.

Steaks, incidentally, are slabs cut at right angles to the backbone. Fillets are slices, boneless or nearly so, cut lengthwise down along the ribs away from the backbone.

FISH CHOWDER

You can prepare for this before you take to the woods by packing and sealing dehydrated equivalents of the following or similar ingredients, except for salt pork and fish, in a plastic bag, or you can make a quart of it on the spot with:

       1 cup diced potatoes
       ½ cup diced carrots
       2 tablespoons diced salt pork
       1 tablespoon chopped onion
       ½ cup dry milk, whole or nonfat
       1½ tablespoons flour
       2 cups liquid (cooking liquid from vegetables plus
           water or fluid milk)
       2 cups flaked cooked fish

Cook potatoes and carrots until tender in enough boiling water to cover. Drain and save liquid. Fry salt pork until crisp, adding onion for the last few minutes.

Add milk powder and flour to the liquid and beat until smooth. Cook over low heat, stirring constantly until slightly thickened. Then combine all ingredients and heat thoroughly.

FISH CAKES

       1½ cups cooked fish
       1 small onion, chopped fine
       3 cups diced, boiled potatoes
       ½ teaspoon salt
       ¼ teaspoon black pepper
       1 tablespoon dried egg in ½ cup water
       2 tablespoons butter or bacon fat

Fry the onion a little. Then mix with fish, potatoes and seasoning. Stir in the egg, water, and edible fat. Form into small cakes ¾ inch thick and fry in a greased pan or in hot deep fat.

TRAVELING WINTER TRAILS

On an outdoor trip anywhere, especially across ice and snow in weather so cold that the breath makes a continual fog, food is a consideration second only to water. The more drastic the conditions that may be encountered, the more essential it will be to plan the meals intelligently beforehand.

On short enough journeys, time and effort on the trail can be saved by cooking as much of the food as possible before heading into the whitened wilderness. You may find it worthwhile too, to keep ahead of your appetite all the way by cooking the next day's meals at the previous night's camp. This is particularly true in regions where fuel is scarce, as in the northern Land of Little Sticks.

Certain dried foods, augmented so as better to meet winter conditions, may as well be carried ready mixed. Flour, baking powder, salt, and sugar in proportions for individual bannocks can be stowed in closed containers. In extremely cold weather, use more than the accustomed amount of shortening in these bannocks to provide extra nourishment and to prevent the breadstuff from freezing hard. You'll appreciate a larger proportion of sugar, too.

Here are a few suggestions for rations for winter trails, tried out by one or both of us above the frost-furred tree line in tall mountain country or up under the aurora borealis in the Far North. They are recommended, too, by the world's oldest trading corporation for use by its own men in and about the some two hundred red-roofed trading posts it still operates in the North. We are speaking, of course, of the H.B.C. which was a century old before these United States were more than an absent-minded dent in one of Paul Revere's teapots.

ONE-DISH BEAN STEW

Bean stew makes a nourishing and palatable dish, particularly when the still white cold is so extreme that smoke, instead of coiling, spreads above the campfire like an enormous banner. The preparation of this one-dish meal is commenced back at the base by soaking dried beans overnight. Partially bake or boil these. Mix in any kind of fresh or canned meat cut into very small segments. Add canned tomatoes. Flavor with molasses, spices, and if you want some beef extract.

Cook until the beans and meat are well done. Then pour the mixture into a shallow pan and allow to freeze. When frozen, break into small pieces and carry in a cotton bag. To use, simply heat up what you want in a pan along with a little water.

When carrying frozen foods under such conditions, be sure to keep them frozen hard until they are required for use. Do not take any more of an item than you immediately require into a heated place. Leave the remainder in the cold, out of the way of hungry animals both small and large.

CARRYING FOOD IN COLD WEATHER

Any bacon should be sliced before one sets off on such a trip. It may also be partly cooked beforehand. The slices, in either event, can be frozen separately and carried this way until needed. Potatoes freeze into something resembling marble, so if you want to pack some of these along, boil them until they are a bit on the hard side. Slice thinly and put out to freeze in individual pieces. Carry the frozen chips in a cotton food sack. They will go well heated in the fat from fried bacon.

MEAT BALLS

Meat balls will provide another one-dish repast. Mince up venison or any kind of meat. Add a little milk, some bread crumbs, potatoes, any other vegetables you want, and whatever spices you prefer. We like to include grated cheese and tomato catsup. Shape into flattened meat balls. Partially cook and then freeze these. They will be ready to eat on short notice on the trail or in camp. Merely thaw them out and heat them in a pan with some water. You can prepare fish balls in the same general manner, substituting fresh or canned fish for the meat.

H.B.C. PLUM PUDDING

If you're going to be hunting in the bush with a friend or two on Thanksgiving and want to have something a little special for that occasion, you may be interested in going prepared to make one of the aromatic Hudson's Bay Company puddings that—traditionally varying in accordance to what ingredients have been at hand—have crowned many a holiday feast in the silent places since the Company was founded 2d May, 1670.

The following components can be mixed at home and sealed in a plastic container:

4 cups flour
4 teaspoons baking powder

½ teaspoon cinnamon
½ teaspoon nutmeg
1 cup brown sugar
½-cup white sugar
¼ cup fine mixed peel
2 cups seedless raisins
1 cup currants
4 tablespoons whole egg powder
6 tablespoons whole milk powder
¼ teaspoon powdered lemon juice

When the memorable day arrives, shake and stir all these ingredients together along with two cups of minced suet. This can be either beef suet brought for the occasion or animal suet obtained on the spot. Add sufficient water to make a cake batter. You will have also carried along a heavy cotton bag and this you will have just wrung out in hot water and sprinkled inside with flour. Pour the batter into this. Tie the top tightly, leaving plenty of room for expansion.

Place this immediately in a pot filled with suffiicent boiling water to cover. Keep it boiling for three hours, turning the bag upside down when the pudding starts to harden so that all the fruit will not settle to the bottom. As the cooking continues, shift the bag occasionally so that it will not scorch against the sides of the receptacle. At the end, dip this cloth container briefly in cold water and carefully remove the fabric so as not to break or crumble the pudding.

Serve this plum pudding hot with some appropriate sauce. Butter and sugar, flavored with some spice such as nutmeg or an extract such as lemon powder, will suffice. So will the thick juice from boiled dehydrated fruit. Everytime I enjoy one of these in the bush, I think of Voltaire acidly describing the North two centuries ago as, "A patch of snow inhabited by barbarians, bear, and beaver." He should have seen the top of the continent when it's in a holiday mood.

CHAPTER 30

WATER and WASHING

WATER FROM SPRINGS and streams that flow from clean and uninhabited North American country can usually be considered safe for drinking and cooking. In the wilderness lake regions of northern United States and Canada, the water from these bodies, unless there are many camps on the shores or along the courses running into them, is also usually pure. This does not always hold true, however. Even if it did, we are not always familiar enough with a region to know what the condition of a watershed may be a short distance away.

Whenever you have the slightest doubt about whether or not water is pure, it should be treated as though unsafe. This includes not only the water you drink. It also involves the water you use for cooking and for washing both cooking utensils and your person.

Cooking and eating implements that have been washed in contaminated water can carry disease germs even though the cooking water is pure or is boiled in the process of cooking. In some localities, uncooked vegetables such as lettuce and radishes are unsafe. Water can often be cleared by letting it seep into a hole dug a few feet from a shore, but such filtration does not assure purity.

PURIFYING WATER

The easiest and most practical way to sterilize doubtful water is to boil it. At or near sea level, hard boiling for five minutes will do the job. For every additional one thousand feet altitude increase the boiling time one minute.

CHLORINE

Or you can use halazone tablets which may be secured at most sporting goods stores. A small two-ounce bottle containing one hundred tablets costs about fifty cents and takes up less room than a 12-gauge shell. Because this process depends on the release of chlorine gas, the tablets should be fresh and the container kept tightly closed.

Dissolve one tablet in a quart of water and let it stand for half an hour. If the water is murky or particularly doubtful, both the time and the number of tablets should be doubled. Slosh a little of this water over the lips of the container after the first few minutes to sterilize these. Then cover the receptacle as tightly as possible.

IODINE WATER PURIFICATION TABLETS

In Mexico and other semitropical and tropical regions, chlorine-releasing compounds can not be depended upon. Water should either be boiled or, when this is not convenient, treated with Iodine Water Purification Tablets. These may be secured from Wallace and Tiernan, Inc., 25 Main Street, Belleville, New Jersey. This manufacturer sells fifty tablets for one dollar.

Iodine Water Purification Tablets, containing the active ingredient Tetraglycine Hydroperiodide, were developed by Harvard University working on a project for the National Research Council. Wallace & Tiernan, Inc., collaborating with Harvard, synthesized the compound and manufactures the tablets. They have been adopted in the United States as standard for the Armed Services.

These tablets are effective against all the common water-borne bacteria as well as the Cysts of Endemoeba Histolytica and the Cercariae of Schistosomiasis. As manufactured by Wallace & Tiernan, they are packaged fifty tablets in a glass bottle with a wax sealed cap. Each tablet is slightly less than a quarter inch in diameter and weighs approximately 120 milligrams. Upon addition to water, each tablet liberates eight milligrams of iodine which acts as a water purification agent. One tablet will purify one quart of water.

It is important to keep these tablets dry. The bottle therefore, should always be kept tightly capped. Following are instructions for use:

1. Add 1 tablet to one quart of water in container with cap.
2. Wait 3 minutes.
3. Shake water thoroughly and allow a little water to leak out to disinfect the screw threads. Then tighten container cap.
4. Wait 10 minutes before drinking or adding beverage powders. If water is very cold, wait 20 minutes.
5. If water contains rotting vegetation or is dirty and discolored, use 2 tablets per quart.
6. Be sure that the iodine-treated water disinfects any part of the container which will come in contact with the drinker's mouth.

A COMMON MISTAKE ABOUT LIQUOR

We've all seen individuals drinking water from dubious sources with the idea that the liquor they were adding to it rendered it safe. This is not the case. The addition of alcohol to water does not rid the latter of germs.

ICE

Ice is no more pure than was the water from which it was frozen. Although heat destroys bacteria and parasites, cold very definitely does not.

COOLING WATER

In warm country, water may be chilled without ice to a temperature that makes it fairly palatable by the use of water-cooling bags. These hold up to several gallons and are slightly porous so that a little fluid continues to seep out and to wet the outside. This exterior moisture evaporates in the air and so lowers the interior temperature.

The process may be quickened by hanging the bag in a breeze. This water you can purify at the same time by dropping in the necessary tablets.

THE TRUTH ABOUT SNOW

The only precaution that need be taken with pure snow in the wilderness is to treat it like ice cream and not put down too much at once when overheated or chilled. Aside from that, clean snow can be safely eaten any time we are thirsty in the bush.

Wilderness snows, after all, afford in flake form the purest of distilled water obtainable from the atmosphere. Snow's primary drawback is that a considerable amount proportionately is required to equal the desired quantity of water. You soon learn to break off sections of any available crust. Heavy granular snow from former storms, you find, is usually more convenient still.

This low water content is quickly evident the first time you melt snow in the noon tea pail. Particular care has to be taken not to burn the utensil, particularly as snow also acts as a blotter. This is the second reason why a few mouthfuls seem actually parching. The safest technique when you want to boil the kettle, is to melt snow in small quantities until the bottom of the container is protected with several inches of water. You can then begin filling it with the more, more, and more snow usually necessary if anything like a capacity amount of liquid is desired.

These shortcomings are more than compensated for by the fact that snowfall makes water readily available throughout the woods, mountains, plains, and the desert it whitens. All one has to do is scoop up clean handfuls while walking along. The body requires a great deal more water in cold weather than most of us would ordinarily expect, for the kidneys then have to take over much of the process of elimination otherwise accomplished by the perspiration glands. Snow so used, far from being harmful or dangerous, is therefore an extremely healthful convenience.

WASHING UP AFTERWARDS

Washing dishes is not really much of a chore if you have some system about it and if you always clean up immediately after a meal. With your cook kit, you'll find it helpful to include such items as a bar of laundry soap, two small tough dishcloths, a little dish mop, and scouring pads that combine steel wool with soap. While you are eating, have your largest kettle over the fire heating dishwater.

At the jump-off-place, buy a cheap tin dishpan if you've the room and ditch it when the trip is over. This will not take up much space if you select a model into which other items in your outfit will nest.

If you prefer, however, you can take along a small canvas wash basin. Such a seven-ounce affair that one of us has carried for years is four inches high and twelve inches in diameter. It squashes down flat to pack. You can even get by with a square of plastic, digging a hole every time you want to use it, and pressing the plastic within to serve as the wash pan. If you're short on receptacles, fill this with water while the meal is cooking, drop in a few pebbles for insulators, and using a bent green stick as tongs, set in several large clean stones from the fire to heat the water. The tin basin, however, is handier than either of these.

Every fellow, as he finishes his meal, scrapes his plate into the fire. When you are through with the frypans, fill them with water and put on the fire to boil. Do the same with any kettle containing the sticky residue of mush.

Down at the creek or lake shore you will find clusters of grass growing, with mud or sand adhering to the roots. Pull up a clump and use it to scour the outside of pots and also both the interior and exterior of the frypans before you wash them. Pans in which cereals like rolled oats have been cooked are particularly bothersome. If you will put a little square of butter or oleomargarine in the water when you are preparing the cereal, it will make the pot ten times easier to clean.

If you have a pet aluminum pot, whose exterior you want to keep bright, coat the outside with a thick film of soap before you place it on the fire. All trace of black will then quickly wash off clean as a whistle. Eventually, most kettles get thoroughly darkened on the outside with soot, which sticks most tenaciously and which can scarcely be removed by anything short of steel wool. But this soot does no harm whatever and even makes food in such a kettle cook faster. If you scour with sand or muddy grass as suggested, very little will rub off on other things when you pack. It is customary to have a canvas bag in which to stow the nest of kettles. This helps to keep them from blackening up other articles in the outfit.

It has been the experience of a great many of the old sourdoughs in Alaska and the Northwest that when a utensil used for cooking meat is washed with soap, they get bad digestive disturbances akin to poisoning and that this ceases when such washing is stopped. One way to clean a steel frypan is to heat it very hot, then quickly plunge it into cold water. If this does not remove all the dirt, then scrub with sand and rinse in clear boiling water. Another way of loosening grease is to fill the pan with water into which some wood ashes have been dropped and allow the whole thing to come to a boil beside the blaze.

GETTING READY TO GO AGAIN

Every outdoor trip is divided into three parts; the excitement of getting ready, the adventure itself, and finally the deep down pleasure of reminiscence.

Although you may not plan to hit the trail again for a month or until next year, you will be missing one of the keenest joys of all if as soon as one such excursion is over you do not begin preparations for the next. You'll be passing up the pulse-quickening satisfaction of keeping your equipment ready, of purposely thumbing catalogs and maps, and of scrawling terse reminders in a worn notebook carried for those moments when inspiration fires. Even in the midst of the steel bones and asphalt veins of the big city, all this can keep you mighty close to those other days and to those freer ones soon to come.

Then once again, almost before you know it, the wilderness night begins bulging from the west in a deep blue flood that drenches all but the last few waning embers of the sunset. Sweet ebony fumes lift from ready birch bark, and then the dry poplar with its clean medicinal odor catches hold. By you, in the forest's untroubled space, is everything you need; gun, fishing gear, camping outfit, grub, shelter, and friendly warmth. Life is very good.

"All this is perfectly distinct to an observant eye, and yet could easily pass unnoticed by most."

Next to last entry in Thoreau's
Journal.   September 3rd, 1861.

APPENDIX

Bake	To cook by dry heat, as in a reflector baker or oven.
Baste	To moisten food while cooking by pouring over it melted fat, drippings or other liquid.
Boil	To cook in water, or liquid mostly water, at boiling temperature (212° F. at sea level). Bubbles rise continually and break on the surface.
Braise	To brown in fat, then cook in covered pan, with or without added liquid, over fire, in reflector baker, Dutch oven or other oven. Larger pieces of meat cooked by braising are called pot roasts.
Broil	To cook uncovered by direct heat over an open fire.
Deep-fry	See french-fry.
Fricassee	To braise individual serving pieces of meat, poultry, or game in a little liquid—water, broth, or sauce.
French-fry	To cook in a deep receptacle, in enough hot fat to cover or float food.
Fry	To cook in fat or oil until brown and tender.
Grill	See broil.
Marinate	To let foods stand in a liquid (usually mixture of oil with vinegar or lemon juice) to add flavor or make more tender.
Pan-broil	To cook in very lightly greased or ungreased heavy pan on top of stove. Any fat is poured off as it accumulates so food does not fry.
Pan-fry	See sauté.
Parboil	To boil until partly cooked.
Plank	To cook and serve on wooden slab or board.
Pot-roast	See braise.
Roast	To bake in hot air, in reflector baker or turning over open fire, without water or cover.
Saute	To cook in a small amount of fat or oil, keeping the food moving until brown and tender.
Scald	To heat to a temperature just below the boiling point.
Sear	To seal surface by exposing it to intense heat.
Simmer	To cook in liquid just below the boiling point. Bubbles form slowly and break below the surface.
Skewer	To pierce with pointed stick.

315

Steam	To cook food in steam over boiling water. Food is steamed in a covered container, on a rack or in a perforated pan above boiling water.
Steep	To extract flavor and other values by soaking in hot but not boiling water.
Stew	To boil or simmer in a small amount of liquid. Meats are stewed at simmering temperatures.
Toast	To brown, and occasionally blacken, by dry heat.

ONE INGREDIENT FOR ANOTHER

For these	Substitute these
1 whole egg, for thickening or baking	2 egg yolks. Or 2 tablespoons dried whole egg plus 2½ tablespoons water.
1 whole egg in a batter	2 tablespoons of fresh dry snow, stirred in just before baking.
1 cup butter or margarine for shortening	⅞ cup of rendered bear or other animal fat, with ½ teaspoon salt. Or 1 cup hydrogenated fat (cooking fat sold under brand name) with ½ teaspoon salt.
1 square (ounce) chocolate	3½ tablespoons cocoa plus ½ tablespoon fat.
Nut meats	Similar amount of browned rolled oats. Peanut butter will do, too.
1 teaspoon double—acting baking powder	1½ teaspoons phosphate baking powder. Or 2 teaspoons tartrate baking power.
Baking soda in breadstuffs	Equal amount of the white of hardwood ashes.
Sweet milk and baking powder, for baking	Equal amount of sour milk plus ½ teaspoon soda per cup. (Each half teaspoon soda with 1 cup sour milk takes the place of 2 teaspoons baking powder and 1 cup sweet milk).
1 cup sour milk, for baking	1 cup sweet milk mixed with one of the following: 1 tablespoon vinegar. Or 1 tablespoon lemon juice. Or 1¾ teaspoons cream of tartar.
1 cup whole milk	½ cup evaporated milk plus ½ cup water. Or 4 tablespoons dry whole milk plus 1 cup water. Or 4 tablespoons nonfat dry milk plus 2½ teaspoons table fat and 1 cup water. Or 1 cup skim milk plus 2 tablespoons melted table fat or salad oil.
1 cup skim milk	4 tablespoons nonfat dry milk plus 1 cup water.
1 tablespoon flour, for thickening	½ tablespoon cornstarch, potato starch, rice starch, or arrowroot starch. Or 1 tablespoon granulated tapioca.
1 cup cake flour, for baking	⅞ cup all-purpose flour.
1 cup all purpose flour, for baking breads	Up to ½ cup bran, whole-wheat flour, or corn meal plus enough all-purpose flour to fill cup.
Commercial jelling agent for jelly making	1 level teaspoon Epsom Salts for each 5 pounds of fruit.

MEASURING FOODS

Part of cup	A compact nest of aluminum measuring spoons will enable accuracy and can also be used for eating. Measure dry ingredients before liquids.

Cup	Check at home the relationship of nesting drinking cup to standard measuring cup. If necessary, mark.
Molasses, syrups	These will bother less with clinging and sticking if you'll either first chill the measuring implement in cold water or lightly grease it.
Sugar	Pack brown sugar firmly into cup or spoon. Press or sift any lumps out of granulated sugar and measure like flour.
Solid fats	When fat comes in one-pound rectangular form, 1 cup or fraction can be cut from pound which measures about 2 cups. With quarter-pound rectangles, each of these equal ½ cup or 8 tablespoons. You can measure a cupfull, too, by packing firmly into cup and leveling off top with knife. Water method may be used for part of cup. To measure ½ cup fat, put ½ cup cold water in 1-cup measure. Add fat, pushing under water until water level stands at 1-cup mark. Pour out water and remove fat.
White flour	Sift once, onto piece of plastic if that is most convenient. Lift lightly into cup. Don't pack. Don't shake or jar cup, or it'll settle down again. Level off top with knife.
Other flours	This also includes fine meals, fine crumbs, dried eggs, dry milks. Stir instead of sifting. Measure like flour.
Baking powder, etc	Cornstarch, cream of tartar, and spices are included in this group. Stir to loosen. Fill spoon lightly to overflowing. Level with spatula or straight knife.

COMMON U.S. FOOD MEASURES

A dash, pinch, etc. .... less than ⅛ teaspoon
3 teaspoons .... 1 tablespoon
2 tablespoons .... 1 fluid ounce
4 tablespoons .... ¼ cup
6 tablespoons .... ⅜ cup
8 tablespoons .... ½ cup
16 tablespoons .... 1 cup
1 cup .... 8 fluid ounces
2 cups .... 1 pint
4 gills .... 1 pint
1 pint .... 16 fluid ounces
2 pints .... 1 quart
1 quart .... 32 fluid ounces
4 quarts .... 1 gallon
1 pint milk or water .... 1 pound

CANADIAN LIQUID MEASURES

1 cup .... 8 fluid ounces
1 pint .... 20 fluid ounces
1 quart .... 40 fluid ounces
1 imperial quart .... 1¼ U. S. quarts
4 imperial quarts .... 1 imperial gallon
1 imperial gallon .... 5 U. S. quarts
One imperial quart, figured exactly, equals 1.2003 U. S. quarts.

DRY MEASURES

2 pints .... 1 quart
8 quarts .... 1 peck
4 pecks .... 1 bushel
British dry quart equals 1.0320 U. S. dry quart.
Legal weights of a bushel of corn, barley, potatoes, etc. vary in different regions.

ORDINARY AVOIRDUPOIS WEIGHT

```
16 drams ............................................... 1 ounce
16 ounces or 7000 grains ............................... 1 pound
14 pounds ............................................. 1 stone
2000 pounds ........................................... 1 short ton
2240 pounds ........................................... 1 long ton
```

This chart may be used, as suggested in the preceeding food chapters and particularly in the one about Provisioning For Camping, for scientifically figuring out a light and compact grubstake made up largely of high-energy rations.

The nutrient values, based on the official researches of two governments with standard United States and Canadian foods, will vary somewhat in different localities. Dehydrated products will, naturally, differ to an even broader extent, depending not only on the original raw products but also on the methods of processing. Seasonal variations have not been noted, either, being minor in the aspects here considered.

PROVISIONING TABLE

Calories	1-Lb. Portion	Outfitting Data
2709	Almonds, shelled, dried	1 cup shelled—5-1 3 oz.
1254	Apples, dried	1 lb. dried—7 lb. fresh
1190	Apricots, dried	1 lb. dry—5½ lb. fresh
1047	Bacon, back	3 slices, 2½″ diam. x. ¼″—3½ oz.
2855	Bacon, side	1 lb.—20 to 24 slices
		2½ to 3 slices—2 oz.
1219	banana, dried	3½ oz. dried—about 1 lb. fresh
1536	Barley, brown, whole	2 tbsp. dry—1 oz. yield ½ cup cooked
1525	Beans, dried, kidney	1 lb.—2-2/3 cups
		1 lb.—7 cups cooked
1512	Beans, Lima	1 lb.—2-1/3 cups
		1 lb.—6½ cups cooked
1535	Beans, Navy	1 lb.—2-1/3 cups
		1 lb.—6 cups cooked
977	Beef, corned, canned	3 slices 3″ x 2½″ x ¼″—3½ oz.
922	Beef, dried or chipped	2 thin slices—1 oz.
1004	Bologna	1 slice—4½″ diam. x. ⅛″—1 oz. 16 slices to 1 lb.
3248	Butter	1 lb.—2 cups
1587	Cabbage, dehydrated	1 lb. serves 50
		1 serving—1/3 oz.
1641	Carrots, dehydrated	1 lb. serves 25
		1 serving raw—4 oz. cooked
2619	Cashews	4 to 5 nuts—½ oz.
1804	Cheese, cheddar	1 lb. cheese grated—4 cups
1676	Cheese, cheddar processed	
433	Cheese, cottage	1 lb.—2 cups, serves 8
		1 serving, ¼ cup—2 oz.
1684	Cheese, cream	2 tablespoons—1 oz.

Calories	1-Lb. Portion	Outfitting Data
1679	Cheese, Swiss	1 slice, 4½" x 3½" x ⅛"—1 oz.
905	Chicken, canned, boned	½ cup—3½ oz.
2273	Chocolate, bitter	1 lb. melted—2 cups
2282	Chocolate, milk, plain	
2413	Chocolate, milk, with almonds	
2403	Chocolate, bittersweet	
2136	Chocolate, sweetened, plain	
1329	Cocoa, dry	1 lb.—4 cups
	Coffee, roasted	1 lb.—5½ cups finely ground, makes 50 cups. Contains, in solid state, 1316 calories.
1577	Cookies, Fig Bars	22 cookies to 1 lb.
1649	Cornmeal, yellow	3 cups weigh 1 lb.
4013	Corn oil	1 lb.—2 cups
1642	Corn Starch	1 lb.—3½ cups (stirred)
4013	Cotton Seed Oil	1 lb.—2 cups
1287	Dates, dried, pitted	1 lb. pitted and cut—2½ cups
655	Egg, fresh, whole	1 doz. extra large—27 oz. up
		1 doz. large—at least 24 oz.
		1 doz. medium—21 to 24 oz.
2688	Egg, dried, whole	5 oz. powder & 1½ cups water—1 doz. fresh eggs
1530	Farina, dark	3 tbsp. dry—1 oz. yield ¾ cup cooked
1677	Farina, light	1 lb.—approximately 2-2/3 cups dry
357	Figs, fresh, raw	2 medium—4 oz.
514	Figs, canned in syrup	½ cup weights 3½ oz.
1223	Figs, dried	3 cups (44 figs)—1 lb.
2838	Filberts, shelled	1 cup—4¾ oz.
1643	Flour, Buckwheat, light	1 cup—4¼ oz.
1574	Flour, dark	1 cup—4¼ oz.
1659	Flour, rye, light	1 lb. rye flour—about 4½ cups
		1 lb. sifted—5-2/3 cups
1442	Flour, rye, dark	
1632	Flour, wheat	All purpose flour—4 cups per lb. sifted
		Cake flour—4¾ cups per lb. sifted
		Pastry flour—4¾ cups per lb. sifted
1586	Flour, self-rising	4 cups per lb. sifted
1510	Flour, whole	Whole wheat flour stirred—3¾ cups per lb.
317	Fruit Cocktail, canned	No. 2 can—1 lb.
1739	Gelatin, desert powder	2½ cups per lb.
		1 oz. pkg. makes 4 to 6 servings
1643	Hominy, grits	3 cups per pound
		3 tbsp. raw—2/3 cup cooked
1400	Honey	1 lb.—1-1/3 cups
1262	Jam, assorted	3 level tbsp.—2 oz.
4091	Lard	2 cups per lb.
		1 oz. measures 2 tbsp.
1530	Lentils, dry	2-1/3 cups per lb.
		2½ tbsp. dry—1 oz.—yields ½ cup cooked
1928	Liverwurst	1 slice 3" diameter ¼" thick—1 oz.
1723	Macaroni	1 lb. 1" pieces—4 cups
		1 lb. cooked—12 cups—weighs 4 lbs.
3266	Margarine	1 tbsp.—½ oz.
624	Milk, evaporated	1 lb. tin & equal water—1½ pts. fresh milk

Calories	1-Lb. Portion	Outfitting Data
2231	Milk, powdered, whole	1 lb.—3½ cups
		4 tbsp. level & 1 cup water—1 cup fresh milk
1642	Milk, powdered, skim	1 lb.—4½ cups
		4 tbsp. & 1 cup water—1 cup fresh skim milk
1142	Molasses	1 cup weighs 11 oz.
107	Mushrooms, fresh, raw	4 large or 10 small—3½ oz.
1728	Noodles, containing egg	1″ pieces—6 cups to 1 lb.
		1 lb. yields 11 cups cooked
1794	Oats, meal or rolled	1 lb.—5-2/3 cups
		1/3 cup makes 1 cup porridge
4013	Olive Oil	1 lb.—2 cups
308	Peaches, canned in syrup	2 halves & 3 tbsp. juice—4 oz.
1207	Peaches, dried	1 lb. dried—5½ lbs. fresh
2613	Peanut Butter	1 lb.—2 cups
1219	Pears, dried	1 lb. dried—5½ lbs. fresh
193	Peas, fresh	2.2 lbs. whole—1 lb. shelled (3 cups)
1540	Peas, dried, green	2 tbsp. dry—1 oz. yields ½ cup cooked
1562	Peas, split	2¼ cups—1 lb.
3159	Pecans, shelled	1 lb. in shell yields 1/3 lb. meats
3410	Pork, salt, fat, with rind	2 slices 4″ x 2″ x ⅜″—3½ oz.
318	Potatoes, fresh	1 lb. as purchased—3 to 4 servings
1620	Potatoes, dehydrated	1 serving—1 oz. dry—4 oz. reconstituted
1034	Prunes, dried, with pits	sizes—large 20 to 40 per lb.
		medium 40 to 60 per lb.
		small 60 to 100 per lb.
1217	Raisins, dried	seeded, 3¼ cups—1 lb.
		seedless, whole, 2¾ cups—1 lb.
1648	Rice, brown	2 tbsp. dry—1 oz. yields ½ cup cooked
1629	Rice, white	1 lb.—2⅛ cups. 7 cups when cooked
1682	Rice, wild	1 lb.—3 cups
		1 oz.—3 tbsp.—1 serving
1787	Salad Dressing, French	2 tbsp.—1 oz.
3211	Salad Dressing, Mayonaise	2 tbsp.—1 oz.
1531	Sardines in oil	15 sardines 3″ long—5 oz.
784	Sardines in tomato sauce	
1817	Sausage, salami in casing	1 slice 4½″ diam., ⅛″ thick—1 oz.
1164	Sausage, wieners, raw	7 to 9 per lb.
4010	Shortening, vegetable Crisco, Spry, etc.	1 lb.—2¼ cups
1719	Spaghetti	1 lb. broken—4¾ cups—serves 15
3437	Suet	1 lb. ground suet—3½ cups
1676	Sugar, brown	2 cups (firmly packed)—1 lb.
1747	Sugar, granulated, white	1 lb.—2¼ cups
1747	Sugar, icing	1 lb.—3½ cups
1747	Sugar, loaf	flat tablets, 100 to 1 lb.
1580	Sugar, maple	1 piece 1″ x 1¼″ x ½″—½ oz.
1299	Syrups, corn	1-1/3 cups per lb.
1123	Syrups, maple	1½ cups per lb.
1633	Tapioca, dry, pearl	2¾ cups raw—7½ cups cooked
	Tea	1 lb.—6 cups dry makes 200 to 300 cups
2969	Walnuts, shelled	1 lb. in shell—½ lb. meats
		1 lb. halves—4½ cups
1639	Wheat, germ	1 tbsp.—1/6 oz.
1544	Whole wheat, dry	1/3 cup dry—1 oz.—¾ cup cooked

WHAT YOU CAN DO WHERE

Regulations governing pothunting, varmint shooting, and every other phase even vaguely connected with the instinctive compulsions of fishing and hunting vary greatly throughout the United States, Canada, and Mexico. Seasons often differ from year to year. So do limits.

Some localities require licenses for certain animals, birds, and fish. Others not only do not, but pay bounties for such prey as mountain lion, bobcat, fox, wolf, lynx, coyote, a few of the predatory birds, and even for the otherwise widely protected porcupine.

The most satisfactory way to secure the latest specific information is to write the sources listed below. If after receiving the regulations you have any doubts about pertinent points, and there are sometimes conflicting interpretations as well as differing local exceptions, it will be well to secure as definite an analysis of these as possible from official sources before you start to hunt.

Where to Write for Fish and Game Laws

Alabama: Division of Game & Fish, Montgomery.
Alaska: Alaska Dept. of Fish & Game, Juneau.
Arizona: Game & Fish Commission, State Bldg., Phoenix.
Arkansas: Game & Fish Commission, Little Rock.
California: Dept. Fish & Game, State Office Bldg., Sacramento.
Colorado: Game & Fish Commission, 1530 Sherman St., Denver.
Connecticut: Board of Fisheries & Game, Hartford.
Delaware: Board of Game & Fish Commissioners, Dover.
Florida: Game & Fresh Water Fish Commission, Tallahassee.
Georgia: Game & Fish Commission, State Capitol, Atlanta.
Hawaii: Division of Fish & Game, Honolulu.
Idaho: Dept. of Fish & Game, Boise.
Illinois: Dept. of Conservation, State Capitol, Springfield.
Indiana: Dept. of Conservation, 311 W. Washington St., Indianapolis.
Iowa: Conservation Commission, E. 7th & Court Sts., Des Moines.
Kansas: Forestry, Fish & Game Commission, Pratt.
Kentucky: Dept. Fish & Wildlife Resources, Frankfort.
Louisiana: Commissioner of Wildlife & Fisheries, Civil Courts, Bldg., New Orleans.
Maine, Dept. of Inland Fisheries & Game, State House, Augusta.
Maryland: Dept. of Game & Inland Fish, Munsey Bldg., Baltimore.
Massachusetts: Division of Fisheries & Game, Ashburton Place, Boston.
Michigan: Dept. of Conservation, Lansing.
Minnesota: Division of Game & Fish, State Office Bldg., St. Paul.
Mississippi: Game & Fish Commission, Woolfolk Bldg., Jackson.
Missouri: Conservation Commission, Monroe Bldg., Jefferson City.
Montana: Fish & Game Commission, Helena.
Nebraska: Game, Forestation & Parks Commission, Lincoln.
Nevada: Fish & Game Commission, Reno.
New Hampshire: Fish & Game Dept., State House Annex, Concord.
New Jersey: Division of Fish & Game, State House Annex, Trenton.
New Mexico: Dept. Game & Fish, Santa Fe.
New York: Dept. of Conservation, Albany.
North Carolina: Wildlife Resources Commission, Raleigh.
North Dakota: Game & Fish Dept., Capitol Bldg., Bismarck.
Ohio: Dept. Natural Resources, State Office Bldg., Columbus.

Oklahoma: Game & Fish Dept., State Capitol Bldg., Oklahoma City.
Oregon: Game Commission, Portland.
Pennsylvania: Game Commission or Fish Commission, Harrisburg.
Rhode Island: Division of Fish & Game, Veterans Memorial Bldg., Providence.
South Carolina: Wildlife Resources Dept., Columbia.
South Dakota: Dept. of Game, Fish & Parks, State Office Bldg., Pierre.
Tennessee: Division of Game & Fish, 166 18th Ave., N., Nashville.
Texas: Game & Fish Commission, Austin.
Utah: Fish & Game Commission, Salt Lake City.
Vermont: Fish & Game Commission, Montpelier.
Virginia: Commission of Game & Inland Fisheries, Richmond.
Washington: Game Commission, 509 Fairview Ave., N., Seattle.
West Virginia: Conservation Commission, Charleston.
Wisconsin: Conservation Dept., State Office Bldg., Madison.
Wyoming: Game & Fish Commission, Cheyenne.
Canada: Govt. Travel Bureau, Ottawa, Ontario.
Alberta: Dept. Lands & Forests, Edmonton.
British Columbia: Game Commission, Burrard St., Vancouver.
Manitoba: Dept. Mines & Natural Resources, Winnipeg.
New Brunswick: Dept. Lands & Mines, Fredericton.
Newfoundland: Dept. Mines & Resources, St. Johns.
Nova Scotia: Dept. Lands & Forest, Halifax.
Ontario: Dept. Lands & Forests, Parliament Bldgs., Toronto.
Prince Edward Island: Dept. Industry & Natural Resources, Charlottetown.
Quebec: Dept. Natural Resources, Quebec.
Saskatchewan: Dept. Natural Resources, Regina.
Yukon & Northwest territories: Northern Administration & Lands Branch, Dept.
    of Mines & Resources, Ottawa.
Mexico: Secretaria de Agricultura y Fomento, Direccion Forestal y de Caza, Ignacio
    Mariscal No. 11, Mexico, D. F.

WHERE TO GET IT

We have had countless letters from our readers over the years asking where certain articles of equipment that we have recommended may be obtained. Many of these especially desirable items are not regularly handled by the average sporting-goods store and retailer. The following list gives the names and addresses of dealers from whom such specialized equipment may be secured, with a short summary of the types each handles. There are doubtless other firms who can supply similar goods, but these are unknown to us at date of publication. When corresponding with any of the below concerns, please mention this book. The outfitter will then understand better what you want and give you better service.

Abercrombie & Fitch Co. Madison Ave. at 45th Street, New York 17, N. Y. Camp equipment and clothing of every kind, guns, fishing tackle, all general sporting goods.

Alaska Sleeping Bag Co. 334 N.W. 11th Ave. Portland, Ore. Sleeping bags of many descriptions, down-insulated clothing.

Eddie Bauer. 417 East Pine St., Seattle 22, Wash. General camp equipment, sleeping bags, down-insulated clothing.

L. L. Bean, Inc. Freeport, Maine. Outdoor clothing and shoes of all kinds, Bean's "Maine" hunting shoes, camp equipment, dehydrated foods.

Bernard Food Industries. 217 North Jefferson St., Chicago, Ill., and 1208 E. San Antonio St., San Jose, Calif. Dehydrated foods, about 90 varieties, packed for campers.

Camp and Trail Outfitters. 112 Chambers St., New York 7, N. Y. Equipment for hikers, back packers, alpinists, light tents and sleeping bags, frame rucksacks, packboards, clothing, aluminum cooking utensils, shoes, hob-nails.

Corcoran, Inc. Stoughton, Mass. Large assortment of camp equipment, clothing, shoes, etc.

Gerry. Ward, Colorado. Equipment for hikers, back packers, and mountaineers. Light tents, sleeping bags, clothing, boots with vibram and defour soles, imported aluminum utensils, materials for making some of your own equipment.

Hamley & Co. Pendleton, Ore. Sawbuck and Decker pack saddles in sizes for horses, mules, and burros.

Megden Industries. 6708 Marshall Road, Upper Darby, Pa. Dehydrated foods packed specially for campers.

Morsan Tent Co. Route 17, Paramus, N. J. Large assortment of tents and tarpaulins in many materials. General camp equipment of all types.

Potomac Appalachian Trail Club. 1916 Sunderland Place, N. W., Washington 6, D. C. Send 50 cents for their booklet: "Hiking, Camping, Mountaineering, and Trail Clearing Equipment," containing names and addresses of all firms handling such equipment, with weights, dimensions and prices of each item.

Ramsey Manufacturing Co. 7353 Deering Ave., Canoga Park, Calif. Oven for gasoline stoves and outdoor wood fires. Has thermometer and is 13″ square and folds to 2 inches thick, weighs 9 pounds.

Sims Stoves. Lovell, Wyo. Sheet-steel folding, wood-burning stove for tents and cabins.

Smilie Outfits. 536 Mission St., San Francisco 7, Calif. Equipment for hikers, mountaineers, and horse and burro packers. Light tents and sleeping bags, aluminum cook outfits, small aluminum folding reflector bakers, "sheep-herder" stoves, dehydrated foods.

Norm Thompson. 1805 N.W. Thurman, Portland 9, Oregon. Hats, clothing, shoes, frame rucksacks for mountaineers and hikers.

Trailwise. 1615 University Ave. Berkeley, Calif. Equipment for hikers, back packers, and alpinists. Frame rucksacks, pack boards, mountain boots with vibram lug soles, light tents and sleeping bags, imported aluminum cook kits, materials for making some of your own equipment.

Le Trappeur. 438 Stuart St., Boston 16, Mass. Imported equipment for Alpine climbers and skiers. Frame rucksacks and ski and mountain boots with lug soles.

Woods Manufacturing Co. Ltd., Ottawa, Ontario, Canada, and Ogdensburg, N. Y. Superior down-filled sleeping bags and robes of all weights. Their 3-Star robe is one of the most famous throughout all the Far North.

> Be present at our table, Lord.
> Be here and everywhere adored;
> Thy creatures bless and grant that we
> May feast in Paradise with Thee.

INDEX

325